THE NATURE OF PHILOSOPHICAL INQUIRY

The Nature of

Philosophical Inquiry

EDITED BY

Joseph Bobik

UNIVERSITY OF NOTRE DAME PRESS
Notre Dame   London

Copyright © 1970 by
University of Notre Dame Press
Notre Dame, Indiana 46556
Library of Congress Catalog Number: 77-85347
Printed in the United States of America
  by NAPCO Graphic Arts, Inc.

CONTENTS

PREFACE

In academic year 1966–67, the Reverend Ernan McMullin, chairman of the department of philosophy at the University of Notre Dame, inaugurated what has come to be called the Perspectives in Philosophy Lecture Series. As he envisioned the series, each year four or five outstanding men in the field would come to stay at Notre Dame for a week (a different week for each), and deliver three public lectures on a topic selected for that year, lead two or three seminar discussions in between, and talk more informally with graduate students and faculty members. Their stays were to be scheduled roughly a month apart, and between stays the coordinator of the lectures for a given year would direct seminar discussions of selected works of the lecturer about to come.

Father McMullin appointed me coordinator for 1966–67, and that is my connection with this volume. The topic for that year was the nature of philosophical inquiry, and the scholars invited were Stephan Körner of the University of Bristol, England; Martin Versfeld of Cape Town University, South Africa; A. J. Ayer of Oxford University, England; Stephen Pepper of the University of California, Berkeley; and O. K. Bouwsma of the University of Texas, Austin. Josef Pieper and Karl Popper were also among those originally invited, but unfortunately they were unable to come. (Someone joked that if they had come, the series could well have been called the Pieper-Pepper-Popper Series.) For all concerned, the lectures of 1966–67 were admirably successful, and they were followed in 1967–68 by a series with the general topic, approaches to ethics; and in 1968–69 the general topic was the historiography of philosophy. Epistemology was the topic selected for 1969–70.

Prior to choosing the nature of philosophical inquiry as the topic for the first year of the Perspective lectures, Father McMullin had enjoyed the opportunity of being effectively instrumental in selecting the same topic for the annual convention of the American Catholic Philosophical Association, which met on the Notre Dame campus during Easter week, 1967. With the Perspectives lectures and the convention, the nature of philosophical inquiry had a year of intense study at Notre Dame. A natural question was asked: Why not share some of the fruits of the year's study with others? And so the idea of a volume was born.

As it happened, there were four particularly good convention papers—those of Professors Rorty, MacQuarrie, Harris, and Johann. In a sense these were the key papers of the convention, presenting themselves as natural candidates for publication. The original plan was to record the efforts of the five Perspectives lecturers and of the four convention contributors, all of whom spoke on the nature of philosophical inquiry. But since the papers of the convention contributors were published in the Proceedings of the A.C.P.A.

the volume in its present form contains fifteen papers all together—three by each of the Perspectives lecturers: twelve of them printed in toto, and three of them condensed into one by their author at his own request.

Without Father McMullin's efforts, neither the Perspectives lectures on the nature of philosophical inquiry nor this volume could have ever come to be. Both the lectures and the volume are in different ways the children of this singularly gifted man of ideas. To him, thanks and acknowledgments and special words of laud and commendation.

My thanksgiving would not be complete if I were not to thank each of the five Perspectives lecturers. They gave of themselves and of their thoughts with the singular determination of Jainist monks. Lastly, my thanksgiving would be incomplete if I were not to thank my wife, Teresa. She has always—but especially in this first year of the Perspectives Series—most heroically, and *philosophiae causa,* endured my prolonged absences from home and children and things.

Joseph Bobik

INTRODUCTION

It is well known that philosophers have always disagreed about many things; perhaps it can even be said that there is nothing on which they have ever completely agreed. Whether or not that is the case, it certainly is the case that they do not agree about the nature of their own subject.

Such is the case with the five philosophers who have authored the papers recorded in this volume. We have here five different views on the nature of philosophical inquiry, no two of which are in complete agreement with one another. Versfeld and Pepper agree in the claim that philosophy talks about the world, but for Versfeld, the utterances of philosophy are characterized by necessity. For Pepper, they are characterized by probability. For Körner, Ayer, and Bouwsma, on the other hand, philosophy talks not about the world, but about talk, and for each of them the function of philosophical talk about talk is different. For Körner, the function of the highest sort of philosophical talk (the meta-

1

physical) is to exhibit and modify the categorial frameworks presupposed—but left unexhibited—by phenomenology and analytic philosophy, and beyond that to invent and to propose new categorial frameworks. For Ayer, philosophical talk has the function of a critical and clarifying analysis of concepts, whether ordinary or scientific or mathematical or logical, and of their theoretical backgrounds. For Bouwsma, philosophical talk has the function of dispelling illusions of sense where there is no sense; i.e. illusions of sense in what has been put forth by its authors, but wrongly, as instances of philosophical talk itself. If any two of these views come close to occupying the same philosophical orbit, they are perhaps those of Körner and of Ayer, as the diligent reader will see.

Stephan Körner, who visited Notre Dame during the second week of October, 1966, was the first of the Perspectives lecturers. He has found it convenient to condense his three lectures into one which "contains the substance of three talks," as he says, on his "conception of philosophy." In the first section of his paper, he is critical of certain methodological theses of Descartes. Pointing out what he takes to be serious difficulties in Descartes' doctrines of intuition, deduction, necessary connection, and the relation between intuition and deduction, he concludes that Descartes "misunderstood the nature of the activity which he so brilliantly pursued," and that this misunderstanding was "bequeathed not only to his later rationalist followers, but also to the empiricists, Kantians and most others who came after him." Whereas Descartes rejected as ill-founded all philosophical efforts which did not yield absolutely certain truths and claimed to have discovered a method which would yield just such truths, Körner argues that Descartes' method is beset by difficulties which are serious enough to render it if not impossible, at least one which is incapable of producing the expected yield.

In the second section, Körner turns to examine the most obvious of the descendants of Descartes' methodology, the phenomenological method of Husserl, and argues that it cannot claim the autonomy which Husserl and his followers attributed to it. Not only does it not possess the means for producing statements which are purely descriptive (that is, with no admixture of interpretation), it does not have the means for distinguishing between interpretations which permit alternatives, on the one hand, and unique interpretations, if any, on the other hand.

The third section examines analytic philosophy. In one way of putting it, Körner concludes that whatever else may be true about analytic philosophy, it is not true that analytic philosophy is the whole of philosophy or that it is autonomous. Of the two types of analysis engaged in by analytic philosophers, exhibition-analysis—like phenomenology—cannot yield pure descriptions of linguistic phenomena without interpretative assumptions. Replacement-analysis, the second type of analysis in which all analytic philosophers engage at least sometime—whether they know it or not—is dependent in theory as well as in practice on certain metaphysical directives guiding the choice of criteria of the defectiveness of concepts, and criteria of replacement. And so there is such a thing as metaphysics, something over and above analytic philosophy, at least in the sense of these underlying interpretative assumptions and metaphysical directives.

Whereas the third section *argued for* a certain sort of metaphysics—metaphysics in the sense of interpretative and regulative (directive) propositions which underlie all theoretical inquiries, including even analytic philosophy—the fourth and last section *argues against* metaphysics of another sort, metaphysics as an attempt to construct transcendental arguments which are absolute in character, arguments which would bring to the light of day *the* absolutely indispensable categories of *all* human thinking at *all* times. The sort of metaphysics which Körner accepts is one which is for the most part concerned with the "exhibition, modification and speculative proposal of categorial frameworks." It exhibits the categorial frameworks presupposed, but left unestab-

lished, by phenomenological description and by exhibition-
and replacement-analysis. But it goes beyond such exhibition
(which is merely empirical or at the level of simple discovery) to become inventive, to innovate by modifying the
exhibited categorial frameworks and by speculatively proposing "new metaphysical theses to thinkers who have not
accepted them as absolute [Collingwoodian] presuppositions
and so far have not even tried to make up their mind about
accepting them."

The method of Descartes cannot produce a metaphysics.
And the descriptive method of phenomenology, as well as
the exhibition and replacement methods of analysis, presuppose a metaphysics, a categorial framework. The metaphysical task, as Körner sees it, is both empirical and inventive:
empirical, in that it exhibits the categorial frameworks presupposed by the various methods which are employed by
philosophers; inventive, in that it modifies the presupposed
categorial frameworks which it has exhibited, and beyond
that proposes entirely new ones.

The second of the Perspectives lecturers, Martin Versfeld,
presented his papers during the second week of November.
In his first lecture, "Metaphysics in Our Time," he begins by
noting that one cannot argue, as contemporary analytic philosophers have tried to do, from the essence of metaphysics
to its nonexistence. Such an attempt presupposes that metaphysics has an essence, some one essence, which is simply
false. Metaphysics does not have an essence capable of definition, nor can the various manifestations of metaphysical
thinking be reduced to some one generic concept. Versfeld
then presents and subscribes to what he takes Plato's view
of philosophy to be. Philosophy, under the name of dialectic (the highest of human pursuits), has the task of giving a rational account of the hypotheses assumed, and left
unexamined, by the special sciences. These hypotheses are
not only theoretical, but practical—moral, political, social—
as well. The pursuit of the metascience, dialectics, results
in a growth in rational self-consciousness. To know oneself

in the human situation, i.e., to lay bare all the hypotheses assumed by oneself in pursuing the special sciences, is to do philosophy. To philosophize is to come ever closer to a fuller knowledge of the human self in the totality of its concrete situation.

To Plato's insight that to philosophize is to come to know oneself, the modern world—under the impact of Hebrew and Christian thought—has added a further dimension, a strong sense of history and of the significance of time. One can know oneself only partially, very partially indeed, if one has not examined both man's and one's own history, and if one has cut himself off from history, from events and thoughts of past time.

But history is not philosophy or metaphysics, though history is in a sense metaphysical. History is not the ultimate science, because history itself always impels us towards the meta-historical. History is only partially self-conscious, and always assumes a philosophy. History, like physics, does not make statements about itself. Only philosophy, as the attempt to come to know oneself, makes statements about itself. Whereas physics seeks the truth about matter, and history seeks the truth about contingent events, metaphysics seeks the truth about truth. And this is why it is concerned with its own truth, and so becomes the science of itself. But this means that metaphysics moves to science about truth from a certain basic awareness of a nescience about it. Metaphysical knowledge rests upon one's knowledge of non-knowledge. One "knows oneself," and so has become engaged in the doing of metaphysics when, and only when, he can assert with understanding, "I know that I do not know." To know myself fully is to know that I do not know; and to know that I do not know is to know being—being as it reveals itself to me. Metaphysics is not a conceptual framework invented by man; it is the handwriting of being on the human self. As Versfeld puts it, "Metaphysics is not a conceptual framework, or a device for creating 'explanatory' nonentities, but the objective unfolding of being in time."

If metaphysics is man's attempt to know himself fully, it is also an attempt which is frustrated by an inherent impossibility of complete fulfillment. In his second lecture, devoted to the idea of philosophical truth, Versfeld pursues at length the source of this frustration. He describes metaphysics as being concerned with knowing about knowing, or (which is the same thing), with the truth about truth. What is knowing?—or perhaps better, What is truth?—therefore, is the question which is constitutive of philosophy. None of the special sciences asks this question. The answer to this question is the source of the frustration of philosophy. We all know that there is such a thing as truth, but knowing *what truth is* is quite a different thing.

"Philosophy cannot separate knowing about knowing from knowing about being. It has as it were to catch itself in action." The philosopher knows knowing in the measure in which he knows being. But he can never fully know being, and so he can never fully know knowing; he can never fully know the truth about truth. Truth is being in possession of itself, and man (though by nature seeking self-possession) can never fully achieve it. Self-possession is the possession of God alone. Truth is a Person. Hence man's frustration; hence philosophy's frustration. Man is left to philosophize with nothing more than the hope of self-possession; this is the "mark of a being whose knowledge has the quality of nescience."

Versfeld's third lecture is an exposition of, and a commentary on, the classical doctrine of truth as *adequatio*. The reason for pursuing this doctrine lies in his claim that whatever he has said in his previous lectures "stands or falls with the notion of ontological truth with which the *adequatio* theory is inseparably bound up." It is not that he is trying to play off the *adequatio* theory against other theories of truth, like the coherence theory. It is just that if there is such an enterprise as metaphysics, i.e., a search for the truth about being, then *adequatio* is the only description of the nature of metaphysical knowledge. The coherence theory of truth is adequate for a certain level of thinking (that of the modern sciences), but not for that of metaphysics. Modern science views human knowledge as an instrument of man, as something by which man can become the master and the possessor of nature, as something which is in man's power and not in the power of things. Such an instrument must be to a very large extent man-made, to a very large extent the construction of formal patterns. Metaphysics, on the other hand, views human knowledge as an instrument of being, as something in the power of being and not that of man, as that by which being becomes the master and possessor of man, thereby enabling man to achieve the highest degree of self-possession of which he is capable. Such an instrument must to a very large extent be made not by man, but by being. Whereas metaphysics is the handwriting of being on the human self, modern science is the handwriting of the human self on being.

Metaphysics is a realism; it is a knowledge about things "as they are." It is not the knowledge of something which intervenes between the human knower and being—not about a Cartesian idea, or about a Hobbesian or Humean association of sensations, or about the language of contemporary analysts. Metaphysics is "primarily a *verbum cordis* which expresses the essence of things, a commensuration with, rather than an instrument for handling the appearances of, being."

Truth is not simply logical truth, i.e., a quality of propositions, as Hobbes and Kant and many others have thought. If there is logical truth, it is only because prior to it there is ontological truth. The *adequatio* theory asserts, indeed, that truth is a quality of propositions; but it also asserts that there is a more radical sense in which truth is a quality of things, that quality in them by which they imitate their Creator, by which they acquire their identity as beings over against other beings and over against nonbeing, thereby becoming capable of being known, of writing on the human self with a writing which reveals them as they are.

A. J. Ayer, the third of the Perspectives lecturers, visited Notre Dame during the second week of January 1967. Very

early in his first lecture, Ayer points out that his aim is to
identify the special province of philosophy—assuming for
the time being that it has one—and that a good method for
this task is the method of elimination. He begins by eliminating the view that what uniquely distinguishes the philosopher
(thereby differentiating him from the scientist) is that he is
occupied with reality as a whole. Next he argues against the
view that philosophy is an attempt to show by a priori reason-
ings that the world in its deeper reality is quite unlike it
appears to be. Third, he eliminates the view that the philosopher is a sage, that is, one who tells us how we ought to live.
Fourth, he casts doubt on the view, dominant since Descartes, that the role of the philosopher is that of a judge; that
is, the view that the main task of the philosopher is to stand
in judgment over the views of others, whether scientists or not
—to ask questions within the context of the basic question:
What can we really be certain of? Linguistically, the question is: What statements can we significantly make? He mani-
fests his doubts concerning this fourth view by employing an
argument which he attributes to G. E. Moore, though Moore
himself did not explicitly advance it.

If the philosopher is not in a position to compete with the
scientist in giving a description or explanation of the world
(views one and two); and if the philosopher can be neither
a sage nor a judge (views three and four); what, then, is left
for philosophy? What is philosophy good for? What remains
is the attempt to elucidate or to clarify the meanings of the
propositions uttered by thinking nonphilosophers—ordinary
men, scientists, mathematicians, logicians, etc. The only
genuine "contribution that the philosopher can hope to make
to the advancement of knowledge is through engaging in
philosophical analysis." But, notes Ayer, philosophical analysis is not a homogeneous enterprise. He concludes this lecture
by distinguishing eight different procedures which count as
analysis, and he notes that they are not put forward as competitors; different procedures may suit different problems or
different persons.

In his second lecture, Ayer takes another look at the argument which he presented in his first lecture as underlying Moore's defense of common sense—the argument which rests on the premise that every type of statement has already built into it certain accepted criteria by which we decide when it is true or false. From this it follows that there is no place for philosophy as a judge. What Moore and his followers overlooked is the fact that all words, even the most ordinary words of our language (or all concepts, if one prefers to speak of concepts), bear with themselves a certain theoretical load—some more, some less. Since we can make the distinction between the application of a word and its theoretical background, and beyond that recognize that a word has application without committing ourselves to the acceptance of its theoretical background, Moore's argument loses a good deal of its force.

Since we can recognize the applicability of a word without accepting the conceptual system which is its theoretical background, the question arises as to how we are to assess different backgrounds as to the grounds on which we decide which system to adopt. He pursues this question in terms of some examples of philosophical systems, each of which he interprets as an attempt to replace one conceptual system with another. He chooses four examples, all of which differ significantly from our present-day common sense conceptual system: (1) absolute idealism, (2) any system in which things are supposed to happen by divine agency, (3) that part of the system of Berkeley in which he attempts to replace physical objects by collections of sensible qualities which, by definition, exist only when perceived; and (4) materialism in the sense of physicalism, the attempt to eliminate states of consciousness or at least to reduce them to physical processes.

The weakness of the absolute idealists, points out Ayer, is that when they reject the common sense view of the world, what they put in its place is unintelligible. As regards any religious, divine agency, view of the world, "the explanations which they furnish of the course of events are always ex post facto. We are given no criteria for determining what the gods intend other than the observation of what actually happens, and this means that the explanations in question are empty." And so, emptiness of explanation and unintelligibility are adopted as criteria for the rejection of a conceptual system.

Ayer's third lecture turns to the third and fourth of his examples of conceptual systems, that is, to part of the system of Berkeley and to physicalism. He begins by asking how Berkeley's denial of the existence of matter is to be construed. He suggests that Berkeley is not to be taken literally, that Berkeley is not telling the plain man that "his world is entirely different from what he takes it to be." Neither is Berkeley trying to tell us what we really mean when we talk about physical objects like sticks and stones and tables and chairs. If one considers the argument which led Berkeley to this conclusion, suggests Ayer, one might be able to see how to interpret him. Ayer analyzes the argument at length—in terms of its validity, in terms of the meanings of its key expressions, in terms of its assumptions. What Berkeley is doing, concludes Ayer, is claiming that the common sense interpretation put on what is given immediately in sensory experience is illegitimate. "What he [Berkeley] rejects is the common sense view of the way in which statements go beyond the data by which they are verified, and the reason why he rejects it is that he thinks it impossible to conceive of material things as existing apart from the data of sense." In the end, Ayer concludes, it seems that one accepts a conceptual system in terms of how one chooses to look at the world and what picture one prefers to form of it. "There would be no question of truth or falsehood here but only of convenience." For example, Ayer thinks that "the adoption of a realistic view is necessary for the progress of a science at certain stages of its development."

That accepting a given conceptual system seems to be grounded in convenience is illustrated again in Ayer's consideration of his fourth example, physicalism. If mental processes can be identified with (or in some way reduced. to) physical processes, one does not have to suffer the inconvenience of explaining what warrants we can have for making an inference from people's overt behavior to the mental processes or states which are said to underlie them. Similarly, if one believes that all that happens in the world can be explained by the laws of physics, one has the great convenience of economy. One also has the convenience that a physicalistic view simplifies the problem of personal identity.

And so Ayer has provided us with three criteria: two for the rejection of a conceptual system (the criteria of unintelligibility and of emptiness of explanation), and one for the acceptance of a conceptual system—the criterion of convenience. In his treatment of the four examples, he has also provided us with an extended instance of philosophical inquiry in operation.

The picture of philosophy which emerges from Ayer's lectures is that of an enterprise with at least three functions: (1) elucidating or clarifying empirical concepts (whether ordinary or scientific), and mathematical and logical ones; (2) replacing the theoretical backgrounds, or conceptual systems, which underlie empirical statements (whether these backgrounds are explicit or only implicit), by other conceptual systems on the basis of the criterion of convenience; and (3) analyzing conceptual systems, with a view to constructive criticism or rejection or acceptance, as the need may be.

The fourth Perspectives lecturer, Stephen C. Pepper, spoke at Notre Dame during the third week of February, 1967. In his first lecture, Pepper gives an account of his own actual philosophy, of how he thinks philosophy ought to be done. The method of philosophy is not the method of certainty, as some have thought. Pepper does not give a detailed justification for rejecting the method of certainty. He simply notes that the bases of certainty from which various philosophers have, as a matter of historical fact, attempted to build firm views of the world have been so copious and mutually contrary, that throwing out the whole batch seemed to be the only reasonable thing to do; and he adds that "there will be occasion to consider the matter of the futility of the appeal to certainty in a concrete instance at a later lecture."

The method of philosophy is rather the method of hypothesis, and the underlying attitude is that of a healthy partial skepticism. The hypotheses of philosophy are world hypotheses, i.e., wholly *un*restricted hypotheses, hypotheses which take into account all evidence. A world hypothesis has all things within its scope, including the special sciences and everything else, however unreal these things may be claimed by some to be. It is in the absolute comprehensiveness of its scope that a world hypothesis differs from a scientific one. The aim of a world hypothesis is comprehensiveness of insight.

As philosophy is now done, observes Pepper, it performs some tasks outside the central one of comprehensive understanding. These other tasks he describes as mostly "leftovers" from the special sciences after they broke away from philosophy. Some of the examples he gives are the philosophy of science or scientific method, the philosophy of history, the philosophy of state, the philosophy of mind, and conceptual analysis. But the heart of philosophy is, and will continue to be an attempt at comprehensive understanding, an attempt at the construction of world hypotheses.

The guiding concepts of a world hypothesis are called categories, and these have their source in what Pepper calls a root metaphor—some striking or intense experience which suggests itself as promising for interpreting the whole of experience. The adequacy of a world hypothesis is judged in terms of the scope and precision of its guiding concepts. "Lack of scope happens whenever certain areas of evidence do not submit to consistent interpretation in terms of the guiding concepts." Also, "Lack of precision . . . occurs when more than one interpretation is consistent with, or worse, demanded by, the guiding concepts."

Pepper notes that in the whole of the history of philosophy, he has found only four world hypotheses which have proved to be relatively adequate: (1) formism, based on the root metaphor of similarity, and associated with Platonism and Aristotelian developments; (2) mechanism, built on the root metaphor of bodies in interaction, or parts of machines in interaction, and associated with the thinking initiated by Leucippus and Democritus and later developed by Galileo, Descartes, Hobbes, and others; (3) organicism, built on the root metaphor of a dynamic organic whole, associated with Hegel and his successors; and (4) contextualism (or pragmatism), based on the root metaphor of the passing historical event in its biological and cultural context, and associated with Dewey and his followers.

One of the main claims of this lecture is that he had come upon a new root metaphor, the metaphor of what he calls selectivism, and that it seemed to him to be more adequate than the root metaphors of formism, mechanism, organicism, and contextualism. He explained this new metaphor in terms of what is commonly called the means-end relation, but viewed in terms of the critical dynamic relation of the "drive for the end charging the drive for the means." If the drive for the end is not satisfied by the drive for the means, the drive for the end automatically selects both for and against certain means—against the incorrect ones and for the correct ones.

In Pepper's first lecture he describes philosophy as an attempt to devise the most adequate, that is, the most comprehensive and most precise world hypothesis, and attempts to defend the claim that selectivism, based on the root metaphor of purposive activity, is more adequate than any other known form of world hypothesis. But his second and third lectures turn to a consideration of ordinary language philosophy and of existentialism, for he had not taken these two movements into account either in his *World Hypotheses* (published early in 1942), or in any other of his publications since that time.

In his second lecture, actually delivered as the third one, Pepper examines linguistic analysis by concentrating on what he takes to be its vital core, the "ordinary language movement." His purpose is to relate this movement to the standpoint of his *World Hypotheses*. After a brief historical survey of ordinary language philosophy and of its origins in logical positivism, Pepper points out how this movement differs from *World Hypotheses* in its treatment of the disclosures of common sense and the meanings of ordinary language. Whereas this movement sets them up "as ultimate philosophical criteria over a wide range of experience," *World Hypotheses* describes common sense as a rich source of cognitive insight and of root metaphors, though common sense is nonetheless in itself a domain of confusion and vagueness and contradictions. And so this domain is never to be appealed to as to ultimate criteria; rather it is to be cognitively refined by what Pepper calls multiplicative or structural corroboration. This means that "the ultimate cognitive criteria are to be sought in the highest refinements of science, mathematics, and philosophy, including those most nearly adequate comprehensive syntheses which are world hypotheses."

In J. L. Austin, Pepper finds "the first inkling of something positive of fairly massive proportions to be found in the ordinary language program." Austin is of the view that the results of ordinary language philosophy are not the last word; they are not what Pepper calls the ultimate cognitive criteria. In fact, in his actual procedure Austin appeals to the dictionary, which is the repository not of the ordinary man's language alone, but of something much more, like "the large vocabulary and sensitive discriminations of a highly experienced author like Henry James." Austin also appeals to the usage of lawyers, psychologists, and anthropologists. Pepper commends Austin for making some approach to the procedure of *World Hypotheses* in that "Austin has made the important gesture of accepting data from special sciences and other institutions of experts even when these data have not as yet been hallowed by ordinary language." Austin's whole approach, notes Pepper, is positive and constructive rather than negative and destructive, as so much of the ordinary language program, and nearly all of Wittgenstein's, has been.

Roughly the last third of Pepper's lecture is devoted to a consideration of the results of ordinary language philosophy "in relation to those of synthetic philosophy as outlined in *World Hypotheses*." He chooses for this purpose Antony Flew's two series of selections in *Logic and Language;* this seems to him to offer a fair sampling of the extensive literature regarded as representative of this school. The destructive papers in these volumes—destructive in the sense of aiming at annihilating metaphysics—represent, according to Pepper, the weakest phase of the ordinary language movement. The destructive analyses are challenging but hardly ever decisive, and the perennial problems of metaphysical philosophy are still with us. As regards the constructive phase of the ordinary language movement, Pepper notes that he has been informed and stimulated in a number of respects. Nonetheless, the techniques of the ordinary language school will never be able to replace direct factual analysis or the need for synthetic philosophy and world hypotheses. It is only the path followed by the selection and employment of the root metaphor method that can be expected to provide us with what at least one ordinary language practitioner, J. J. C. Smart, calls "the tentative adumbration of a world view," which he sees as a function of philosophy over and above its simply unravelling conceptual and linguistic muddles.

Pepper's third lecture is an evaluation of existentialism as a world hypothesis; that is, existentialism as found in Sartre's *Being and Nothingness*. He restricts himself to Sartre since he believes Sartre to be most responsible for the initiating impulse of this movement. Besides, for his purpose of comparing the approach of existentialism in philosophy with that of *World Hypotheses,* "we cannot do better than to concentrate upon this one book"; even though he realizes that the movement has extended far beyond Sartre and that it "now has many branches, many orthodoxes and heterodoxes."

Pepper finds Sartre's existentialism defective for at least two reasons. First, there is its obsession with, or its over-concern for, certainties and indubitabilities, for the proper attitude underlying a world hypothesis is one of a healthy partial skepticism. "Sartre's appeal to certainty is comparable to the ordinary language school's appeal to common sense as a philosophical ultimate." Nonetheless, there is this basic difference: as far as Pepper can see, the linguistic movement evolves no system; Sartre's *Being and Nothingness,* significantly subtitled *An Essay on Phenomenological Ontology,* does reach out towards an unrestricted hypothesis, or complete ontological system.

Nonetheless, Sartre's existentialism is like mysticism in that it lacks scope. That is, it simply does not take into account all the facts, as an adequate world hypothesis must do. Sartre "denies outright that there is anything like the Freudian 'unconscious' connected with his for-itself." This is Pepper's second reason for claiming existentialism to be defective. And this lack of scope shows up even in the practical outcome of this philosophy, namely existential psychoanalysis. Sartre's denial of the Freudian unconscious has the consequence "that existential psychoanalysis is limited in its treatments to what can be found in the central voluntary area of consciousness." This restriction "cuts the existential analyst off from tracing back in depth to the traumatic incidents in the patient's past history, and the untangling of the drives progressively tangled up since then."

In spite of this overconcern for indubitabilities and this lack of scope, there is—according to Pepper—something fruitful in existentialism: its concern with the human situation, and its descriptions and analyses of *human purposive activities.* And Pepper would lift out bodily all that Sartre has to say on the human situation—excepting, however, the distorted and overdramatized, overanguished *way* in which Sartre presents it—and put it into his own world hypothesis, because what Sartre has to say on this point is wholly in line with the root metaphor of selectivism. This conclusion, Pepper admitted after the lecture, came as a surprise to him.

All in all, existentialism has much more to offer to world hypotheses than has ordinary language philosophy. Not only does it strive to construct a comprehensive view (which ordinary language philosophy does not), but it has even hit upon the root metaphor which seems to Pepper to be the most fruitful yet: the root metaphor of selectivism.

O. K. Bouwsma, the fifth and last of the Perspectives lecturers for the year 1966–67, delivered his lectures during the second week of March. Whereas his predecessors in the series approached the nature of philosophical inquiry by looking at it and describing what they saw, Bouwsma's approach is not primarily one of looking at and describing. Each of his lectures is designed mainly to *exhibit* philosophy (what *he* takes philosophy to be) in action. Bouwsma's aim in these lectures is to focus—not to defend but to focus—and to help avoid some possible misunderstandings about Wittgenstein as a philosopher.

His first lecture, a most inventive and artful one, can be described as having been delivered in *plain talk* (i.e., plain, ordinary, everyday, understandable English) about two other sorts of talk, in order to throw light on still another sort of talk. Throwing light on this last sort of talk meant dispelling an illusion of sense and understanding where there is no sense and understanding. Bouwsma talks first about double talk. He presents, and analyzes, a most entertaining piece of double talk which he composed himself. Double talk is *disguised* nonsense. Then he presents and analyzes a version of Jackie Vernon's story about his friend, the watermelon. This watermelon talk is *patent* nonsense. Then in terms of the distinction between disguised nonsense and patent nonsense he moves on to try to throw light on a certain sort of *ordinary* philosophical talk (as opposed to Wittgensteinian philosophical talk) which asks and tries to answer questions of the form, What is . . . .? Bouwsma uses the question, What is consciousness? as his example. He offers a piece of patent nonsense as an answer to the question, What is consciousness?, "in order to nudge one into examining the question," thereby coming to see that the question is a piece of disguised nonsense. "I offered patent nonsense in answer to a question which was disguised nonsense, as a step in the task of clarification." And so philosophy emerges as the art of spotting and dispelling illusions of sense and understanding where there is no sense and understanding.

Bouwsma devotes the last ten pages of his lecture to looking at and describing what he, proceeding as Wittgenstein would, has done in the preceding thirty. He describes what philosophy has as its task in a number of slightly different ways. The following seems to express it especially clearly: "I think I see now better than I ever did before what Wittgenstein has done and why it had to be done in this way. His task [as a philosopher] was to dispel a whole order of illusions, illusions which proceed from what Wittgenstein describes as 'misunderstandings' concerning the workings of our language." Although Wittgenstein is certainly concerned with philosophical questions, he does not treat them in any ordinary philosophical way. That is, he does not answer them; he questions them.

Bearing in mind that the main task of philosophy, in Wittgenstein's view and in his own, is to dispel (by various uses of plain talk) illusions of sense and understanding where there is no sense and understanding, Bouwsma turns in his second lecture to pursue that philosophical task with Descartes' *cogito, I think,* as the target.

He does three things. First, he tries to awaken an uneasiness or stir up a suspicion concerning what Descartes does with "I think" and with "I." By skillful and imaginative uses of plain talk, he indicates that the *I* of Descartes' "I think" is quite unlike the *I* of plain talk, that is, the *I* who speaks out of a mouth, the one we are all familiar with; so much so, in fact, that there are, in the end, two *I's*. There is the one *I,* Descartes, who speaks out of his mouth; but there is another one, the one that gets in and *thinks,* and by thinking mixes things up. The trouble, according to Bouwsma, is that there are two *I's,* but only one mouth. There ought to be a mouth for every I. At any rate, this is the case for the *I* of plain talk, the *I* we are all familiar with. And so, the thinking I is a mouthless I, and hence a shadow, not a human being.

Secondly, Bouwsma tries to show how it is that Descartes

comes to do what he does with *I think*. And he suggests that Descartes came to do it because of a tangle of what Wittgenstein describes as "grammatical" confusions. Descartes maintained that "I think" is both indubitable and true, and further that it is true because indubitable. Bouwsma calls to our attention three different ways of interpreting the distinction between the dubitable and the indubitable, which are already found imbedded in plain talk, and tries to show that most uses of the expression "I think" are indubitable in such a way that it does not make any sense to say that they are true, let alone to conclude that they must be true, as Descartes did with his "I think." "What is more natural, since it [i.e., "I think"] is indubitable, than to conclude [as Descartes did and wrongly] that it is true?; especially since it is sometimes used in such a way that it is true and furthermore has the form of many sentences which are true."

Thirdly, Bouwsma tries to show how Descartes would want us to understand his "I think." Descartes' "I think" is an "I think" in isolation. It is what remains after all dubitables have been removed; that is, the sky, the earth, all bodies, other minds. And what remains is "I think," though "not the words, but the wordless fact." This means that the *I* of "I think" is an embarrassed *I*, an *I* which finds itself in new and dumbfounding surroundings, so new and dumbfounding that the I "neither believes nor doubts nor imagines nor supposes nor sees nor fears nor guesses though it has a suspended capacity for doing all these things. And that is what "I think" is, suspended capacities."

In his third lecture, Bouwsma pursues the philosophical task, as he sees that task, with St. Anselm's ontological argument as the target. He takes a close look at five sentences in Anselm's argument, in order to "unscramble the scramble" in each of them—the scramble which grows and grows as Anselm goes on. As regards the first sentence, "We believe that thou art a being than which none greater can be conceived," Bouwsma argues at length the claim that the sentence mixes up the grammar of sentences of praise with the grammar of statements of belief. To put it differently, St. Anselm lifted a fragment of the language of praise out of the context of praise, and put it into a sentence stating a belief which looks like the result of a comparison in which Anselm discovered that God was greater than all conceivable things by a review of the praises of them all. But this confusion, according to Bouwsma, is only a transitional confusion.

There is another and similar confusion which operates in the argument proper, according to Bouwsma, and he tries to bring it to light in his look at the other four sentences, namely: "The fool hath said in his heart, there is no God"; "this very fool . . . understands what he hears"; "what he understands is in his understanding"; and "that than which nothing greater can be conceived cannot exist in the under-standing alone." Here too, according to Bouwsma, St. Anselm lifted scriptural talk about the fool out of its scriptural sur-roundings, so that his fool is not the fool of Scripture, and put this talk into a sentence stating the conclusion that God cannot be a mere idea or image or sensation, a conclusion which looks very much like the result of comparing God with mere ideas and images and sensations.

Bouwsma's conclusion, in summary, is that St. Anselm's argument is a collection of sentences which have been lifted out of their appropriate surroundings in Scripture (surround-ings in which they are at home and cause no difficulty) and have been placed into new and strange surroundings (those of an argument) in which they cause all sorts of difficulties—difficulties which make the argument very similar to the *I* of Descartes, the one without a mouth.

Like the mouthless *I* of Descartes, which is what remains after all the surroundings of the *I with a mouth* have been removed—sky, earth, all bodies, all other minds—St. Anselm's ontological argument is based on what remains of God and of the scriptural fool after their scriptural surroundings have been removed. The ontological argument cannot talk, for both its God and its fool are without a mouth.

STEPHAN KÖRNER

jur. Dr., Ph.D., F.B.A., was born on September 26, 1913, in Ostrava, Czechoslovakia, where he lived until 1939. He was educated at a classical gymnasium, then at Charles University in Prague, and Trinity Hall, Cambridge. His army service consisted of two periods, 1936–39, and 1943–46. In 1946 he was appointed to a lectureship in philosophy, and in 1952 to a professorship in philosophy (which he has held ever since), at the University of Bristol, England. He was visiting professor of philosophy at Brown University in 1957, at Yale University in 1960, at the University of Texas in 1964, and at Indiana University in 1967. He has been editor of the journal Ratio *since 1961. He was president of the British Society for Philosophy of Science in 1965; president of the Aristotelian Society in 1967; and is currently (1969) president of the International Union of History and Philosophy of Science.*

His principal books are Kant *(1955),* Conceptual Thinking *(1955, second edition, 1959),* The Philosophy of Mathematics *(1960),* Experience and Theory *(1966). He was editor of* Observation and Interpretation *(1957). He has also contributed to* Mind, Proceedings of the Aristotelian Society, *and to numerous other philosophical journals.*

DESCRIPTION, ANALYSIS AND METAPHYSICS

This essay contains the substance of three talks in a series of lectures given by philosophers of widely different backgrounds who were asked to explain their conception of philosophy. Philosophical thinking, more than any other intellectual activity, involves a great deal of conscious and deliberate reflection on its general aims and methods, which not infrequently gives rise to more or less elaborate methodological pronouncements or, at least, brief methodological *obiter dicta*. In explaining the conception of philosophy which has emerged from one's own work and reaction to the work of others, it is thus not only necessary to look back but also difficult to avoid repeating oneself.

The following remarks are divided into four sections. Section I contains a discussion of some well-known Cartesian theses to the effect that philosophy consists in the application of a special method which results in the establishment of indubitable propositions and which, *a fortiori*, protects philosophical inquiry against the intrusion of mere speculations and assumptions. In sections II and III the allegedly autonomous methods of phenomenology and analytical philosophy are examined. It is argued that their application is not free from assumptions which—whether or not one regards them as "metaphysical"—are neither indispensable to everybody's thinking nor in fact made by everybody. In section IV an account is given of metaphysics as being largely concerned with the exhibition, modification, and speculative proposal of categorial frameworks. This account, which is comparatively new, grew out of a critical examination of Kant's Transcendental Deduction of the Categories and of later versions of it in post-Kantian and contemporary philosophy.[1] On the other hand much of the material of section II and III is not new.[2]

I

Although by no means the only begetter of modern philosophy, Descartes is rightly regarded as one of its founding fathers. He has influenced his successors not only by his own extreme doctrine of the nature and function of philosophical thinking, but also—indirectly—by some of the more moderate and modest implications of his views. It seems useful to start this essay with a critical examination of his more extreme methodological theses. Decartes rejects all philosophical speculation which does not lead to absolutely certain results as ill-founded, and claims to have discovered a method by which incorrigible philosophical truths can be discovered. The gist of the method is formulated in the following passages of the *Regulae ad directionem ingenii*.[3]

(I) "In the subjects which we propose to investigate one should search for . . . what can be seen clearly and with self-evidence or deduced with certainty" (Rule III).

(II) "By *intuition* I understand, not the fluctuating assurance of the senses nor the fallacious judgment based on misleading imaginary constructions but the conception which emerges in an unclouded and attentive mind so easily and distinctly that no doubt is left about that which we understand" (comments on Rule III).

(III) *Deduction* is based on the recognition of necessary connections—a connection between things being necessary "when one is implied in the other in a confused manner so that we cannot conceive either of them distinctly if we judge them as separate from each other" (comments on Rule XII).

(IV) To bring intuition and deduction into play, a preliminary *analysis* is required which consists in "reducing obscure and complicated propositions gradually to simpler ones and afterwards in starting with the intuition of the simplest things. . . ." (Rule V).

The Cartesian doctrine of intuition gives rise to serious difficulties. The indubitability of an intuition is assumed to guarantee its intersubjectivity. Yet what seems indubitable to one person may seem dubious to others. If, however, intersubjectivity is used as a criterion for the distinction between apparent and genuine intuitions, the doctrine of intuition becomes viciously circular. Similarly the indubitability of an intuition is assumed to guarantee its truth or, more precisely, the truth of any statement which correctly describes an intuition. Yet what seems indubitable may turn out to be false. If, however, truth is used as a criterion for the distinction between apparent and genuine indubitability, the doctrine becomes viciously circular once again.

Descartes tries to avoid these pitfalls by proposing to "start with the simplest things" (IV above). This injunction seems to require an analysis of all complex propositions into explicit, logically equivalent conjunctions, the members of which cannot be further analyzed in this manner. But even in the case of such "simple" propositions the distinction between apparently indubitable and genuinely indubitable propositions may be controversial. Another *prima facie* more promising sense of the injunction, which is also found in Descartes' writings, equates simplicity with freedom from interpretation. A proposition is simple in this sense if it correctly describes what is given in consciousness just as it is given. The idea of absolute description is central to Descartes' phenomenological successors and will be examined below.

According to Descartes no set of indubitable propositions, i.e. no set of propositions correctly describing intuitions, is sufficient for the systematic development of any branch of philosophy or science. Nor is it sufficient to enlarge this set by its *logical* consequences, since "as regards logic its syllogisms and the major part of its other instructions serve on the whole the purpose of explaining to others what one already knows."[4] It makes the content of the premises explicit without adding to it. Cartesian deduction is not, or not merely, logical deduction; and the necessary connection on which it is based (see III above) is not a logical implication. What it is, is not clear, and is (as we shall see), made not much clearer by the historical observation that its influence can be seen in some post-Cartesian transcendental, dialectical, phenomenological, and other philosophical arguments.

The Cartesian notion of necessary connection is first of all exposed to the same objections as the Cartesian notion of intuition: the indubitability to a thinker of a necessary connection is supposed to guarantee its intersubjectivity and truth, although intersubjectivity and truth have often to serve as criteria for distinguishing between apparently and genuinely necessary connections. Analysis of large inferential steps from Cartesian antecedent to consequent into a sequence of simple steps (after the fashion of formal deduction), will not remove the objections to the notion of Cartesian deduction; just as analysis of complex propositions into explicit conjunctions of simple components will not remove the objections to the notion of Cartesian intuition.

A further difficulty attaches to the relation between Cartesian intuition and Cartesian deduction. On the one hand Descartes demands that philosophical reasoning should start with propositions which are clear and distinct (see II above). On the other hand, philosophical reasoning involves the recognition that its premise cannot be conceived clearly and distinctly in separation from the conclusion (see III above). But then the reasoning either cannot start (because the premise is only confusedly apprehended), or else it is superfluous (since, if the premise is clearly apprehended, its connection with the conclusion and the conclusion itself is also clearly apprehended). Its Cartesian deduction would then at most "serve the purpose of explaining . . . what one already knows." This dilemma seems to have been recognized by some of Descartes' successors. Thus Brentano, who substantially takes over the Cartesian doctrine of intuition, does not pretend to employ any but the normal deductive and inductive methods of inference. As against this, Hegel and the adherents of a coherence-theory of truth (who substantially take over the Cartesian doctrine of deduction) hold that clarity, and even truth, is reached not at the beginning but only at the end of philosophical reasoning, when all (non-logical) necessary connections have been laid bare and their whole network has been uncovered.

Descartes conceives philosophy, mathematics, and even science as intellectual discovery, and not as in any way invention. Although his own philosophy, like every other, is inseparable from metaphysical assumptions, it is so in fact and not in intention. He misunderstood the nature of the activity which he so brilliantly pursued. And it is this misunderstanding which he bequeathed not only to his later rationalist followers, but also to the empiricists, Kantians, and most others who came after him.

II

The most obvious descendant of Descartes' methodology is Husserl's phenomenological method.[5] For our purpose it is not necessary to show that the so-called phenomenological reduction is supposed to yield Cartesian or near-Cartesian intuitions, and the so-called eidetic reduction of Cartesian or near Cartesian necessary connections. Whatever the outcome of this comparison may be, Husserl claims to have discovered both a method for the exhibition of what is given in consciousness and quite separated from any admixture of hypothetical interpretation, and a method for the expression of what is so given in purely descriptive propositions.

In order to appreciate the usefulness of Husserl's method for philosophy, it is convenient to separate the strong claim that it is possible to formulate purely descriptive propositions in the knowledge that one has done so, from the implied weaker claim that it is possible to distinguish within some pairs of propositions the more interpretative (less descriptive) from the less interpretative (more descriptive) member. Both claims are rather vague; but the weaker claim can be made more precise and justified. Consider two concepts P and Q, each of which is applicable to perceivable objects. Let us call P and Q "co-ostensive" if, and only if, the applicability of P to an object entails the applicability of the same perceptual characteristics to it as does the applicability of Q. For example, the concept 'x is a table,' as employed in ordinary life, and the sophisticated concept 'x is a table as conceived by Plato' (as conceived by Leibniz, Hume, Kant, the adherents of some physical theory, etc.) are all co-ostensive. Yet the sophisticated concepts are more interpetative than the everyday one. The reason for this gradation is that the applicability of each of the sophisticated concepts to an object entails, but is not entailed by, the applicability to it of the ordinary concept.

Briefly, if in the case of two co-ostensive concepts P and Q, the applicability of P to an object unilaterally entails the applicability of Q to it, then P is more interpetative than Q. In order to make these explanations more complete one would have to make the sense of 'entails' and of 'perceptual characteristic' clearer, and to admit that neither of them has a sharp demarcation. Since this admission would, however, only strengthen the points I wish to make, the further clarification may be omitted. For similar reasons I shall not attempt to answer the question: How far could concepts which are not co-ostensive and concepts which do not stand in entailment-relations be compared with respect to their relative degree of interpretativeness?[6]

However, even if such relative comparisons were always possible, this would imply neither the existence of nor the availability of a criterion for absolutely descriptive concepts and absolutely descriptive propositions. The applicability of 'less than' does not entail the applicability of 'absolutely least,' and, more particularly, the applicability of 'less descriptive' does not entail the applicability of 'absolutely least descriptive.' Statements which appear to be purely descriptive may turn out to contain avoidable interpretations. Another difficulty about absolute descriptions is connected with the problem of translation from one language or conceptual framework into another. Phenomenologists assume that absolute descriptions of the same phenomenon are expressible in different languages, including their own. Yet unless two statements have absolutely the same meaning, at least one of them is not an absolute description of the phenomenon. The notion of absolute sameness of meaning and the question of criteria for its applications are, if anything, even more problematic than the notion of absolute descriptiveness and the question of criteria for its application.

Let us assume that a concept P is mistakenly regarded as absolutely descriptive. This means that one has overlooked the possible employment of a more descriptive concept Q such that P and Q are co-ostensive, and such that the applicability of P to an object unilaterally entails the applicability of Q to it. If the applicability of P to an object unilaterally entails the applicability of Q to this object, then there exists as a matter of logic (the possibility of defining) a concept—say, I such that P is equivalent to the conjunction of Q and I; i.e., such that the applicability of P to an object entails, and is entailed by, the joint applicability of Q and I to it. Since P and Q are co-ostensive, I is not a perceptual characteristic. It is, as it were, the nonperceptual, purely interpretative or a priori difference between P and Q.

Co-ostensive concepts, such as the concepts of a Platonic,

Humean, or Leibnizian table, may differ from each other by mutually exclusive a priori components. In the case of these particular concepts, their interpretative differences are unlikely to be overlooked. Yet when no alternatives are available or for the time being conceivable, their possibility may easily escape notice and a particular interpretation may be regarded as the only possible one. The phenomenological method not only lacks the means for yielding absolute descriptions, but also the means for distinguishing between interpretations which admit of alternatives, and interpretations (if any) which are unique. It is thus not immune against the intrusion of assumptions which change from one person or group of persons to another and are, therefore, not indispensable to everybody's thinking. And it gives no account of the source and function of these assumptions.

The phenomenological method falls short of the autonomy which Husserl and his successors ascribed to it. But there can be little doubt about the usefulness of occasionally pushing the distinction between relatively descriptive and interpretative concepts and propositions further than is normally done in daily life or in scientific thinking. In failing to do so, one may miss opportunities for the critical examination, reconstruction, or total abandonment of habitual modes of thought which are inadequate to old purposes or to new ones. For example, a more radical distinction than is usually made between the impression of a limited freedom of action and its interpretation in the light of deeply rooted religious, scientific, or other assumptions, is a precondition of many philosophical attempts to make sense of the apparent conflict between freedom and natural necessity.

III

In spite of some antagonisms between the phenomenological and the analytical movement in modern philosophy, both these movements hold fast to the Cartesian ideal of philosophy as the nonspeculative clarification of experience.

The rejection of speculative metaphysics is common to all analytical philosophers. So also is the restriction of the subject matter of philosophy from the clarification of all phenomena of human experience to that of linguistic or conceptually organized phenomena. Philosophy is conceived as linguistic or conceptual analysis—the analysis of natural languages, of theories, and sometimes of a preferred natural language, often called "ordinary language." Most analytical philosophers are skeptical about Cartesian intuitions, at least outside mathematics; but many of them have revived the unclear Cartesian notion of necessary connection under new names such as 'conceptual necessity' or 'coherence.'

"Philosophical analysis" covers at least two very different types of philosophical activity, the confusion of which may give rise to serious errors. It may, in particular, give rise to the wrong impression that both types of analysis are independent of metaphysical assumptions. The difference between the two types of analysis is connected with an ambiguity in the use of the term 'clarification,' which may imply on the one hand that what is being clarified is merely recognized more clearly; on the other hand, that what is being clarified is thereby also modified. Both kinds of clarification could without too much artificiality be traced back to Descartes.

Since I have explained the nature of exhibition- and replacement-analysis and their differences elsewhere, I can put my points very briefly. The task of exhibition-analysis is, roughly speaking, the exhibition of the meaning of concepts which a person or group of persons employ in their thinking. It consists in the explicit formulation of rules (or other criteria reducible to rules), conformity to which constitutes for the person or group of persons the correct employment of the concepts in question. An exhibition-analysis thus results in empirical propositions to the effect that the person or group of persons has adopted such and such rules in his thinking or language. The adoption of a rule, or the intention to satisfy it, may be implicit and does not imply that the person who has (implicitly) adopted a rule is capable of formulating it himself. The implicit adoption of a rule, i.e., the implicit intention to satisfy it, may manifest itself in the person's ability "instinctively" to distinguish between correct and incorrect performances in such a manner that he regards a performance respectively as correct or as incorrect if, and only if, it conforms to or violates the rules which the exhibition-analysis has brought to light. The exhibition-analyst's inquiry is thus empirical in the same sense as the inquiry of a scientific linguist or anthropologist.

As a philosopher the exhibition-analyst is, of course, not equally interested in all the rules which are adopted by a person or a group of persons, but only in those which have some bearing on philosophical questions which have exercised him or others. The problems of exhibition-analysis are frequently far from trivial—for example, when one has to show that philosophically relevant rules which are established by an appeal to every person's thought or language are in fact not adopted as widely as assumed, or are not adopted at all. The application of the so-called Socratic method, displayed in some Platonic dialogues, and of Kant's regressive method are examples of exhibition-analysis.

Exhibition-analysis resembles phenomenology in aiming at description without interpretation, even though the phenomena it is intended to describe are exclusively linguistic. In this connection, it is of some interest to note that the late Professor Austin once suggested that the term "linguistic phenomenology" might be a better name for his way of doing philosophy than "linguistic" or "analytic" philosophy.[7] Like Husserl's phenomenology, exhibition-analysis or linguistic phenomenology is not immune from the intrusion of unnoticed assumptions and has no means to distinguish indispensable linguistic features, if any, from those which change from one person or group of persons to another. Theoretical linguistics criticize the philosophical practitioners of exhibition-analysis for lacking any theory of language. But the absence of an explicit theory does not imply that the conceptual apparatus used in linguistic descriptions is free from dispensable interpretative concepts and assumptions admitting of alternatives.

Even if one conceded, for the sake of argument, that exhibition-analysis yields pure descriptions without interpretative assumptions, analytical philosophers in their practice rarely rest content with exhibition-analysis. For this type of analysis frequently reveals that the exhibited rules are inadequate for their purposes or, at least, capable of improvement. It may reveal confusions, gaps, and even contradictions where none were suspected. The classical examples of unsuspected contradictions are found in "naïve" set-theory (and those parts of the natural languages in which a similar notion of set is employed). Briefly, when the attempt at clarification without modification reveals defects in the linguistic phenomena which are to be clarified, modification becomes necessary. Exhibition-analysis gives way to reconstruction, which often takes the form of replacement-analysis.

A replacement-analysis consists in the replacement of a defective concept (or a set of concepts) by a concept which is free from the defects of the former, and stands to it in a relation which guarantees the suitability of the new concept for the purposes for which the old one has been employed or intended. For example, the concept of a set as defined in Russell's simple theory of types is the result of a replacement-analysis of the original Fregean concept of a set and its cognates in other theories and natural languages. Let us write A for the concept which is to be replaced, the so-called 'analysandum'; X for the so-called 'analysans,' i.e. the concept, if any, which is to replace A; 'D' for the criteria by which the defectiveness or otherwise of concepts is being judged; and R for the so-called "analyzing" or "replacement-relation" which guarantees the suitability of X for the purposes for which A has been employed or intended. The form of a problem in replacement-analysis can then be generally expressed as follows: Given A which is defective according to D, to find an X which is not defective according to D, such that X stands to A in the relation R.

Although the differences between exhibition- and replacement-analysis are fairly obvious, it is worthwhile to emphasize at least some of them. First, the answer to a problem of exhibition-analysis is always—as has been mentioned already —an empirical proposition. The answer to a problem of replacement analysis may be a nonempirical proposition, the truth of which depends on the meaning of rules rather than on empirical facts. Second, every problem of exhibition-analysis has one, and only one, solution; whereas a problem of replacement-analysis may have no solution or more than one—depending on the criteria of defectiveness and on the replacement relation in terms of which the problem is stated. This fact is easily overlooked when the problem is not clearly formulated, i.e., when it is rather vaguely characterized as an attempt at rational reconstruction or explication. Third, since replacement-analysis differs from exhibition-analysis in presupposing criteria of defectiveness which may change from one group of philosophers to another, replacement-analysis raises the question as to the provenience of these criteria.

They may have their origin in fairly common needs or desires. Thus most people will regard internal inconsistency and misleading vagueness as defects of concepts and conceptual networks and try to eliminate them. On the other hand the criteria of defectiveness may have their roots in more or less idiosyncratic convictions, such as religious and metaphysical doctrines. A person who is committed to a monotheistic faith cannot without qualifications employ concepts which imply that there is no God. Nor can a metaphysical materialist employ without qualification concepts whose correct application implies the existence of mental substances. Clearly, one analytical philosopher's metaphysical criteria of defectiveness may be another analytical philosopher's metaphysical criteria of soundness. But it does not follow that since every analyst can dispense with some other analyst's criteria of defectiveness, and thus with some metaphysics, every analyst can—or cannot—dispense with all metaphysical criteria of defectiveness and thus with all metaphysics.

IV

Phenomenological description, exhibition- and replacement-analysis are not autonomous philosophical methods,
since each of them employs tacit or at least unquestioned
assumptions, which it does not establish. Phenomenological
description and exhibition-analysis involve the application of
purely interpretative a priori concepts and thus the assumption of their applicability. Replacement-analysis presupposes
criteria of the defectiveness of concepts which go beyond
the demands that their application should be consistent with
sense experience and should not lead to contradictions. Thus
it, too, rests on assumptions which are in some sense a priori.
Even though few philosophers have tried to demarcate the
class of metaphysical propositions or at least some philosophically important subclass of them by means of a definition, unquestioned "a priori" assumptions of the sort entering
the allegedly autonomous methods of phenomenological
description, exhibition- and replacement-analysis have usually
been regarded as "metaphysical." Exceptions are Hume's
doctrine of the meaninglessness of all nonempirical and non-
logico-mathematical propositions, Kant's account of synthetic
a priori propositions, and Collingwood's theory of absolute
presuppositions.

I shall here say nothing about the Kantian or the Humean
account. The former will be seen to be partly (the latter
wholly) incompatible with the subsequent discussion of
categorial frameworks. A few words, however, about Collingwood's identification of metaphysical propositions with absolute presuppositions seem appropriate in the present context.[8]
According to Collingwood "every statement that anybody
ever makes is made in answer to a question" and involves a
"presupposition . . . from which it directly and immediately
'arises'." A presupposition is "either proximate or absolute."
Whereas a proximate presupposition "stands relatively to one
question as its presupposition and relatively to another question as its answer," an absolute presupposition "stands rela-

tively to all questions to which it is related, as a presupposition, never as an answer." It is thus not a true or false answer to any question. "Metaphysics," according to Collingwood, "is the attempt to find out what absolute presuppositions have been made by this or that person or group of persons, on this or that group of occasions, in this or that piece of thinking."[9]

Among the merits of Collingwood's account are that the absolute presuppositions which he identified with metaphysical theses need not be empirical or logical—at least not in Hume's and the logical positivists' sense; that such presuppositions are made by all thinkers, including scientists and logicians; and that they are not exempt from change and replacement in the course of history. Yet his account is both too narrow and too wide. It is too narrow in regarding metaphysical thinking as a species of exhibition-analysis, aiming at the discovery of absolute presuppositions. It excludes metaphysical speculation and innovation; that is to say, the proposal of new metaphysical theses to thinkers who have not accepted them as absolute presuppositions and so far have not even tried to make up their mind about accepting them.

Collingwood's account is too wide since principles of any kind could be absolute, unquestioned presuppositions; for example, the law of excluded middle, the principles of Aristotelian or Newtonian physics, all kinds of religious dogma. The reason for this is that Collingwood defines metaphysical principles by the manner of their acceptance, rather than by their content. This does not mean that Collingwood's conception of a historical science of absolute presuppositions is in any way illegitimate. Its usefulness to general history, anthropology, and sociology can hardly be questioned. It might, however, be better not to call it "metaphysics," but, for example, "historical dogmatics," or—more clumsily—"exhibition-analysis of unquestioned presuppositions."

It is possible, I believe, at least to demarcate a central concern of metaphysicians from Aristotle to the present day in a philosophically illuminating manner by concentrating on the attention which all of them have given to the categorization of the universe or possible experience, to the articulation of categories of the highest kinds, the *summa genera,* to distinguishing these categories from each other, to exhibiting their interrelations, and to explaining their role in commonsense and scientific thinking. The result will be a definition of metaphysics in a narrow sense, as the exhibition, modification and speculative proposal of categorial frameworks. We might call this kind of metaphysics "categorial metaphysics" or "framework-metaphysics."

A categorization of the universe in the sense of everything there *is* or *is knowable* is, as it were, merely the highest level of a classification. It determines the highest genera in terms of which a person or group of persons think, or might think, about the world. Concerning each category of entities—i.e., the category, *if any,* of external phenomena, of facts, of processes, of mental acts, of angels etc.—metaphysicians have asked two questions; namely (1) what constitutes an entity of the category, and (2) what individuates an entity of the category, i.e., what makes an entity of the category a distinct individual belonging to it. They thus aimed at determining the "constitutive" and "individuating" attributes of one or more categories of objects.

An attribute is *constitutive* of the entities of a category if, and only if, (a) the attribute is applicable to the entities of the category, and (b) the applicability of the attribute to an entity logically implies that the entity belongs to the category. An attribute is *individuating* for the entities of a category if, and only if, (a) the attribute is applicable to every entity of the category, and (b) the applicability of the attribute to the entity logically implies the entity's being a distinct individual belonging to the category. To every constitutive or individuating attribute associated with a category of entities, there corresponds respectively a "constitutive" or "individuating" principle expressing the applicability of the attribute to the entities. A categorization of the universe together with the individuating attributes and principles which are associated with each category will be called a categorial framework.

Strictly speaking, the logic in terms of which "logically implies" (as used in the above definitions) is defined, should also be made part of the definition of a categorial framework. But I omit this qualification.[10]

The definition of a categorial framework reminds one both of Kant and Collingwood. Kant's Transcendental Aesthetic exhibits the individuating attributes and principles; Kant's Transcendental Analytic the constitutive attributes and principles of the category of external phenomena, employed in the common sense and science which he investigated in the *Critique of Pure Reason*. These individuating and constitutive principles were Collingwoodian, absolute presuppositions of Kant's thinking. Kant, however (unlike Collingwood), not only could not conceive that these principles might ever be abandoned or modified, but even attempted a proof, the so-called "transcendental deduction of the categories" to the effect that they could never be abandoned because they are indispensable to all thinking about an objective experience of the external world.

A metaphysician may be concerned with categorial frameworks in a number of ways; the following three are of special interest. First of all, he may approach a categorial framework from the outside with the aim of exhibiting the associated constitutive and individuating principles employed by a group of thinkers. This historical or anthropological approach results, as a species of exhibition-analysis, in empirical statements to the effect that such and such constitutive or individuating principles are in fact employed by a group of thinkers. Secondly, he may for a variety of reasons try to construct a new, or radically modified categorial framework. This constructive or speculative approach results in the proposal of a new categorization of the universe with new constitutive and individuating principles or at least in the proposal of new constitutive or individuating principles.

The third, or transcendental, approach results in claiming to have established the individuating and constitutive principles as incorrigible, synthetic a priori principles, a claim which is largely illusory. The principles are indeed synthetic since each implies an existential statement to the effect that a (constitutive or individuating) attribute is not empty. They are also a priori *in the limited or relative sense* that no statement about objects, as constituted by the constitutive attributes and individuated by the individuating attributes of a categorial framework, can be incompatible with the constitutive and individuating principles *of this particular framework*. The principles are synthetic a priori with respect to the categorial framework with which they are associated. However, they are not therefore synthetic a priori with respect to every categorial framework. Kant confused relative with absolute constitutive and individuating principles. It is in the main this confusion between relative and absolute synthetic a priori propositions, which invalidates his transcendental deduction of the Categories and some subsequent versions of it.

Insofar as thinking employs a classificatory scheme, i.e. class and relational concepts, it employs categories. If the entities belonging to a category are the bearers of constitutive and individuating attributes, then the thinking in question takes place in a categorial framework. Its associated constitutive and individuating principles appear to the thinker who confines himself to his classificatory scheme or at least to the categories of this scheme, as incorrigible (synthetic a priori) propositions. This internal incorrigibility, however, must not be confused with incorrigibility *simpliciter*. It does not, as is borne out by the history of philosophy and even more strikingly by anthropology, preclude conceptual change—in particular the change of categorical frameworks. Since constitutive and individuating principles are (on almost all accounts of metaphysics) metaphysical propositions, and since much common sense thinking (and all scientific thinking as we know it) takes place in categorial frameworks, metaphysics forms an integral part of common sense and science.

It is equally clear that the application of the allegedly autonomous philosophical methods, examined earlier, takes place within classificatory schemes, and thus, normally, within categorial frameworks. The individuating and, in particular the constitutive principles associated with a particular categorial framework thus naturally enter phenomenological description, exhibition-analysis, and replacement-analysis. Every phenomenological description presupposes a classification and categorization of the described phenomena; every exhibition-analysis a classification and categorization of the exhibited linguistic rules and regularities. Again, the individuating and constitutive principles associated with a particular categorial framework may function as criteria of soundness for replacement-analysis. Indeed, replacement-analysis is frequently the means for resisting conceptual change by transposing (not translating!) statements from one categorial framework into another.

Constitutive and individuating principles do not, of course, exhaust the class of propositions which by general (or almost general) consent are regarded as metaphysical. There are the "transcategorial" principles, which are constitutive of any object, whatever category it may belong to. Examples are Leibniz's principle of sufficient reason and Berkeley's *esse est percipi,* and—at least on Aristotle's view—the principles of logic. Again some logical consequences of constitutive in conjunction with other principles would be regarded as metaphysical. An example is the principle of continuity, which Kant deduces from his constitutive principle of causality and the assumption that "neither time nor what appears in time consists of smallest parts."[11] If one were to put forward general criteria which should be jointly satisfied by metaphysical propositions, one might propose the following: (1) A metaphysical principle should be corrigible in the sense of possibly conflicting with other propositions such that the conflict is resolvable by abandoning the principle in favor of some alternative. (2) It should not be a substitution instance of a logical principle, which is what Kant meant by calling metaphysical principles synthetic. (3) It should not be empirical in the sense that its truth or falsehood is decidable by experiment or observation. This is part of what Kant meant by calling metaphysical propositions a priori. (4) A metaphysical proposition should be comprehensive in the sense of referring to all entities of at least one category. The constitutive and individuating principles associated with a categorial framework satisfy all these conditions.

Once the mistake of confusing the internal corrigibility of these (and other) metaphysical principles is recognized, it becomes fairly easy to refute some favorite metaphysical arguments, such as transcendental and dialectical "deductions." It also becomes obvious that the so-called arguments which consist in accusing another philosopher of a "category-mistake" are frequently no more than an invitation to abandon his categorization for that of his opponent. A proper discussion of these matters would, however, take more room than can be decently claimed on this occasion.

NOTES

1. See "Transcendental Tendencies in Recent Philosophy," *The Journal of Philosophy* LXIII, no. 19 (1966), 551–561. Also, "The Impossibility of Transcendental Deductions," *The Monist* LI, no. 3, 317–331.

2. See, for example, "Broad on Philosophical Method," *The Philosophy of C. D. Broad*, ed. Paul Arthur Schilpp (New York: Tudor, 1959), pp. 95–114.

3. René Descartes, "Regulae ad Directionem Ingenii," *Oeuvres de Descartes* X, Adam-Tannery edition (Paris: Cerf, 1897–1913), pp. 359–469. Cf. Leslie John Beck, *The Method of Descartes: A Study of the Regulae* (Oxford: Clarendon Press, 1952).

4. René Descartes, *Discours de la Méthode* VI, Adam-Tannery edition, p. 17.

5. H. L. Van Breda, ed., *Cartesianische Meditationen und Pariser Vorträge,* in *Husserliana,* collected works of Edmund Husserl, vol. I (Haag: Martinus Nijhoff, 1950).

6. This might be done along the lines of *Conceptual Thinking* (Cambridge: University of Bristol Press, 1955), chapter XVII.

7. J. L. Austin, "A Plea for Excuses," *Proceedings of the Aristotelian Society* LVII (1956–57), p. 8.

8. R. G. Collingwood, *An Essay on Metaphysics* (Oxford: Clarendon Press, 1940), especially chapter XVI.

9. *Ibid.,* p. 47.

10. See "Transcendental Tendencies in Recent Philosophy," *op. cit.* Also *What is Philosophy? One Philosopher's Answer* (London: The Allen Lane Penguin Press, 1969).

11. Immanuel Kant, *Critique of Pure Reason,* A 209, B 254.

MARTHINUS VERSFELD

was born on August 11, 1909, in Cape Town, Republic of South Africa. He was educated at the South African College School, and the University of Cape Town (1927–31), where he took the degrees of B.A. and M.A. in philosophy. He pursued further studies at the University of Glasgow (1931–34), where he received his Ph.D. Shortly thereafter, he was appointed to the department of philosophy at the University of Cape Town, where his present rank is that of associate professor of philosophy. He was elected to the Suid-Afrikaanse Akademie in 1965.

Among his published books are the following: An Essay on the Metaphysics of Descartes *(1940),* Oor Gode en Afgode *(1948),* The Perennial Order *(1954),* A Guide to the "City of God" *(1958),* The Mirror of Philosophers *(1960),* Rondom die Middeleeue *(1962),* Berge van die Boland [with W. A. de Klerk] *(1947, 1965),* Wat is Kontemporêr? *(1966), and* Klip en Klei *(1968). Besides this array—a good portion of which was written in Afrikaans—he has done translations, contributed chapters to books and articles to encyclopedias, and written innumerable essays which have appeared in professional journals the world over.*

METAPHYSICS IN OUR TIME

It is impossible to say what metaphysics is from the outside and from the outside to affirm that it is an invalid kind of knowledge. The latter attempt would be rather like singing a demonstration, that there was no such thing as music, in Gregorian chant, though one might expect that under such circumstances the rules of the chant would not be very well known. If the raising of the question: what is metaphysics, assumes that one can take up an "objective" and uninvolved attitude, the answer is already settled, at whatever price in self-contradiction: there is no such thing. It is well enough known how the manner of putting the question determines the answer.

There is a curious little book called *The Nature of Metaphysics*[1] written by members of the British analytical school, which illustrates the case in point. It reminds one of the lines in the Lay of St. Gengulphus: "They put him in mind of a Council of Trent engaged in reviewing a diet of worms." One might say that it gives a cockatrice's eye view of metaphysics. Or one might recall the story of the emperor's clothes, with a difference. You have people declaring that the empress has no clothes, and discussing her anatomy while she is present fully dressed. This is rude and may be risky.

What one senses is a certain insulation from the matter at hand. If the corpse does not smell too bad it is because the thought is so antiseptic. "When I speak about modern philosophers and modern philosophy," says Miss Murdoch, "I shall be meaning that present-day version of our traditional empiricism which is known as linguistic analysis."[2] For example, "Fog on the Channel; Continent Isolated," as the headlines put it on one occasion. Mr. Warnock mentions "the assumption that its (positivism's) classification of types of significant discourse is complete."[3] The assumption extends further than positivism.

At the back of this endeavor to discover the nature of metaphysics lies a false assumption, that you have to do with a nature capable of definition or that you can reduce various manifestations of metaphysical thinking to a generic concept. To put it differently: that the word 'metaphysics' can be used univocally. It is like lumping men together under the concept of humanity, at the price of losing the capacity to see the living person. The language behavior of some existentialists is very similar. Thus Chestov writes as though 'rational discourse' means the same thing when applied to Plato, St. Thomas, Leibniz, Hegel etc. The fact there may be irrationalist philosophies like his own and like Hegel's thus entirely escapes his attention, just as the fact that there may be antimetaphysical metaphysics is not observed by the analysts. The analysts, in fact, make the same mistake about metaphysics that Hegel makes about being, when he thinks of it as a genus. As a consequence, a flavor of old fashioned Hegelian essentialism clings to these modern philosophers, and the body under inspection is decorously bedecked with lavender and old lace. Such a metaphysics is indeed a "metaphysical entity," so that it is no wonder that it displays the anat-

omy which has been foisted upon it. No wonder that so
many modern philosophers know the meaning of certain
ethical, metaphysical, and theological propositions better
than the proponents themselves. They have reached the conceptual clarity which becomes possible when we *decide* what
things are to mean for our purposes. Thought is to be in
terms of concepts which dictate to things; or the real is
the rational, and metaphysics is described as a conceptual
framework.

What one has to do with, consequently, is a sort of effete
Platonism, which has very little to do with the Platonism of
Plato. It is as well to remember that if the British tradition
is empirical it has also been, at least since the time of Grosseteste, Platonic, and the empiricism and Platonism have
some curious links. The links exist at the price of conceptual-
izing Plato, so that one encounters the curious phenomenon
of Plato being used to attack Plato, and of metaphysical
entities being used to condemn metaphysical entities.

Thus Professor Walsh tells us that Plato did not know
what metaphysics was, meaning I suppose that he had not
succeeded in defining an essence; and indeed that he was
obscure about what philosophy was.[4] It is true, we may comment, that Plato did think that it was a kind of wisdom, but
then, as Socrates said at his trial, "Perhaps, gentlemen, only
God is wise," so that Plato was perhaps intentionally nescient
in matters philosophical. We should consider whether the
nescience of Plato was not perhaps intentional, and that he
must have known a great deal to know that he knew so little.
There is such a thing as what Jaspers, in his excellent account
of Plato, calls a knowledge of nonknowledge, but it will never
be possible to those who think that they can exhaust essences
in clear and distinct ideas. Plato held that we cannot grasp
the essence of philosophy. It is true that Professor Walsh
wrote in Edinburgh under the Christian dispensation so that
what philosophy is may have been revealed to him. Hegel,
too, endeavored to import the divine self-consciousness into
human reason. Rationalism is a pretension to divinity. It is

perhaps precisely in his reticence and inclusiveness that the real conclusions of Plato must be sought, and perhaps we ought to consider the possibility that it is not we who are to judge metaphysics, but that it is metaphysics which judges us. In the last resort it is not we who question being, but being which questions us, and if, as Professor Ryle says, "ontology is out," it is because ontologism is in, and because he is arguing from the essence of metaphysics to its nonexistence. But this is merely bad theology. An imperialism of the mind seems to be the ghost left in the broken-down machine of the Empire.

To pretend to know what philosophy is or what metaphysics is, is to pretend that you have to do with essences which can be clearly and distinctly conceived, and this is to out-Plato Plato. According to Plato, a science is defined by determining with what subject matter it has to do. Philosophy has to do with reality, and since it is itself included in its object, it is itself included in the independent reality which is the object of thought, and is thus in a radical way always beyond itself. It is always striving after a self-consciousness which eludes it. Socratic self-knowledge and Socratic nescience are closely connected. That is why Socrates can say that only God is wise, or that only God knows what wisdom is, an insight expressed by St. Thomas when he says that only in God are essence and existence identical. Philosophy is knowledge *in via*.

For Plato, this insight is expressed by the word *philosophy* itself. It is not wisdom, but a love of wisdom. It expresses a condition of the will as much as of the intellect; a submissive and not a dominative condition. When he says that it strives towards the Good, which is the object of desire, he implies that its insights cannot possibly be stripped of all "emotive" elements, but that they are the insights of the integrated and not of the eviscerated man. There are things which we cannot know unless we are united to them by love. In the *Republic* and *Symposium* as well as in the Bible and the fathers, the words 'knowing' and 'conception' have sexual resonances.

The *Republic* speaks about union, marriage and offspring. That is why both Plato and Aristotle insist that the intellectual virtues are founded upon the moral virtues, and presuppose a universe of moral intelligibilities. It would be insufficient to say that for them scientific propositions rest upon ethical propositions. For them, moral virtue consists in the information of the passions by reason, which in its turn is supported by the emotions rightly formed. For them, a philosophy divorced from the moral virtues and from the passion for the good would be simply absurd. In our own times, it is Nietzsche, Freud, and Scheler who have rediscovered this.

In the *Republic,* Plato is speaking about a metascience called dialectics, meaning by "science" in the word "metascience" the body of special sciences achieved at the level of intelligence which he calls *dianoia.* I shall use the phrase "special sciences" to indicate these knowledges. The special sciences are not intelligible at their own level. The reason is that they rest upon unexamined assumptions, and build out bodies of coherences which are not rationally *bene fundata in re.* "If your premise is something you do not really know and the intermediate steps are a tissue of things you do not really know, your reasoning may be consistent with itself, but how can it ever amount to knowledge?" We speak of these special sciences as branches of knowledge only from force of habit, but they should be called by some other name. Further, it is not enough to achieve a comprehensive view of their relations and affinities, and to establish, as it were, a unified science. We have to be able to give "a rational account" of them, before they become intelligible—properly speaking.

It would follow that to give an account of the metascience, or even of the rest of the special sciences in terms of the results or procedures of any one of the latter—for instance, in terms of its logic or procedures of verification—would be absurd. Reality is prior to logic, and Plato is *not* a proto-Hegelian.

In what, then, does a "rational account" of the special sciences consist? It does not seem to me that most commentators give sufficient weight to the fact that Plato's account of the metascience occurs in the middle of a work on politics, which like Aristotle, he refuses to separate from ethics. The sciences are the work of a political animal. Hence scientific intelligibilities rest upon political intelligibilities. The intelligibility of the objects of the special sciences rests upon a prior intelligibility of human relationships. We have to remember that for Plato the political order mediates between the individual and the cosmos. If a man is society writ small, so, too, society is the cosmos writ small. We cannot understand reality if its order and structure is distorted in passing through the medium of an unjust society. Justice is a precondition of truth, and any undermining of ethical propositions will cause the whole structure of the special sciences to topple. Thus we cannot, like Hume, give an account of human relationships in terms of any of the special sciences, but must in fact reverse the procedure.

There is, then, a close connection between metascientific intelligibilities and moral intelligibilities. If you cannot love your neighbor you cannot love the good, and the shadows of this incomprehension will obscure your work as a special scientist. If political and moral relations do not lie open to rational comprehension, then neither do mathematics or astronomy. If dialectics "enables us to see the connections between things," it must first enable us to see the connections between people.

On this account it would be a great mistake to put asunder the ethical and the metaphysical approaches to the Good in the thought of Plato. The master of dialectic "must be able to give an account of the essence of each thing." But there are many essences which are not considered by the special scientists. In particular they do not study such forms as justice, beauty, and goodness, the forms in which moral and political life participate, and to which the special sciences must be related. After dianoetic investigations it still remains to relate their results to society, which remains their unexamined assumption. They are well-founded only when this assumption is explicitly grasped, and validated by reference to the transcendence which gives human relations a meaning.

At the risk of repetition let me restate this point. The pursuit of any science takes place within a certain political and moral complex. The scientist "assumes" the society within which he is working, and its structure is not the explicit object of his science. Further, he is assuming the validity of a number of value judgments; for instance, that it is *good* for him to pursue his work, that truth is something which must be sought, and that he must be honest in estimating and communicating his results. Even were he to achieve the unification of the sciences by means of a philosophy of science, then as long as his unification has to do only with the world of the special sciences and not with the wider social and moral world which lies behind it, the sciences would not yet be *bene fundata*. The scientist would not yet fully know *what* he is doing because he would not yet fully know *why* he is doing it. He could not answer the question why he pursues his activities in any fundamental way. He could not "give an account of the essence" of his science. The morality of science is not extrinsic to its substance whatever formal distinctions we may have to make. Aristotle distinguishes between the moral and the theoretical virtues, but he maintains that the rational soul actualizes the potentialities of the animal soul, with which moral virtue has to do; and assumes it into itself not by destroying it but by raising it to a higher power of itself. In this way the sciences assume morality. For Plato this morality is a morality which rests upon the Socratic injunction that we should know ourselves, so that the pursuit of the metascience is a growth in rational self-consciousness. It is only when we know ourselves in our human situation that the pursuit even of sciences such as mathematics and astronomy are not themselves the pursuits of a dream world which has not fully awakened to consciousness of itself.[5]

Science, then, is human science and its limits are the limits of human self-consciousness. There can not be an integration of science which does not involve personal and political integration and this integration is a metascientific or metaphysical activity.

We may say, then, that metaphysics is the desire and pursuit of the whole. For Plato the pursuit of *to ontos on* is also the individual's pursuit of himself. The urge behind dialectics is the urge to agree with oneself, and the urge to agree with one another without calling in a judge from the outside. It is a kind of thinking in which the subject himself is involved, and in which he puts himself in question. A unified self and a unified world are correlative, and since interpersonal conflicts are the source of neurotic disintegration, both imply a unified social order. Bad metaphysics or antimetaphysics are always accompanied by patent political correlates, and that is why Plato regarded dialectics as an individual and political *therapeia*. A man who cannot agree with himself cannot agree with others, and he cannot agree with others because he is trying to live in several worlds at once. The metaphysical urge in man is his incurable urge to sanity, and the root of all communication.

We may put it differently by saying that metaphysics seeks the concrete and we may count it as one of the fascinating perversions of human thought that the contrary opinion ever gained credence. Plato's critique of the special sciences is a critique of abstractions. The object of a special science is always an object qualified in a certain way, or taken under a certain formality. This is quite clearly stated in *Republic* IV, 437–438, a passage which has always to be kept in mind in the exegesis of *Republic* VII. The object so qualified is the object of a desire correspondingly qualified. If philosophia is an unqualified desire for unqualified truth, any special science requires a qualified love for a certain kind of truth. Hence the critique of the special sciences involves a critique of the emotional contractions which have to be practiced in order to achieve the necessary narrowing of vision. A vision confined to the level of *dianoia* would bring with it a kind of erotic failure. In agreement with the conception of philosophy as a *love* of wisdom, the critique of the special sciences requires a critique of our loves, of the kind which is carried out in the *Symposium*. For Plato, to regard metaphysical or ethical truths as "emotive," and "scientific" statements as emotionally neutral would argue a singular absence of self-knowledge and lack of empirical acumen. All knowledge has a motive, and that motive is the love which constitutes our interest in the object known. At the level of dianoia we are apt to tell ourselves lies about this since the conscious union of knowledge and love belongs to the level of *noesis*. There is some substance in the linking of metaphysics with poetry: they share a common truthfulness about the human condition. There is no such thing as nonemotive language. Restrained or suppressed emotion is not absence of emotion. But there is such a thing as the lie in the soul when we make emotional attacks on metaphysics. And there is a kind of Olympian disembodiedness and pseudo-detachment which incorporates the very parody of Plato which it attacks.

When Aristotle speaks of metaphysics as the knowledge of *ens qua ens,* his expression embodies the same concern with the concrete; that is, with the total subject from which the intellect abstracts in accordance with its need and interests.

Amid all this chatter about "metaphysical entities" let us remember that *all* entities, even books by antimetaphysicists, are metaphysical. Aristotle remains within the Platonic conviction that truth has to do with being, and unqualified truth with unqualified being. *Ens qua ens* is the object seen in the round, and the knowledge of it is the knowledge of the man who has achieved ripeness. Metaphysics is not objective knowledge in the sense that the condition and situation of the knower is indifferent to it. The special scientist has to practice a kind of self-attenuation, amounting to depersonalization, in order to construct the kind of an intersubjective world and the kind of public communication which his discipline requires. He tends to support this with a spurious metaphysical pantheism of pure reason, necessary to make the world safe for abstractions and for the human ghosts which are their correlates. Kant and especially Hegel represent the ultimates in this direction. Hegel is the greatest of all the antimetaphysicists, and this is nowhere more apparent than in that sentence in the *Logic* where he says that "man ought in an interior way to elevate himself to that abstract generality where his own existence becomes indifferent to him." Marx and Kierkegaard were contributing vastly to the rediscovery of metaphysics when they reemphasized the role of personal passion and ethical commitment in knowledge. Both are more Platonic than Hegel. Hegel's treatment of death as the negation of a finite determination of the absolute is much worse metaphysics than Plato's arguments for immortality, since the latter imply a concern with the existing individual. Unfortunately, Oxford is in some respects more Hegelian than it was in the days of Bradley. The attenuations have gone further, and the desire and pursuit of the whole man have suffered further suppressed emotional obscurations. "Unde et multi naturam animae ignorant, et multi etiam circa naturam animae erraverunt. . . . Hoc igitur est quod primum de intellectu intelligitur, scilicet ipsum eius intelligere. Sed circa hoc diversi intellectus diversimode se habent."[6]

I have suggested, then, that the metascience has something to do with human relations and with human action, and that Plato was deeply aware of this. For the special sciences are themselves modes of human action, and as such have to be evaluated in order to be intelligible. As John MacMurray remarked in his Gifford lectures: "The term science refers primarily to a personal activity of intellectual reflection . . . for the production of science is one of the manifestations of the 'I do'. It is itself matter of intention, and not merely matter of fact."[7] Further, it is a social activity because the 'I do' is located in the 'we do.'

The modern world however, has added a further dimension to Plato's insight, and that is a much stronger sense of history and of the significance of time. It is a commonplace of commentators that Plato has difficulty in representing human affairs on the move, and that he is more concerned with the essence of society than with its dynamics. I should not care to exaggerate this, but, it is true that under the impact of Hebrew and Christian thought, there has been a growing sense of history and of personality. As a consequence it becomes necessary to bring the notion of a metascience into closer connection with history.

The relation between science and history is in fact a very lively theme in contemporary thought. We are all acquainted with the Marxist position, and with Comte's attempt to elevate dynamic sociology to a metascience. Attempts are not lacking to elevate history into a metascience, and if Bertrand Russell could write a book, *The Impact of Science on Society,* the contemporary thinker is more likely to write on the impact of society on science. In a book entitled *History and Science,* Hugh Miller wrote: "Rest in peace, Philosophy! You did your work well. May your progeny, the historico-theoretical natural sciences, do you honor!"[8] We may comment on this that if it is intended as a proposition of historico-theoretical natural science, then the latter looks uncommonly like what used to be called philosophy; and that if it is intended as a philosophical statement it has written its own epitaph. As Gilson remarks, philosophy has a way of burying its own undertakers.

However that may be, the modern metaphysicist has to take history seriously. C. F. von Weizäcker's Gifford lectures are dominated by this conviction. In the eighteenth and nineteenth centuries one heard a great deal about the contribution which science had made and, above all, was going to make to history. This culminates in the ideal of controlling history scientifically. This remains a dream of those eminent Victorians, the Marxists. But we ought to take note of a fundamental ambiguity in the phrase: science's contribution to history. Clearly science makes a vast contribution to actual history, insofar as it influences men's ways of thought, and changes the material conditions in which they live and act. But in another sense the mathematical and natural sciences make no contribution to history whatever. The propositions of the special scientist are very different from the propositions of the historian. As occurrences the former are historical events. The fact that they are formulated is a factual occurrence in history, and is part of the corpus of historical evidence. But they do not themselves interpret the evidence which they provide. They do not themselves make any statements *about* history. A "scientific" statement about a scientific statement would be different from a historical statement about a scientific statement. Thomas Hobbes, for instance, endeavors to make scientific statements about scientific statements, and by reducing them to motions of matter he transfers them from historical to physical time. Hume sets out to make scientific statements about historical events, and thus reduces history to a system of atemporal generalizations. That Newton formulated the law of gravity is an historical fact, but the law of gravity is not a statement about history. The historian can make statements about it and about Newton, but it makes no statements about itself. If as an historian I look at the structure of Newton's thought, I can locate it as belonging to a certain society in a certain century. It can be recognized as belonging to a certain milieu. Thus apart from its intrinsic intelligibility as a body of coherent propositions, a special science has to be transcended to achieve the intelligibility which it enjoys by being seen in the concrete complex of existential occurrences with which history has to do. Hence, that Newton's theory has a certain place in human history and society is a metaphysical statement. The metaphysical statement has to do with the physical statement *qua ens.* For an abstract generalization can itself be taken *sub specie entis,* though only by virtue of a formality which is not its own. What may be asserted as being true for all time can be asserted only in time, and it is only in time that it actually influences our intelligences.

What I am laboring is one of those very obvious truths which are difficult to apprehend just because they are so obvious, for as Whitehead remarked, it requires a large mind to take an interest in the obvious. I am concerned with this truth: that there is a science called physics is a historical and not a physical statement. The truth of this historical statement is assumed by every physicist as the absolute precondition of his activity as a physicist. He assumes that he is not mad, and that his activities exist significantly. This is his basic assumption, his *hypothesis,* in the Platonic sense of the word. Let us put it with formal succinctness: There is a science called physics which makes statements about matter. This is not a statement about matter (unless *modo Hobbesii,* we reduce physics to matter). Therefore it is not a statement of physics. Statements about physics are made from outside physics, and so is the judgment that we do right to study physics. That bodies have weight is a statement of physics, but the statement that bodies have weight is a statement of physics, is not itself a statement of physics, but a metaphysical statement without which no physicist could carry on his work for a moment. It implies some classification and evolution of experience which is prior to the pursuit of the special science. Physics makes no statements about physics but provides evidence on which such statements can be made.

It would appear, then, that Plato was right, and that ultimately no special science can render itself intelligible. Its intelligibility is derived from the intelligibility of the historical and social process, so that what we make of it will depend, in part at any rate, upon our philosophy or theology of history. This completely inverts attempts to explain or to explain away philosophy or religion in terms of any special science, or even in terms of a history modeled on the latter. We have to relate the abstract to the concrete, not to explain away the concrete in terms of the abstract. This also does away with the false humility of some modern philosophers who offer and limit their unwanted services to changing the diapers of the special sciences.

Whatever may be the weaknesses of Plato's historical sense, he does make the point that intelligibility rests upon evaluation, and that to render the dianoetic sciences intelligible we have to refer them to a source which is constitutive of the meaning of our moral and political actions also. The neutrality of science with respect to values is itself a value, which is why it is so often passionately defended. The pressing moral and political problems raised by physical and biological science are simply insoluble unless we use these distinctions and perspectives. The prevalence of positivist and nonmetaphysical views of science, let alone of ethics, simply sinks us further into the morass of the meaningless, by removing us from the concrete which is the domain of action, history, and metaphysics.

It remains to distinguish metaphysics from history and to relate them to each other. This is a vast undertaking and I intend to attempt only a sketch of the answer.

If history is, in the sense set out, metaphysical, it is nevertheless not the ultimate science, because history itself always impels us towards the metahistorical. While it is closer to actuality and therefore to intelligibility owing to its concern with the concrete, it does not at its own level reach a complete understanding of itself, but uses values and categories of interpretation which it derives from elsewhere. It is only partly self-conscious, and always assumes a philosophy. It may deny this, and declare that it has no philosophy, and that it is simply concerned to relate the facts as they happened. But the policy of having no philosophy remains a philosophical policy, and the reasons why we should be interested simply in the facts as they happened are metahistorical reasons. When Nietzsche made the remark, "This concern with facts —what pessimism lies concealed in it!" he was indicating that the decision for sheer facts was in fact a philosophical decision, and one which was open to question. These metahistorical questions rise within the bosom of history itself, and lead the historian to a concern with historiography, and with the philosophy and theology of history. History cannot fully answer the question, why history? *Qua ens* it has a kind of contingency which is not dealt with by itself.

Neither physics nor history, then, make statements about themselves. Insofar as they are forced by their own exigencies to do so they are becoming philosophical. We are led to ask the question whether there is a science which in the nature of the case asks questions about itself, and whose whole essence, indeed, lies in the activity of self-questioning. Now such a metascience there must be, or we shall be involved in an infinite regress, always seeking to found our intelligibilities in what is *ex hypothesi* not yet intelligible, and relying only on a coherence which, as Plato remarked, is not sufficient.

But if we look within ourselves we find that we do possess the capacity for a knowledge of such a kind. If physics seeks the truth about matter, and history the truth about contingent events, metaphysics seeks the truth about truth; and since it seeks the truth, it is concerned with its own truth. In this sense, it is the science of itself. Thus we are back at the Socratic position that all knowledge rests upon self-knowledge. Let us observe that if the activity of metaphysics is an activity of asking questions about its own truth, then it is in a very real sense a nescience which is aware of itself; so that, if it is the basis of the dianoetic sciences, these must rest upon our knowledge of nonknowledge, and this leads to a view of science as being rather a matter of opening horizons than of closing problems by a final solution.

For Descartes, the true method enables one to solve problems rather than to open them. The roots of this attitude lie in his obsession with certainty, and this certainty reaches back into the clear and distinct knowledge which he has of his own existence. Let us observe that Descartes does not only claim to know *that* he is but *what* he is. He is claiming an identity of essence and existence which St. Thomas had attributed only to God, for only God could be unquestioning self-intelligence. From this point of view Descartes calls in God only to confirm us in our own self-idolatry. In this manner, he set metaphysics back half a millennium, since his attitude developed steadily into that of Hegel, who arrives at the conclusion that we can close the question, and reach a pinnacle of self-consciousness which will be the truth about truth.

For metaphysics remains the love of truth, rather than its possession; and it is its desire to possess itself which spurs it on. It exists as a question about itself, and for this very reason it knows that it is not the answer to its own question. It seeks its own being *qua ens* and is well aware that its *adequatio* can never exhaust its own essence. It always points beyond itself to a wisdom which *is* its own being, and without this reference to a transcendence it would not be what it is. By keeping itself open, it keeps the special sciences open to their own progress. It is precisely as antimetaphysical that Comte and Hegel are fatal to the sciences.

Since I have mentioned Descartes, and since the Cogito is usually referred back to Augustine's *si fallor sum,* it is necessary to point out that in fact their basic attitudes to self-knowledge are radically different. When Augustine says that the essences of things remain unknown to us, he applies this to ourselves and to our own knowledge. Its essence remains unknown to us, and if all our knowledge is human knowledge it is rooted in a being who is an enigma to himself. Let me quote from the *De Trinitate:* "For not only he who says I know, and says so truly, must needs know what knowing is; but he also who says, I do not know, and says so confidently and truly, and knows that he says so truly, certainly knows what knowing is; for he both distinguishes him who does not know, from him who knows, when he looks into himself, and says truly, I do not know; and whereas he knows that he says this truly whence should he know it, if he did not know what knowing is?"[9] There is for Augustine, then, a certainty in nescience which is very different indeed from ignorance. It is the distinction of ignorance from nescience at which Descartes never arrives. Augustine would maintain that you can base science on nescience but not on ignorance. For all science is based on self-knowledge; that is, on the knowledge which knowledge has of itself, and this knowledge can only be oblique but never direct. Truth is always immanent in any particular truth, but always as a background which can never be fully comprehended. Although all knowledge is based on self-knowledge, for nothing is more present to the mind than the mind itself, yet this presence is an imperfect presence rooted in aspiration after a good. "Although it is not known to itself, yet it is known to it how good it is, that it should be known to itself. And this, indeed, is very wonderful, that it does not yet know itself, and yet knows already how excellent a thing it is to know itself. . . . [The mind] feels the more annoyed that it is itself wanting to its own knowledge, wherewith it wishes to embrace all things. And it knows what it is to know; and while it loves this, which it knows, desires also to know itself . . . For it knows that it knows other things, but that it does not know itself; for it is from hence that it knows also what knowing is" (X. III. 5). What we find in Augustine is an essential sense of wonder concerning that knowledge which he considers to be the basis of all knowledge. What the philosopher and the poet have in common, says St. Thomas, is that they both have a sense of wonder. Those who compare St. Augustine with Descartes would do well to observe the incidence of question marks. *Ego sum* in Augustine may put an end to skepticism, but it is just at this point that the world lies open again to questioning. In Descartes we go from doubt to certainty, in Augustine from skepticism to questioning.

The incompleteness of the sciences rests upon the incompleteness of our self-knowledge. I think that Descartes' complete lack of vision with respect to the long future history of science rests upon lack of a sense of inner historicity. He wants to be independent of the childhood of the race and of his own childhood. But to be cut off from the past is to be cut off from the future also. A sense of inner movement is definitive for a sense of outer movement. And here metaphysics again joins hands with history. Cartesian thought is antimetaphysical because it is antihistorical. That is why the Thomist dictum concerning self-knowledge: *intellectus in actu est intellectum in actu,* cannot be given a Cartesian interpretation. Self-knowledge being reflexive is something which snowballs. It is not given in a timeless intuition, but is the knowledge of a being in time and in history. In this way, metaphysics is essentially a historical discipline. It is a principle of endless growth, and will always cultivate a love of its own past in those who pursue it. Not only does it mature progressively in the individual but it matures progressively in the human race. There is an evolution of self-consciousness, a never-ending confrontation of thought by itself. For it assimilates something in each confrontation with itself, which will become an *intellectum* to the *intellectus*. If you like, metaphysics is growing intelligence with its finger on the pulse of its own growth. Its *actus* is a becoming, and that is why when true to itself it can never be dogmatic, but must always keep the question open both for itself and for the special sciences.

There is in metaphysics an essential capacity for relativizing itself, which is founded in human being itself. It is rooted firmly in its own contingency, and rests in a humility which keeps it open to the truth which is immanent in it. It knows what it does not know, and is receptive of the future and of its own mutations because it is open to its own past. It remains the queen of sciences, drawing water from a perennial fountain, because it is nourished not by concepts but by being, and by the being of the thinker. It is the pursuit of rational life. Unless we can distinguish rational being from *entia rationis*, and the truth of his thought from the truth of the thinker *qua ens* we should not presume to talk about metaphysics. Metaphysics requires the distinction between logical and ontological truth. As a thinking being a man has ontological truth, which is the measure of the truths which he discovers about himself. Man is the measure only in the sense that his being is the *mensurans* of his thought. He has to conform his concepts to himself rather than himself to his concepts, and hence he cannot become his own possession in the manner desired by Hegel. And since the degree of his self-possession is the measure of his possession of things, his sovereignty over the world is limited by the limits of his self-

possession. If man is man in the world, his self-knowledge
and his other-knowledge are strictly correlative, and his pro-
prietorship over the world is intimately connected with his
property in himself. An imperialistic attitude to the world
goes together with a metaphysical imperialism of the self. If
I fully possess myself in a clear and distinct concept, it is
inevitable that I should desire to become the master and possessor of nature. A theory of knowledge resting on the claim
of thinking to become fully cognizant of itself will also be a
theory of knowledge orientated by the will to control things
and to control history. Hence metaphysics is not a conceptual
framework, or a device for creating "explanatory" nonentities,
but the objective unfolding of being in time, submissive to
its own entity. It is our effort to become what we are, scrutin-
izing its own operation, and humbly aware that the necessity
to do so implies limits to the depth of that scrutiny. Metaphysics has always to undermine itself, and it is in this pit
that it buries its own undertakers. By its enmity to dogmatism, and its fidelity to a truth which we know that we do not
know, it is a perennial source of refreshment both to history
and to those historical achievements which we call the
special sciences.

It is an Old Testament notion that the knowledge of man
is a to-be-known, a notion picked up again by St. Paul when
he says that beatitude, which includes a share in God's pro-
prietorship of all things, is to know as we are known; that is,
to grasp ourselves in our own essence. That our own *esse* is a
percipi is perhaps the foundation of all ontology.

Idealism rests upon the assumption (or the claim) that
I am the ultimate *percipiens,* and that I have a clear and distinct knowledge of myself. The majestic collective self-deifica-
tions of our times seem to me to rest on this claim. There is
a sense in which man makes and owns himself and his world,
but it is the facture of a factum, and subject to this limitation. In traditional language, it is creation by a secondary
cause, thus a life which makes itself only by finding itself
through the course of time which constitutes the biography

of an individual, and the history of the human race apart from which no biography is intelligible. Nietzsche remarked: "It has gradually become clear to me what every great philosophy up till now has consisted of—namely the confession of its originator, and a species of involuntary and unconscious autobiography." This is true in some respects. But it does not imply that philosophers have always masked or deluded themselves, nor is the process necessarily unconscious. We cannot think about what we are and know, without thinking about when and where we are and know. The only delusion is the claim to an inhuman objectivity, and the hope of prescinding from the situation in which we think and write. In the last analysis it is not philosophies but philosophers who are true or false. Truth in the last resort is a Person.

For if we merely *have* truth it becomes a utility, to be employed by agents who stand outside of it in determining how to employ it. But the only reason for speaking the truth is the truth of reason itself. Philosophy, as Aristotle said, is useless. It is useless because persons are useless and because God is useless. They cannot be treated as utilities. It belongs to the realm of play rather than of work because it is a gratuitous activity. If philosophy is a gift it is because man and philosophy are entirely gratuitous. There is no purpose beyond persons. And what we are as persons is something that we do not know.

We have to put together the two Socratic sayings "Know yourself," and "I know that I do not know." Knowing oneself means knowing that one is ignorant. In the Introduction to *Portable Plato* Scott Buchanan writes that "I know that I do not know" contains a pun as it is pronounced in Greek. As it is written with a choice of accents, spacing and emphasis, it can mean three things: (1) I know that I do not know; (2) I know what I do not know; (3) I know whatever I do not know. It can even mean "I know because I do not know." It suggests that the study of ignorance is the beginning of wisdom."[10]

The originator of Western philosophy was a Silenus figure,

a comic, a humble clown who knew how to die. The spirit of gravity was exorcised from philosophy at its beginning together with the pretence of knowledge. And indeed there is nothing more comic than a grave philosopher. Knowing that one does not know produces a certain light-heartedness. It removes from us the burden of thinking that we are God, which is an unbearable cross. Being serious with oneself involves being not too serious. It means taking the whole vast structure of knowledge which rests upon self-knowledge with a certain levity, and seeing the universe once more as the play of God. Socrates saw that philosophy requires a certain playfulness. Working in the sweat of our brow results, after all, from diabolic intervention. When I look at the vast labors designed to purify philosophy from metaphysics, from poetry, from rhetoric, from myth, and from the traps of ordinary language, I am appalled at this work of negativity, so far from a true skepticism; this endeavor to become, like the devil, a pure spirit. If philosophy is to survive our industry, including the Ph.D. industry, it has to recapture again the earthiness of Silenus, and to walk the streets of Athens with a certain barefooted loafer, who knew that his perplexity was radical, and who had no degree but only a command from God.

"What does it matter to me if someone finds this incomprehensible? I should like him, too, to rejoice as he says: 'What does this mean?' Yes; this is the way I should like him to rejoice, preferring to find you in his uncertainty rather than in his certainty to miss you."[11]

ON PHILOSOPHICAL TRUTH

"I am asking questions, Father, not making statements."
(Augustine, *Confessions, XI*)

In endeavoring to speak about truth we are engaged upon one of the most difficult of human undertakings. Essentially we have to do with a philosophical question, yet it is part of the activity of philosophers to put questions about philosophy itself, and to undercut its own certainties. This is a most curious situation. There is no wisdom without a certain measure of skepticism, yet we should call no one wise whom we did not consider to possess some truth. At the very least we expect a man to be able to show us why it is true that there is no truth, so deepseated is the demand for truth in us.

Let us observe that we are putting a very curious question. We are inquiring about the truth concerning truth. This is a different question from the question about truth concerning other things. In biology we are looking for truth about

66

living beings, in physics for truth about bodies, in philology for truth about languages. But of course it may very well be that we are capable of reaching truth about life, or body, or whatever may be the formal objects of the various special sciences without being able to reach the truth about truth. When we ask questions about the latter we are practicing a curious kind of reflexive inversion which may, in a sense, seem to be unnatural. Of course, we could not say that there is truth in biology or physics (or what have you), without maintaining that there is such a thing as truth; but we might consider it either idle or impossible to inquire further into what, in general, it is. Or again, we might consider it possible to say what truth is in physics, or mathematics or biology, but to hold that we can go no further than to determine what we mean by truth in each of these particular fields. Truth, we may say, is truth only in relation to various fields of intellectual concern: bodies, the phenomena of life, and so on. But to say that truth itself can be the formal object of inquiry is a very different matter. Why should we concern ourselves about truth when it is much more profitable to seek truths about other things? If I know truths about bodies, I can get to the moon. Yet where is the truth about truth going to land me?

And yet I have in the past few minutes been doing the very thing upon which I have been casting doubts. I have been asking questions about truth, and you and I have both been putting the question to ourselves whether what I have been saying is true. Is not this true? Not only do we consider this to be a legitimate wonder, but every one of us considers that there must be an answer to the question whether what I am saying is true. If you consider this to be an untrue statement you must have reasons for saying so, and then my point is proved.

I say we do not doubt that there is such a thing as truth. For anybody who denies that this proposition is true is implying that he knows what is true and what is untrue. Of course, this does not take us very far. If I say that there is such a thing as truth, the word *thing* is very unspecified indeed. Do I mean by *thing* a substance, or a quality of a proposition, or a feeling of assent or persuasion induced by the hearing of certain words? And yet what we are after must lie very close indeed, because what I am saying right now must be either true or untrue, so that somehow what I am after must be right here in these words now.

I confess that I find the situation absolutely baffling, because I hold it to be true that I find the situation absolutely baffling, and yet what baffles me is the clear truth that I find truth baffling. Did I not clearly see the truth that I am baffled about truth, I could not be baffled. If it is true that I do not know what truth is, I nevertheless know it to be true that I do not know what truth is. In fact I could not know that I do not know unless I know. So I do know. Know what? That I do not know what knowing is. I know *that* I am knowing but I do not know *what* knowing is. Yet if I do not know *what* it is, how can I distinguish it from eating, or running, or sleeping?

The difficulty is to know how we can be said to know; that is, to have the truth about anything, if we do not know what knowing is. I say I know that rose is red. If you say to me, How do you know it? the answer is at one level fairly simple. I should say, We have agreed to call objects of this sort roses, and if I look at this one—we all know what looking is—I experience the sensation which we have agreed to call redness. But even this is not nearly so simple as it sounds. One could spend hours just setting out the difficulties which it raises. The psychologist, for instance, would say: as a matter of fact you don't know *how* you know the rose is red. I have spent years in studying the phenomena of perception, and I don't know yet how you perform that apparently simple operation. As to how I think about perception, I find that more difficult still. You see the difficulty. If I say I know the rose is red, I am employing a proposition the meaning of one of whose terms escapes me. If you say nevertheless it is a fact that I know that the rose is red, the fact nevertheless remains unintelligible. We must distinguish, it is true, between knowing the rose, and knowing our knowing of the rose. I might say that I know that I know the rose, and the fact that I don't know what knowing is makes no difference to the fact that I know the rose. But doesn't it? The botanist would say to me: You have only got as far as being able to point at a certain object which convention has agreed to designate as a red rose. I do not call being able to make the "right" noises in a certain situation knowledge. Now I, as a botanist and after long years of work, have some knowledge of what a rose is. What do you mean by calling it knowledge? you ask him. And he will say, I know how to relate it to other plants and other forms of life; I know its chemistry, how it reproduces, what is its evolutionary descent. His reply clearly indicates some knowledge of knowledge; e.g. that it is systematic, that it requires the relation of some facts to other facts, that explanation has a certain logic, and that induction has certain requirements which if not fulfilled would leave us short of knowledge. I know that I know, he says, because as a scientist I have some notion of what botanical knowledeg is. You think you know because you do not know what scientific knowledge is. But I do know, and therefore I would be very wary of saying that I know what a rose is. If I knew exactly what scientific knowledge was, and I knew that what I know about the rose comes up to those requirements, I might be able to say that I knew what a rose was. But in fact I do not.

The point I want to make, then, is that knowing requires knowing what knowing is. We cannot know without having some degree of reflexive knowledge about what knowing is. And yet we have seen the coils in which thinking about thinking apparently lands us. I am well aware that my foregoing meditation may seem almost neurotic, yet I cannot escape the conviction that knowledge requires an awareness of itself, and the highest knowledge the highest awareness of itself.

In fact we do find that this is recognized by the sciences in the course of their growth. A science may commence by employing, say, induction in a naïve and unselfconscious way. The moment is bound to arise when the scientist asks himself: what sort of knowledge am I getting, what is its validity, what weight can be put upon it, and what sort of information is it giving me? To answer this question we must overhaul the processes of reasoning which have gone into the constitution of the science, to investigate the logic of what constitutes a valid induction, to ask what we mean by a law and what we can validly conclude from it, and so on. Thus Crombie in his book on Robert Grosseteste points out that modern physics was made possible by the thought of the thirteenth and fourteenth centuries on the method and general theory of science. In modern physics this need for subjective awareness has become more acute. Thus epistemological considerations have played a considerable part in the formulations of relativity and quantum theory. Or, to take another example, we cannot say absolutely whether light consists of waves or particles but must consider the intentions of the experimenter.

We find in nature what we bring to it, so that the analysis of what we bring to it becomes part of the business of science. In Eddington's phrase, we have to consider our generic subjectivity. "We are not so eager now as we were . . . to eliminate the observer from our world view." This appears to be a somewhat belated and unconscious recognition of the great principle of Thomas Aquinas: *cognitum est in cognoscente per modum cognoscentis;* that is, what he knows is in the knower according to the sort of knower that he is. That is, if we want to know what we know, we had better find out what manner of spirit we are. And if we don't know what we are we don't properly know it, and we cannot assess it. It is the doom and the glory of man to have to be self-conscious. He has to know according to what he is, so that he has both to find out and to be what he is. The sciences and the humanities are indissolubly linked.

My contention, then, is that if philosophy is concerned with knowing about knowing, or with the truth about truth, then the special sciences are bound to become more philosophical as they develop. They will realize that all our truth is human truth, relative to our human condition, and perhaps when we have learned to relativize even our conviction about the relativity of things we shall be nearer that ultimate skepticism which is the beginning of wisdom.

Philosophy is concerned with knowing about knowing, or with the truth about truth. It is this conviction which has led to the description of metaphysics as the queen of the sciences, and it stems largely from Plato's conviction that we cannot be satisfied with a multiplicity of truths, but desire the truth about truths. That is why he required that the special sciences should be completed by dialectic. It is true that the special sciences are concerned with their own knowing, but their own knowing is correlative and adapted to special departments of reality, while knowing as such should be concerned with being as such. I need hardly say that I am aware of how much is implied, and assumed, in this statement. If you like, it begs the question whether there can really be a science of being qua being to which a knowledge which is somehow quintessentially knowledge corresponds.

Philosophy cannot separate knowing about knowing from knowing about being. It has, as it were, to catch itself in action, and this is what makes it look like an exhibition of introverted neurosis to those who are not tough enough to take it. And it is well aware of the imperfection of what it can achieve. I started this paper by trying to take you into the tensions which arise. To have to strive for a knowledge about knowledge is itself an indication, and the surest indication, of the imperfection of that knowledge. For it is a knowledge which is separated and distanced from itself, which is striving to be itself, which is self-conscious about its lack of self-consciousness, which is split into knower and known, which is aware that it is a process, which knows that it wants to know all things *tota simul,* and by the very fact of its want knows that it cannot do so. It is always trying to destroy itself in order to be itself. That is why the philosopher must always swing between the two dangers of self-deification and suicide.

Plato was right when he said that quintessential truth requires quintessential courage. The danger of all knowing is pride unto death.

That is why a dogmatic metaphysics is a contradiction in terms. Metaphysics can exist only in a condition of moral and intellectual tension, knowing only, as Socrates said, that it does not know. Insofar as it is the queen of the sciences it communicates this openness and sense of an impossible finality back into the special sciences themselves, and makes them aware that new truth is essentially an awareness of vistas not yet explored. I have mentioned Socrates. When Socrates was brought to trial on the capital charge of being a know-all about the gods, the Athenians were perhaps dimly aware of the deadly character of philosophical knowledge. Socrates himself was aware that one was only saved from death by presumption by knowing that one did not know. That was why his defense consisted in a confession of a wisdom which was ignorance. The truth of the matter, gentlemen (he said), is that only God is wise. Centuries of philosophers and theologians have elaborated this attitude, and I should like to place myself in the tradition of those who have held that the only final truth is the truth about truth; that is, the truth about being, which is only possible to a being which is so fully his own truth that he does not have to seek it. Truth in the last resort seems to me to be being itself, and since being which has truth about itself is precisely what we mean by a person, I can only conclude that truth must be a Person which all our sciences are trying to reach.

I experience an ever-growing conviction that this conclusion is true. In the last analysis what I have said rests on the classical distinction between ontological and logical truth, and upon the primacy of the former. It is not primarily propositions that are true, but things. Truth is a property of being, and what we do when we think is to unveil a truth which is there. I do not see in what other way the objectivity of our knowledge can be satisfactorily founded. A fuller exposition and defense of this conviction, however, requires a paper to itself.

Modern philosophy is more traditional than some of its exponents realize. It is essentially committed to a meditation upon the words: man-in-a-situation. In this committal it has to go behind the movement in Western philosophy initiated by Descartes. There are two hiatuses created by Cartesian thought which are closely connected: the gap between the thinker and other *res cogitantes,* as well as *res extensae;* and the gap between the present and the past. Every reader of the *Discours* knows in what manner Descartes turned his back upon the past. But it should be noticed that he turned his back upon his own past and upon his own youth. His youth is the period in which he was held by prejudice and tradition, so that his doubt involves the sweeping away of his own youth. He has to recreate himself in a moment of clarity the resources for which lie entirely within himself.

"But as for the opinions which up to that time I had embraced, I thought that I could not do better than resolve at once to sweep them wholly away, that I might afterwards be in a position to admit either others more correct, or even perhaps the same when they had undergone the scrutiny of reason" (*Discours II*). We have to take this passage in connection with the simile of the architect who freely plans a city on the open plains, and with the discussion of the housing difficulties of those who have to find a temporary dwelling while this house is razed for rebuilding.

Descartes thought that by suspending the past by means of doubt, the human mind could come to maturity. But, on the contrary, one may very well ask whether the conditions of growth and maturation have not been obliterated, and whether at the very moment in which Descartes had made a new start, the conditions for moving on from there had not been destroyed. It is, after all, a very adolescent attitude not to wish to accept anything unless it has been proved. Perhaps that is why so many young people feel so isolated and unable to make contact with the world. How do you *prove* that a friend is a friend? How does one *res cogitans* reach out to another?

The thinking substance has in fact no growth. It can explicate its clear and distinct ideas, and this requires time. But what kind of time does it require? Having lifted himself out of historical time Descartes concludes that what this requires is sheer quantity of physical time, so that his problem is not how to grow up and how to grow old gracefully, but how to postpone death indefinitely, while he himself completes the corpus of the sciences necessary to make man the master and possessor of nature. This postponement is to be effected by a science of medicine achieved by the method which will enable you to be *certain* that you will live for centuries. Longevity is to be the surrogate for maturation. The tragi-comedy of Descartes' attempt to subject death to science has been well described by Gilson in his *Unity of Philosophical Experience.*

The ultimate aim of Cartesianism is to achieve an abolition of time by achieving a point of clarity the correlate of which will be a world which is absolutely transparent to human reason. Movement has departed from both the subject and the object, and the price of clarity has been the stopping of growth. Once we admit growth we admit obscurity, and to recognize that we are a becoming in the midst of a universe of becoming is to cease to be a Cartesian.

There is an important positive lesson to be learned from Descartes, namely that the clearness and distinctness with which we know ourselves will be the measure of the clearness and distinctness with which we know the world. Self-knowledge sets the norms for other-knowledge. But this requires as a consequence the idea of man as being-in-the-world, a consequence which cannot be seen by Descartes because he becomes transparent to himself in a concept by a movement of doubt which cuts himself off from the world. I hold, on the contrary, that the notion of man as being-in-the-world involves the recognition of a certain obscurity in both. This obscurity is essentially linked with the fact that our being is a being in time, and that the growth of our knowledge is a maturation in time. I will venture the statement that our being is a being in a maturing universe, of which our search for ourselves is a microcosm.

At the beginning of our philosophical tradition is the
Socratic insight that man exists in a condition of radical
nescience. The injunction, know thyself, does not express any
hope that we can arrive at a clear and distinct idea of ourselves. It is rather an injunction to accept our condition, to
arrive at clear-sightedness about our myopia, to know our
ignorance. With this, St. Thomas concurs. He holds that
intelligibility corresponds to being, and that that which is
supremely being is per se supremely intelligible. God as He
Who Is, is supremely intelligible, but is known as he is only
by himself. He alone can speak the word which comprehends
him. Man, though a spiritual being, is less than God, and
not only has less intrinsic intelligibility but radically fails
to comprehend himself, because as his being is less, so in
proportion is his hold upon that being. In fact, St. Thomas
continues, though bodies have less intrinsic intelligibility
than minds, they are nevertheless more knowable by us than
are our own minds, by virtue of the place which we occupy
in the scale of being. He holds that self-knowledge and knowledge of the world about us are inseparable, and that the
character of the latter depends on man's ontic structure; but
that we cannot have the kind and degree of knowledge of
ourselves which we have of bodies. Created spirit escapes
itself, and the knowledge which we have of bodies is proportional to our nescience. Man exists as a question to himself,
and upon this questionability rests his science.[12]

Since man is a being aware of itself, he poses the question
about himself, about his relation to the world, and his relation to his science. For he is not his own logos, as is God. And
if his truth is proportional to his being, he exists as a question
about truth. That is why he is a philosopher. It is something
built into his being, and if the pursuit of philosophy is something divine, as Plato and Aristotle said, it is because it yearns
after that Wisdom which is a knowledge of itself, and seeks
to be in the same fashion and by the same act by which it
knows. It seeks the union of thought and act. God is the only
absolutely committed person, and if a Socrates or a Kierke-

gaard insists that as we know so must we act, they were expressing an exigency of man as question and as person.

But, however obscurely, man grasps himself in his being, as an entity in which being and truth, and truth and value adumbrate their ultimate identity. This seems to me to lie behind Plato's doctrine that the knowledge of the Good is the copestone of the sciences. We encounter ourselves here, and, as Augustine insists when dealing with the Stoic doctrine of suicide, we find it good to be here. We always experience our *isness* as an *ought to be*. Further, we encounter ourselves as truth seeking a world in which it can be realized, and therefore as committed to the making of a human world. We become mature in responding to this commission.

It is in carrying this out that we construct history. Our being as questioning and questionable is a being in time committed to the construction of our own time and the time of a humanized world. Our being is a being *in via* through a time and through a history which bears the traces of our constructivity. Philosophy must be conscious of its own relative and historical character. It is this which exhibits the image of the divine self-knowledge in it and registers its response to an absolute commission.

If history carries us on, it also conserves. We write history to conserve the past and to lend it a significance reflexively by bringing it into the present and future. It does not befit a philosopher to deny his youth, but to preserve his youth, and the prime and primitive things of the world. That is why it is par excellence the activity of a mature man and a moment in the maturation of the world. It seems to me that the realism and empiricism of St. Thomas is connected with an awareness of this. Much more than the special scientist does the philosopher rely on the accumulation of experience. That is why, in the *Republic,* Plato wishes his philosophers to be men of experience, and why he exhibits so much experience of the ways of men, for instance in *Republic* VIII and IX; and why he is even more empirical in the *Laws* which he was young enough and wise enough to write at the age of eighty.

"Philosophy" said Kant in his old age "is in reality nothing other than a practical knowledge of men." For philosophy is a validation of experience and of history, a process of gathering up what men have done and constructing a world with the materials of the contingent. Only a mature man stays young, and our world matures according as it recovers the freshness of its genesis. Philosophy is closely related to the primordial genesis, when creation stands out in the freshness of being, and it has a commission to regenerate. It is itself at once hoary-headed and newborn, renewing its youth by its everlasting questioning of itself, lest its ways grow old and set.

I am well aware that I may be called rhetorical. I am content. The world itself is a rhetoric spoken by the Logos. It befits a philosopher, if he has any love of wisdom, to be well-spoken and to embody his thought in an action. All genesis is an action. And if our being is a to-be-spoken-by God, it is also a to-be-known-by God. The Old Testament insists that our knowing is a to-be-known-by God, and that is the foundation of the Christian nescience which finds itself at home with Socrates. To know as we are known in the fullness of time, is what St. Paul understands by beatitude; and philosophy is animated by the hope of that beatitude, in which alone we can enjoy the fullness of that science whose intelligibility is correlative with the degree of our self-knowledge. Our being as truth is a search after itself, undermining its pride not by doubt but by question. If I call upon anybody to doubt, then, as Kierkegaard pointed out in Johannes Chinaeus, I call upon my hearer to doubt my call. But if I call upon him to question, I establish our common humanity, and enlist his aid for our mutual progress. That is the essence of Socratic dialogue, and that is the perpetual issue between the true and the false skeptic. The true skeptic is the man who is true to his own human being, and does not try to negate it by doubts which his own historicity prohibits. Only God could be an absolute skeptic. The true skeptic questions, but on the basis of an acceptance of what he is in the world.

Wisdom is skepticism because it is acceptance, and only the *verus scepticus* can carry out the true commission of philosophy which is to construct a world, in hope and humility, which realizes the intentions of the rhetoric which presides at its genesis.

What I have endeavored to do in these two papers is to indicate that there is a difference between the truth about truth and the truth about things. When I say that the specific gravity of iron is whatever it is, I am saying something about iron. Later on, I raise the question about *what* I am saying, and what kind of information I am getting. I ask what I mean when I say that the statement is true. I am then making a statement about a statement about iron, but not about iron.

I remember that what committed me to philosophy when I was still a boy was my suddenly understanding somebody who said to me: In philosophy you ask questions like, What do I mean when I say, this rose is red? I ask then what I mean when I say that this statement is true, hoping to arrive at some true statements about my statement.

But I make a further act of reflection when I start asking questions about these true statements about statements. In due course, I come to ask: What is truth? It does not seem to me that I am asking the same sort of question as when I ask: What is iron? When I ask, What is iron? I am raising a question, but I am not raising a question about questions. The latter kind of question cannot be answered in the same way as the former, and that is why I hold that there is a specific kind of knowledge called philosophical knowledge. This knowledge is the knowledge of knowledge, the *epistēmē epistemōn* of Plato's *Charmides*.

Of course, if we say that the first kind of question is the only reasonable kind of question, and that the only rules for answering questions are those which apply to that situation, then a question like What is truth? is a pseudo-question, and philosophy is a pseudo-enquiry.

I have refused this conclusion, and doggedly pursue my meditations on the truth about truth.

Now the truth about truth must be a statement which completely comprehends itself. It is not a statement about iron or roses but about itself. It refers to itself and not to something out there upon which our interest is concentrated.

This truth about which we are thinking is not an object, and not even a statement insofar as we can treat statements as objects of thought. The distinction between thinking and objects thought about is lifted, as it is in the upper division of Plato's line. As we increase our knowledge of the cosmos it would be wise to increase our knowledge of what we do not know. It is not the function of philosophy to contribute a little more cosmological knowledge to our store, especially if it is of a derived and second-rate kind, but to add to our knowledge of our ignorance. We have only to turn inwards to recognize the abyss to which all our cosmological knowledge is relative.

We come to the conclusion that truth *is* the truth about truth, and at that point the distinction between truth and being vanishes. We arrive at the notion of an interest which is entirely absorbed in itself and generates its own logos. This identity beween being and logos we call God, and insofar as philosophy is concerned about the truth it is concerned about the divine self-knowledge. It does not, however, seek to divinize itself, knowing that the very agony of its efforts to know itself, and the subjection of that effort to temporality, marks a radical gap in man between his truth and his being. Philosophy is a question about philosophy, but God is not a question about God. The Logos is the answer.

We must say then that philosophy is either doomed to radical frustration and should give itself up—which it can't for that would still be a philosophical act—or it can exist only in hope. It is the mark of a being whose knowledge has the quality of nescience. Let me insist again that this is not an absence of knowledge but a quality of the highest knowledge which we can possess. I may say that this qualifies my adherence to the position that philosophy has to do with second order propositions. My position here is Platonic and I agree with Cushman when he writes: "Plato's conception of Wisdom is governed by his conviction that truth relating to ultimate reality resists propositional status. Truth *about* reality is subordinated to truth *as* reality. Where man's relation to ultimate Being is involved, truth and reality are inseparable, for reality is embraced in immediate apprehension."[13]

To know that we do not know is the highest achievement of the human intellect. Thus philosophy roots us not only in hope but also in humility. In philosophy, man is in search of his logos and he knows that he can receive it only as a gift which it is not within the power of philosophy to bestow. In the last resort philosophy waits upon an illumination which is a grace. I think that this is what Socrates and Plato saw, and whatever else we may subsequently have added to that insight, we have taken nothing away from it. Attempts at its diminution are always sophistry.

ADEQUATIO—TRUTH AND THINGS

In this lecture I am going to wander in the realm of the history of philosophy. You will have gathered from what I have said that I am most at home in the atmosphere of existential phenomenology. Yet I have some quarrels with some of its representatives. They lay too much claim to novelty and to new discoveries. I have heard too much denigration of Plato and St. Thomas from some existentialists. The really great philosophers knew what philosophy was, and the bigger and more modern we are, the more clearly we shall see that the fresh things we discover are old things seen anew. The more I know about contemporary philosophy the more I find in it a way to appreciate afresh what was done and seen by the ancients. There is a real sense in which Plato knew more about what philosophy was than I ever shall.

I am concluding my lectures with an exposition of, and comment on, the classical doctrine of truth as *adequatio*. The reason for this is that whatever I have said in my previous lectures stands or falls with the notion of ontological truth with which the adequatio theory is inseparably bound up. Truth requires a certain fidelity of human being to itself, which is a prerequisite of its fidelity to things; and things invoke this fidelity because to be a thing is to display a certain trueness to the fact of concrete existence. As Augustine remarked, they seek to proclaim what they are through us, so that we are—as it were—the vicars of their existence, responsible for the wholeness in ourselves by which alone we can see them whole.

Fundamentally, I am not trying to play off the notion of adequatio against other theories of truth, such as the coherence theory. It is not a question of either-or. If there is such a thing as metaphysics, that is, a search for truth about being, then adequatio is a description of the nature of *metaphysical* knowledge. It is strictly speaking a metaphysical theory which seeks to be consonant with the truth which it is itself proclaiming. It seeks to do justice to its own truth by turning reflexively upon the operation which it is performing. You have to do with the third degree of abstraction.

Philosophy has first to give an account of itself, and then of other activities of the intellect. The coherence theory of truth is adequate to certain levels of intellectual operation but not to the metaphysical. It belongs to the level of the special sciences, and when Descartes made truth the function of a position in an order dictated by the method, he was making the world of intellect safe for science, but unsafe for philosophy. Since science is further removed from being than philosophy, it tends to a greater degree to the construction of formal patterns. That is why brilliant young scientists are quite in order, but a brilliant young philosopher is almost a contradiction in terms. Philosophy knows that the world is a coherence only to God. The seventeenth century system builders wanted to make philosophy scientific, and philosophy can only be philosophical.

There is a place for coherence theory in any inclusive account of the structure of human truth. It is a philosophical theory in the sense that philosophers have a right to work it out, but it is not a philosophical theory in the sense that it does justice to the nature of philosophic apprehension itself. Forced upon metaphysics it can only alienate metaphysics from itself. It represents, then, a failure of philosophic self-awareness. When we seek, with Socrates, to know ourselves we find that we are alienated from ourselves if we try to cast that knowledge into the form proper to physics or mathematics, or attempt to explain ourselves in terms of the patterns by means of which they endeavor to render the world intelligible. If science is to be intelligible in the sense of *bene fundata in re,* then coherence must be founded in adequatio.

Perhaps the great stumbling block to the acceptance of this has been Descartes' lineal descendant, Hegel, who I will dare to say was no metaphysician, precisely because he was so *lacking* in a self-consciousness adequate to the human condition. A philosophy which is perfectly resolved in itself—as thought about thought—lies open to the same criticism as the Cartesian attempt to grasp the essence of the mind in a clear and distinct concept. It becomes system driven to its ultimate, but represents an alienation of philosophy into science, for the nineteenth century version of which it was to make the world safe. This is what Marx grasped in his attack on the philosophers. Philosophy must make way for science, by which man can grasp the contingencies of history itself, enabling mankind to occupy the throne of that Being which is its own Logos, and who has an idea of Himself which is adequate to his existence. Metaphysics, however, requires humility. The foundation of adequatio theory is the identity of God's being and his intelligence, the consubstantiality of the Father and the Logos. It is rooted in the notion of a Being who *is* his truth, in an intellection which in knowing itself knows itself precisely as being, in whom the distinction between logical and ontological truth falls away. Its primary concern is with the problem of self-knowledge, not with the knowledge of "things," or with the attempt to grasp the cosmos as a coherence. Knowing oneself means tracing the image of the divine adequation in oneself, that is, in treating one's own intellection as substance, and not as an activity which distances itself from itself by regarding itself as an instrument or as a series of "merely mental" events; that is, relegating it to the domain of objects.

I am going thus to speak about the Thomist conception of truth, which is summed up in the famous formula that truth is the adequation of thing and intellect. Let me say at once that I approach the subject with some hesitation because I seem so often in the past to have failed to make the conception intelligible. I have been forced to ponder deeply upon the causes of this failure which I cannot ascribe altogether to my own stupidity and lack of facility in expression, and I have come to the conclusion that there are other reasons as well.

And the fundamental reason is that we have here to do with a realist theory of knowledge, not in the sense in which the Platonic forms theory is called realism but in the modern sense which indicates a direct acquaintance with objects "as they are." My difficulties would be less were the fundamental characteristics of Cartesianism more fully grasped, especially in their radical opposition to the spirit of medieval philosophy. While the prejudice persists that we are using the word "metaphysics" in the same sense when we speak about Cartesian and about Thomist metaphysics, I shall simply be flogging the wind.

When I say "realism" then, I wish to indicate an opposition to idealism rather than to nominalism, though I am deeply convinced that the roots of idealism are to be found in nominalism, and that we cannot understand the seventeenth century unless we understand the fourteenth. What nominalism achieved was a break with reality in its metaphysical dimension and a concentration upon those appearances of things which could be handled by means of words. It opened the door to modern science by laying the foundations of the attitude that the object of reason is the sphere of the manipulatable, and therefore of the project to become through reason the masters and possessors of nature. There is a close connection between this project and the prevalence of idealism in modern philosophy; and while it persists as a conscious or unconscious dominant in our social structure, realism will be unpopular.

Having said this I am bound to make clearer what I understand by that Protean word, *idealism*. Fundamentally, I understand by it an action by which a word or an idea or sensation is interposed between the mind and the nature of things. Thus Descartes' position that thinking is about ideas, or Hobbes' that it is an association of sensations, and the related position of Hume, are all idealist actions. The empiricism of the latter is a form of idealism. Again, I regard modern British linguistic analysis as being basically idealistic. Language has been placed between mind and essence. I find the holy war of the analysts upon the Oxford Hegelians merely comic. Both are embarrassed by the principle of identity in a society where the domination of becoming is the basic social premiss.

The key to idealism in my view, then, is the action of *alienation,* and I regard the Cartesian doubt as being primarily an action of this kind. In the form which it takes in the *Discourse* there is an alienation of the mind from sensible being, and, in the hyperbolical doubt of the *Meditations,* an alienation from truth. The certainty of my own existence and the causality of God are called in to close these gaps, but in fact the condition of alienation remains. Mind is affirmed to be really distinct from body, and what is in some ways more important, the ego as universal epistemological subject is not reunited with the existing individual. As a consequence, thought becomes an instrument in the hands of a disembodied and impersonal subject. From this stems the whole sweep of the modern preoccupation with epistemology. How can we determine the limits of and put an edge upon the instrument by which we are to manipulate reality? The hidden premise of the preoccupation is an instrumental conception of mind. Further, although God guarantees the truth of our clear and distinct ideas it remains true that ideas and not things are the objects and terminus of our thought. The mind operates *upon* and *with* ideas.

It may at first sight seem strange that this break between thought and things should have been achieved by a thinker whose intention it was to make us the masters and possessors of nature. What has happened to the contact with nature? The unity between Descartes' theory of knowledge and his practical intentions is to be found in the conception of instrumentality. Thought is something which we must *use,* and we cannot use it unless it is in our own power rather than in the power of things. Consequently, nature for the Cartesian must be regarded primarily from the point of view of what we want it to be. In order that it should correspond with human thought and intention it must be *made* to correspond with them. In the last analysis it is *will* which constitutes reality to be what it is. Becoming masters and possessors of nature thus involves the project of constructing nature in our own image by means of thought manipulated according to a scientific method. In this manner and under the aegis of the instrument, the course is set for the subsequent attempt at human self-deification which reaches such high peaks in Hegel and Marx. In due course, truth, and God (usually in the form of Humanity), will be what we want them to be. And the greatest essay in anthropomorphism in the history of man will have run its course.

In many respects the principles of the process can be better studied in Hobbes than in Descartes. Hobbes is, fundamentally, no less idealist than Descartes, and the Cartesian doubt operates no less deeply in him. One of its chief manifestations is the dissociation of sensation from the motion which gives rise to it. Color, sound, and smell do not inhere in it, and yet thought by which we are to manipulate the generable is to be accounted for by the association of sensations. A parallel situation is thus created: we are to manipulate nature on the basis of a rationality which is thoroughly subjective. And again the solution of the problem of closing the gap between the subject and reality is the same. We think in order to exercise power over nature.

It is here that Hobbes' theory of speech becomes so vital for understanding the course of modern philosophy and indeed of civilization. The proper object of ratiocination is motion, since only the changeable can be the subject of power. The manner in which motion is known and controlled is by means of words attached to images which do not inhere in motions. The word as public currency is a sign attached by a conventional consent to the same image. Further, the manner in which words are to be used and related to each other is also a matter of convention. Reasoning, then, is a manipulation of signs in accordance with conventions agreed upon. I should like to stress the significance of the connection between Hobbes' voluntaristic linguistic analysis and his idealism. I should also like to point out its connection with the formation of scientific terminology. When we decide to call a certain bit of metal an ounce we are not saying anything about that bit of metal "as it is in itself." We are prescinding from the question of essence. What we are doing is to state our determination to use that bit of metal in a certain way, namely, as a weight. We manipulate the results of our weighing by means of certain public systems such as the multiplication table. Hobbes universalizes the procedure and declares that what is good, what is evil, or what is man is decided in the same manner as what is a pound or a quart. Truth and falsity consist in the right handling of signs according to public conventions, and the 'right' manner is determined by Leviathan. It is in the interest of the state that men should speak in the same manner. "Seeing right reason is not existent the reason of some man or men must supply the place thereof; and that man or men is he or they, that have the sovereign power." Or again, "The decision of the question whether a man do reason rightly, belongs to the city." These are the conclusions which Hobbes draws from the thesis that "true and false are attributes of speeches not of things."

We have to take note of these positions if we want to appreciate, in their historical context, what is implied in the rejection of the notion of ontological truth or the truth of things, the reduction of all truth to logical truth, and the rejection of the statement that *ens et verum convertuntur*. I have dealt with these points at this length because I want to make clear what the historical conditioning is which sets up the resistance to the Thomist formula. Where we are dominated by the notion of the instrument, where we identify reasoning with scientific or formal reasoning, where we put the final arbitration on spiritual matters in the hands of the state, where we are cut off from reality by the numerous subterfuges which have become commercial and political vested interests, there we are shut off from an understanding of it. It requires a self-knowledge helped out by an understanding of history.

I am not here attempting a straight exposition of Thomist epistemology. That has been done well many times. I am rather endeavoring to give some bearings on it. While writing I have been haunted by the words, I think of Paulinus, *sine numine nomina,* because it would be a perfect superscription for Hobbes' theory of language; while for St. Thomas it would be truer to say that words are *coram Deo prolata.* I have over my desk a prayer which he used to say before speaking or writing. For St. Thomas the word is primarily a *verbum cordis* which expresses the essence of things, a communication with (rather than an instrument for handling the appearances of) being. It is this point which I should like to bring out.

Another way of expressing that St. Thomas is a realist in theory of knowledge would be to say that in him ontology is prior to theory of knowledge. We cannot determine a priori what the limits of knowledge must be. Epistemology must be a reflection upon what the mind has actually done at the various levels of its employment. Thus it is not for theory of knowledge to determine whether physics is possible or not, or whether metaphysics is possible or not, but rather to make explicit what they have done and what structures of thought and language they have employed. This is an important aspect of his explicit rejection of idealism in the form of the theory that what the mind knows is the species of things. The species is not what the mind knows, but that through which it knows beings. It is not an instrument by means of which we approach being but the way in which being is present in us. The sense of a break with being which we find both in Descartes and in the empiricists is entirely absent in him. That is why both the *Summae* start with demonstrations of the existence of God. These demonstrations supply important and necessary data for any theory of knowledge which is to be faithful to the human intellect in all its employments. We have to be humble in the face of the capacities of our minds, and that is another way of saying that we must have confidence in reason. The proof of that particular pudding is in the eating. The being of the mind in action sets its own limits and you cannot alienate yourself from yourself to set your limits from the outside. The primary act of the mind is to accept being and its own being. Wonder at being includes wonder at our own being. Hence the realism of St. Thomas might also be described as a simple wonder at being and at being St. Thomas. From a Thomistic standpoint one of the fundamental criticisms to be made against Descartes and Hobbes and Hegel and Marx is that they have removed wonder, and (I think) humor from human knowing. They have removed wonder because you cannot wonder at your own artefact. One is not, strictly speaking, thinking but using thought according to a method. You know the world because you have determined a priori or by convention what you can know. As Descartes explicitly puts it, we are to know nature "as we know the various crafts of our artisans"; that is, there is to be no more in it than what we put into it. But philosophy is not primarily a matter of serious purpose but of wonder, and I cannot hope to put realism across to people who take human existence too seriously.

For St. Thomas, then, to think is to be directly in contact

with the natures of things, so I had better say a little about his notion of being. St. Thomas is not a philosopher who is fascinated by the abstract notion of being. On the contrary. Abstraction does not involve the rejection of what is not common to a widely distributed reality, but the subsumption of the latter under a single symbol. The Latin word for being is *ens,* which is a participial form of the verb *esse.* We can, of course, use the word *ens* substantively, as when we speak of "a being." But the philosophy of St. Thomas is a philosophy of the verb rather than of the substantive. His is not a philosophy of being or existence, both of which are abstract nouns, but of existing or existings; that is, it looks at the act by which this pipe or this pencil are posited here and now. Likewise, when we turn to his theory of knowledge we find that it is not concerned with thought generically taken, but with the *act* by which this is grasped here and now. Of all philosophers he has the strongest sense of actuality. The mainspring of philosophy is wonder at there being *something* rather than *nothing.* When, on some glorious day, we are seized with the sense of the absolute gratuitousness of existence, and no longer take for granted that we are standing here looking at that tree, but are overcome with amazement at the total situation being there at all, then we are on our way to the philosophic point of view. When anything—this pipe, this pencil, this tree—suddenly stands out for us from nothingness, in all the wonder of its being a thing and its being itself, we are on our way to realism.

Infusing the philosophy of St. Thomas, then, is his sense of the unique and irreplaceable character of each and every act of existence. The world is a multiplicity of substances each of which is, in a sense, its own, held together by an inner principle of unity which is the act by which it exists. Thus the principle of identity—A is A, being is being—does not serve as a principle of abstract unity or of monism as in Parmenides or Spinoza, but as the charter of the claim to significance of the endless diversity of the empirical world.

We see, then, what are the connections of Thomist realism

with the analogy of being. For the philosopher of abstract being being is the same thing in angels, men, jackals, carrots, bicycles and ideas. If this is true, then being is indistinguishable from nothing, and we must come to the conclusion that the empirical world is *maya*. After all, this is what Hobbes and Hume are saying in their own way, and it does not seem to me improbable that a world constructed on an instrumental view of thought will end by condemning itself as illusion. St. Thomas insists on our right to call things *things*. I doubt whether any modern positivist has really gone further than the Buddha system in reducing objects to sense data. For St. Thomas, by calling a thing a thing we are indicating that it is not another thing. What they have in common is that the being of the one is not the being of the other. Being is always *this* being, in all its concrete determinations; that is, as having whatever makes it *this* and *not that*. Hence we should be careful how we employ the word "existence" which is an abstract noun. As Cajetan remarks, no contradiction is involved in saying that existence does not exist. There can *be* no existence in general. Experience presents us with a diversity of existings, and it would be a contradiction to say that an existing does not exist. You can not separate the being of a thing from its being this thing. Hence in each having its own being, each thing is both like and unlike any other, which is to say that being is analogical in structure. The act of knowing is possible on the basis of the likeness, but it is an occurrence which is itself an act bringing the unlike together in a manner which reveals the natures of both. The intellect is one thing, the thing known another, and in this sense truth belongs to the thing as it is in the mind.

The realism of St. Thomas then rests on an ontology which affirms the organic relevance of all acts of existing to each other. Knowing is a direct existential affirmation of the relevance of the world to me, and of myself to the world. A realist epistemology could, I think, be corroborated by a phenomenological examination of 'importance' and 'relevance.'

Though St. Thomas declares that knowledge is knowledge

of beings, and that all knowledge commences in sense experience, he does not hold that sensations are something from
which we *infer* the existence of some underlying being. Locke
and Hume thoroughly misrepresent the classical doctrine of
substance. Being is directly known by the mind and is given
directly and immediately together with our sense awareness.
Sense and intelligence form an indissoluble unity.

Here we must point out again the importance of realizing
that the theory of knowledge of Aquinas is consequent upon
and not prior to his anthropology. Man is by nature a creature
both of intelligence and sense, and therefore he is both a
metaphysician and an empiricist at the same time. What he
apprehends is sensible being. But this brings us to the large
question of the "abstraction" of the first principles of being,
about which I shall be brief.

Empiricists like Ockham and Hume are forced in a certain
given direction by their nominalist and idealist assumptions
when they have to give an account of principles such as A is
A, and every effect must have a cause. For instance, Hume
shows that if we take his sensationalist empiricism seriously
we cannot claim ontological validity for the causal axiom.
Such principles may be regarded as illusions, tentative empirical generalizations, verbal conventions, devices for handling
experience, but in any event not as ontological laws. They
may be regarded as useful or useless, but in either event we
are looking at them from the viewpoint of utility or of the
instrument; that is, from the point of view of the will to control rather than to recieve. Now Aquinas holds that while the
human mind as an embodied mind is dependent on sensation, yet man has intellect as well as sense. But it is the function of the intellect to go beyond the appearances of things.
As he puts it, intelligere equals *intus legere*. Now the inside
of things is their being, and we can say of Hume that for him
things have no insides, and that man has no intelligence.
There is no self to *be* an intelligence, but only a capacity for
imaginative self-deception existing in vacuo. For St. Thomas
we cannot experience things without grasping them—and

ourselves—in their substance or in their being, and without grasping in an inchoate way the general principles of being.

For instance, I see this pencil. I immediately grasp that it is this pencil and not this pipe. I immediately intuit not only that this pencil is this pencil, but I rise immediately to the insight—which may be quite unformulated and unattended to—that *to be,* anything must be itself and not something other. I intuit this as something absolutely universal and necessary, and as not admitting of any possible exception. Thus, that A is A, and that A cannot at the same time be both A and not-A is given to me together with my sensible experience of any object, as a primary ontological law. Identity, noncontradiction and causality are primarily neither logical nor empirical but metaphysical principles. Hence there is no reason why the empirical scientist should not cut loose from the principle of causality which is a principle of substance and not of appearance, nor why the logician should interpret identity existentially. Logically it is a tautology, metaphysically a synthetic proposition, and there is no contradiction in this if we preserve the formalities.

It may not be out of place here to call to mind Kant's reference, in § 12 of the *Critique of Pure Reason,* to the Scholastic position: *quodlibet ens est unum, verum, bonum.* The principle, he says "has proved very meagre in consequences, and has indeed yielded only propositions that are tautological." He goes on to say "these supposedly transcendental predicates of *things,* are, in fact, nothing but logical requirements and criteria of all *knowledge* of things."[14] Kant is here opposing the conception of ontological truth, and aligning himself with the Hobbesian position that "true and false are attributes of speeches, not of things." The reason for his doing so is the same, and you will find it in the Preface to the Second Edition. "[The physicists] learned that reason has insight only into that which it produces after a plan of its own, and that it must not allow itself to be kept, as it were, in nature's leading-strings . . . but must constrain nature to give answer to questions of reason's own determining."

Physics must adopt as its guide "that which it has itself put into nature."[15] The Kantian philosophy, too, marches under the banner of the dominative will. Man imposes his creativity upon nature, and this is the ultimate source of Kant's doctrine of the autonomy of pure reason.

The question at issue between idealism and realism is also the question of human autonomy. Their anthropologies are radically different, and here it is apropos to point out that the epistemology of St. Thomas is the epistemology of a *creature*. It expresses the status of man as a being dependent on God. In this sense it is true that it is an epistemology which is theologically conditioned, though whether it is true or not should be decided on rational grounds. It would be misleading however, not to point out that the entire philosophy of St. Thomas deploys within the conviction that this is a created universe.

I pointed out earlier in what sense the *adequatio* formula asserts that truth is a quality of propositions. But there is a more radical sense in which truth is in things rather than in thoughts or words. Here Aquinas is moved by considerations not unlike those of Plato when the latter proposed the forms as having the kind of being which can be known. It is because a thing cannot be both itself and its contrary that it can be known, and it is in this veracity, in this consistency with itself, that its possibility of being known consists. Only the true can be known, and only that can be known which has the ontical property of being itself. The demand for consistency and coherence in the thinker himself arises from the demand of his own being to be itself.

Now what makes a thing itself, is its being creatively thought by God. There is one God who has made and sustains a diversified universe, every being in which is in his image, so that each in its degree reflects or mirrors the uniqueness of God. Each must be one and itself and the center of a power of existence because it resembles a sole Creator who made it like himself in the power of his own undivided act of existence. In other words, things have natures and are causes and therefore are knowable because of the act by which the being of God is his own truth; that is, the act by which he knows and sustains all things. As Professor Pieper has pointed out, there is a fascinating negative tribute to this in Sartre who declares, "There is no human nature, because there is no God to think it." Hence thinking truly or realistically is rethinking the divine thought in the degree possible to a creature, or speaking words which are morsels of the Word.

This gives us the context for understanding the formula that knowledge is *per modum recipientis* which must be taken in the closest connection with the definition of truth as *adequatio*. It is an expression of the conviction that epistemology must be founded on ontology. The *adequatio* definition implies that we can know *what* things are, but it does not imply that we can have an exhaustive knowledge of their essence. We can know them only from the point of view of a creature having its determinate place in the scale of being. God as the creator of beings is the source both of their existence and of their truth. Hence the truth about this pencil or this pipe is hidden in the mystery of God who alone can penetrate their being through and through in the manner to which the gnostics and rationalists lay claim.[16] As utility or as artefact this pencil is knowable through and through, but as creature it remains an ultimate mystery and source of wonder.[17] In this we see the reason why the rationalists' claim to make human knowledge the final arbiter of truth must issue in the conception of nature as the area of utility, and therefore as potentially manipulatable process. In Marxism, history itself becomes manipulatable. When Sartre goes further and finds in consciousness a principle of nothingness he is being quite logical: he is reducing the instrumental conception of the mind to the more than Oriental nihilism which it implies. For St. Thomas our knowledge is true, but it is relatively true. This pencil is green, and it is the pencil which is green, but there is no reason to suppose than an angel or God need see it as green. We see then that the *adequatio* formula serves also to limit human knowledge within its own proper modality. We might describe it as the epistemology of a humanism which is creaturely.

To conclude, then, I should like to say that I am well aware that I may be accused of trapping my hearers in a theology, and that I have ruined the claims of Thomist epistemology to be a rational philosophic theory. My answer is that the position of St. Thomas is no more theological than that of Descartes or Hobbes or Kant; it is also no less. They all have a preepistemological background. They rest on an anthropology. Either God creates man or man creates God, and what we see in the moderns is a struggle with and often a compromise between these positions. Either the will is primarily created and receptive or it is primarily autonomous and creative. The instrumental and self-alienating view of thought is no less theological than the Thomist, and I dislike the self-deceiving pretensions of the idealists, whether absolutists or empiricists to be above all these matters. Had they more coherence with themselves we should hear less of the coherence theory of knowledge. And since St. Thomas explicitly rests his theory of knowledge on his anthropology, and works out its implications, then, if I must choose, I prefer to choose a position which is self-conscious, and which is not controlled by principles which it does not recognize. It is more rational and philosophic.

It may be thought that I am reading modern positions back into St. Thomas, but I do not think so, though I say this with the general *caveat* that I do not think that a great thinker can be held strictly within the bounds of his own words, but that being open to the world he keeps on growing with it. The more faithful we are to his words the more we will find that his principle of growth is our own. Rather, however, I seem to be going back to Plato and St. Augustine, and perhaps especially to those great books of the *De Trinitate* in which self-knowledge is made the key both to our knowledge of the universe and of God.

The *adequatio* theory of St. Thomas is not merely an

attempt to give an account of what happens when I know this pencil or this table. It does not leave us with the *disjecta membra* of manifold acts of cognition. It implies a creative unification of experience from a centre which has made the effort to know and to unify itself. Thus he writes:

> Truth follows the operation of the intellect inasmuch as it belongs to the intellect to judge about a thing as it is. And truth is known by the intellect in view of the fact that the intellect reflects upon its own act—not merely as knowing its own act, but as knowing the proportion of its act to the thing. Now, this proportion cannot be known without knowing the nature of the act; and the nature of the act cannot be known without knowing the nature of the active principle, that is, the intellect itself, to whose nature it belongs to be conformed to things. Consequently, it is because the intellect reflects upon itself that it knows the truth.[18]

He continues:

> The most perfect beings, i.e., intellectual substances, return to their essence with a complete return: knowing something external to themselves, in a certain sense they go outside themselves; but by knowing that they know, they are already beginning to return to themselves . . . That return is completed to the extent that they know their own essences.[19]

No truth, then, without self-knowledge, and without a judgment which takes into account the kind of being which we are, and the kind of operation which we are performing. Philosophy makes the call upon us which it made upon Socrates: to enter into those spaces and times within ourselves which are the subjective correlates of those times and spaces which modern times, and the techniques of rocketry are opening to us. There is no going outwards without going inwards.

Berdyaev remarks:

"The compulsorily perceptible world which is the only real world for prosaic, workaday experience, and the only 'objective' world, is a creation of man. . . . When the ordinary everyday person naïvely says: 'I regard as real only what I perceive with the senses' he is, by so saying, and without being aware of the fact, regarding the reality of the world as dependent upon himself. And that is why philosophical empiricism was a form of idealism. Naïve realism is subjectivism at its worst . . . Man exteriorises his own enslavement, he projects it upon the external, and he pictures it to himself as constraint exercised by an exterior reality."

What we require is that true subjectivism which Kierkegaard inherited from Socrates, and which he was expressing when he said:

> The Law for the development of the self with respect to knowledge, in so far as it is true that the self becomes itself, is this, that the increasing degree of knowledge corresponds with the degree of self-knowledge, that the more the self knows, the more it knows itself. If this does not occur, then the more knowledge increases, the more it becomes a kind of inhuman knowing, for the production of which man's self is squandered.

Philosophy is simply human knowing, knowing which knows how it is human, and in this knowing preserves our humanity and our freedom in a world in which man is his greatest enemy. What is philosophy? is an ultimate question which man puts to himself about himself, and in the openness of the question lies the foundation of his rational freedom.

"When a man has come to be able to think of the nature of his own mind, and to find what is the truth, he will find it nowhere else but in himself. And he will find, not what he did not know, but that of which he did not think."[20]

NOTES

1. D. F. Pears, ed., *The Nature of Metaphysics* (London: Macmillan, 1957).

2. *Ibid.*, p. 99.

3. *Ibid.*, p. 128.

4. William Henry Walsh, *Metaphysics* (London: Hutchinson, 1963), p. 34.

5. This suggests the importance and the scope of a genuine sociology of knowledge.

6. St. Thomas Aquinas, *S. T.*, I, q. 87, a. 1, c., and a. 3, c.

7. John MacMurray, *Persons in Relation,* Gifford Lectures, 1953, *The Form of the Personal,* vol. II (London: Faber and Faber, 1961), p. 42.

8. Hugh Miller, *History and Science* (Berkeley: University of California, 1939), p. 85.

9. St. Augustine, *De Trinitate,* Bk. X, chapter I, *in fine.*

10. Scott Buchanan, ed., *Portable Plato* (New York: Viking, 1948).

11. St. Augustine, *Confessions,* Bk. I, 6, *in fine.*

12. Karl Rahner, *Geist in Welt,* 2nd ed. (Munich: Kösel, 1957), p. 71 ff.

13. Robert Earl Cushman, *Therapeia: Plato's Conception of Philosophy* (Chapel Hill, N. C.: University of North Carolina Press, 1958), p. xviii.

14. Immanuel Kant, *Critique of Pure Reason,* B 113–114.

15. *Ibid.,* B xiii–xiv.

16. *Principia essentialia rerum sunt nobis ignota* (St. Thomas Aquinas, *In I De Anima,* lect. 1, n. 15).

17. Cf. John Henry Newman, *Grammar of Assent* (New York: Catholic Publication Society, 1870), p. 271: "Each of his creatures is incomprehensible to us also, in the sense that no one has a perfect understanding of them but He. We recognize and appropriate aspects of them, and logic is useful to us in registering these aspects and what they imply; but it does not give us to know even one individual being."

18. St. Thomas Aquinas, *De Veritate,* q. 1, a. 9, c.

19. *Ibid.*

20. St. Augustine, *De Trinitate,* Bk. XIV, chapter V, *in fine.*

ALFRED JULES AYER

was born on October 29, 1910, in London, England. Educated as a King's Scholar at Eton and as a classical scholar at Christ Church, Oxford, he then spent a short time at the University of Vienna, where he obtained firsthand contact with the logical positivism of the "Viennese Circle," under the leadership of Moritz Schlick. He became lecturer in philosophy at Christ Church in 1933, and research student in 1935. He joined the Welsh guards in 1940, but served in military intelligence for most of World War II. In 1945 he returned to Oxford, where he became fellow and dean of Wadham College. From 1946 to 1959 he was Grote professor of philosophy of mind and logic at University College, London. He was elected a fellow of the British Academy in 1952, and in 1957 honorary fellow of Wadham College, Oxford. In 1962, he became a doctor honoris causa of Brussels University. Since 1959 he has been Wykeham professor of logic at Oxford and fellow of New College.

He is well known for his radio and television appearances, having appeared on the following programs, among others: "The Brains Trust," "Tonight," and "Table Talk." He has also been a frequent contributor of articles and reviews to various journals, newspapers, and collections of readings.

One of his principal books is the now classic Language, Truth and Logic *(1936, second edition, 1946) in which is found his first full-length presentation in English—with some modifications of his own—of the logical positivism of the Vienna Circle, and of which Bertrand Russell has said, "A delightful book . . . I should like to have written it myself." Other of Ayer's works include* The Foundations of Empirical Knowledge *(1940),* Philosophical Essays *(1954),* The Problem of Knowledge *(1956), and* The Concept of a Person and Other Essays *(1963). He was also a contributor to the eminently successful collection of essays,* The Revolution in Philosophy *(1956). His most recent book is* The Origins of Pragmatism, *an important and full-length study of Peirce and James.*

PHILOSOPHY AS ELUCIDATING CONCEPTS

It is strange, if you come to think of it, that this series of lectures should be taking place at all. You have invited a number of professional philosophers to try to tell you what philosophy is. It might be expected that we should not find this very difficult. Since nearly all of you are either teachers or students of philosophy, it might also be expected that you would not need to be told what it is. Yet not only am I not at all confident of my ability to give a satisfactory answer to the question which you have put to me, but it is very probable that the answers which you obtain from my colleagues will differ quite markedly from my own; it might even be that they are radically divergent.

This disagreement among specialists about the very nature of their subject appears to be peculiar to philosophy. This is not, of course, to say that serious disputes do not occur in other subjects, or that these disputes may not be of a radical character. The disagreements between formalists and intuitionists in mathematics, or between Darwinists and Lamarckians in biology, or between Marxist and other historians provide obvious examples. But in all these cases the debate is staged against a background of accepted doctrine or, at the very least, a stock of accredited facts. This is not so in philosophy. In this respect, though in this respect only, it has something in common with theology. Even so, there is a greater measure of agreement among theologians as to what they are trying to achieve, however great the uncertainty as to whether they are succeeding.

The failure of philosophers to come to an agreement about the purposes of their activity, and the methods by which it should be pursued, has become more marked in recent years and has led, understandably, to a certain crisis of confidence. Philosophers of all schools increasingly feel the obligation to put the value of philosophy in question. Since this crisis has been building up for some time, it may be useful to trace its historical development.

In the main, it is the outcome of the dissociation of philosophy from science. It did not affect the ancient Greeks, since they did not make any such distinction; for them, philosophy covered every kind of human knowledge. Neither was it a problem for medieval philosophers, who were content to take their premises from theology. Looking back, one can see the beginnings of a threat to the position of philosophy in the extraordinary development of the physical sciences which followed the Renaissance, but this was not apparent at the time. Philosophers like Descartes, Leibniz and Spinoza did not look upon their problems as being generically different from those of Galileo and Newton. Even philosophers like Locke, Berkeley, and Hume—who stood further away from the physical sciences—did not distinguish their subject from what we should nowadays call psychology. In particular, Locke was clearly aiming to produce a theory of mind which would be a counterpart to Newton's theory of matter. Kant was himself a distinguished cosmologist, and his *Critique of Pure Reason* is very largely an attempt to supply a foundation for the Newtonian system. Hegel, it must be admitted, was a good deal less scientific, but even he tried to incorporate the science of his day in his all-embracing metaphysical system.

It is in the nineteenth century that philosophy and science begin to take different paths. Indeed, the very word "scientist" is a nineteenth century coinage, introduced by the English philosopher of science, Whewell, in 1840. The need for its introduction marked the growing autonomy of the special sciences; until then they had been content with the title of natural philosophers. The new appellation declared their independence. This was conceded by the philosophers, though not (as we shall see) without some attempts to reassert their sovereignty; they were then left with the problem of finding some territory which they could still count as their private property. That there is such a territory (at least in the sense that there are activities which are distinctively philosophical) is perhaps the only point on which all the lecturers are likely to be in full agreement. It is when we come to the characterization of this territory that the divergencies will appear. All that can be done, in these circumstances, is to describe it in my own way, at the same time setting out as clearly as possible the reasons why I believe this description to be correct.

I start with the assumption that there is some class of true propositions which it is the special business of philosophy to discover, and that their discovery is of some importance; in short, that philosophy is, or is capable of being, a worthwhile cognitive discipline. This assumption is itself not accepted by all contemporary philosophers, but my hope is to succeed in vindicating it. If I did not believe that it could be vindicated, I doubt if I should still be engaging in philosophy. Of course this is not an argument; it is only a confession of faith.

Our aim being to pin down the special province of philosophy (assuming provisionally that it has one), a good method will be to proceed by elimination. I shall try to dispose of various current views and then consider what possibilities remain. The answer at which I shall eventually arrive will be found to raise problems to which I do not know the solution. For our present purposes, I shall be satisfied if I can arouse your interest in the problems.

The first view to examine is that philosophy differs from the sciences only or mainly through its greater generality. The physicist, it is said, occupies himself only with one limited aspect of reality; the chemist with another, and the biologist with another. What uniquely distinguishes the philosopher is that he is concerned with reality as a whole.

There is some truth in this. What is true is that the subject matter of philosophy is not circumscribed in the way that the subject matter of any one of the special sciences may be held to be. On the other hand, it's false to say that the philosopher does the same work as the scientist, only on a larger scale. For what would this amount to? How would he set about depicting the whole of reality except through the depiction of its parts? I suppose that it would be possible to compose an encyclopedia which would set out all the theories and hypotheses which were currently accepted in the various branches of science. It would be a difficult task for any one man to accomplish, and by the time that he had completed it, some parts of the work would almost certainly be obsolete. Even so, if it were well done it would have some utility. However, it is more than mere concern for the dignity of my profession that prompts me to reject the suggestion that the province of philosophy is limited to the compilation of scientific works of reference.

It may be thought that this is unfair to the view under consideration. What it requires of the philosopher is not that he should merely assemble the scientific theories of his time but that he should integrate them into a world picture; but again it is not clear what such a world picture could be. Perhaps one could envisage something of the following kind. It might turn out that physics could be unified; that is, a means might be found to fulfill Einstein's aim of constructing a unified theory of the utmost generality, incorporating both quantum theory and the theory of relativity. It might then be shown that the other sciences were all reducible to physics.

To some extent this has already been achieved: there is good reason to think that chemical laws can be derived from those of physics and biological laws from chemical laws. If it could be shown that the laws of psychology and sociology were derivable from biological laws, the program would be complete. If it were completed, one might then regard the ultimate physical theory (in terms of which everything else was explained) as affording a general picture of the world. Since the theory would be bound to be entirely abstract, it could only yield a very schematic picture; but it seems to me all that could be significantly looked for in this way.

But now it is surely clear that the question whether any program of this kind is feasible is one of a highly technical character. Only a practicing physiologist could be in a position to decide whether it is possible to construct a physiological theory which would account for what are ordinarily classified as mental phenomena. Equally, the question whether biochemistry provides a satisfactory bridge between the organic and the inorganic sciences is one that can be answered only by someone who is working in this field. Such questions certainly cannot be answered by a philosopher in his armchair, contemplating concepts. If any philosopher pretends to be able to answer them on purely a priori grounds, you should not listen to him.

You should listen to him even less if he claims to be introducing you to a different reality from that which is explored by science. This is an idea that has been most prevalent in the East, but it was also adopted by some Western philosophers in the nineteenth century, and still finds some adherents in the West. Among Western philosophers it has mainly taken the form of an attempt to show by purely a priori reasoning that the real world is quite unlike the world that we ordinarily believe in; that, for example, space and time and matter are illusory. In oriental philosophy, there is less that one can recognize as argument; you are exhorted rather to penetrate beyond appearances to a deeper level of being where everything is one.

I am afraid that this is just nonsense. There is no way of

finding out what the world is like except by putting up hypotheses and testing them by observation. When people talk of a deeper reality, you will find that they are using the word "reality" in such a way that no sense can be attached to it; there are no criteria, in this usage, for determining how it is to be applied. It is the same with the contention that everything is one (where this is construed not as implying that the stuff of which the world is made is homogeneous), or that everything is subject to the same laws, but that all distinctions are ultimately unreal. In any ordinary sense, it is just not true that I am identical with this glass, or this watch, or this chair, or that they are identical with one another. Perhaps by the use of drugs or by some other method, one could get into a state in which one had the feeling that everything, including oneself was merging into everything else, but this feeling would have no cognitive import; it would have nothing to do with any matter of fact. It may, indeed, happen that things which seem to be distinct are not really so, as when some persistent object reappears under a disguise, but in all such cases there are recognized criteria for deciding whether or not identity has been preserved. To say that everything is one, in default of any criteria of identity, is to say nothing significant. I have chosen extreme examples, but the same objection would apply to any talk of an ultramundane reality.

A more intelligible view of the function of philosophy is that in which the philosopher is cast as a sage. What is expected of him is that he should (as Plato put it) tell people how they ought to live. This view, still very prevalent, was popularized by the Stoics who are also responsible for the popular usage of the word 'philosophical,' in which to take something philosophically is not to mind about it. The idea is that the sage has his attention so firmly fixed upon higher things that he is not troubled by any of the ordinary cares of life. There is no particular reason to expect those who study philosophy to be philosophical in this sense of the word.

The role of the sage is one that philosophers can and sometimes do play; but it is not their professional perquisite.

It is not anyone's professional perquisite, for the sufficient reason that morals is not a subject. This does not imply that it does not matter how people behave or that if one is in doubt about one's proper course of conduct there may not be persons from whom it is sensible to seek advice. Certain persons may be said to have good moral judgment, in the sense that the conduct of their lives or the verdicts which they pass upon the conduct of others command one's moral respect. What is meant by saying that morality is not a subject, is that there is no such thing as being learned in morals. It is not possible to have specialized knowledge in the field of morals, in the way that a chemist or an ornithologist has specialized knowledge. There is no repository of moral doctrine to which a philosopher, or anyone else for that matter, could have privileged access. To have had a philosophical training may be of advantage in helping one to see whether one's moral attitudes are self-consistent, and also perhaps in enabling one to discount prejudice. The study of moral philosophy may lead to a better understanding of the role of moral concepts and of the relation of judgments of value to statements of empirical fact. Insofar as a philosopher may be expected to think clearly about such matters, his moral pronouncements may be held to carry a little extra weight. Even so, if he does set up as a moral counselor, his claim to our attention will depend rather on his character and his experience of the world than on his strictly professional attainments.

I come now to the conception of the philosopher's function which has played the most prominent part in the history of Western philosophy since the time of Descartes. This is the conception of the philosopher as a judge. The idea is that the philosopher does not investigate the world at first hand, but rather assesses the evidence which others set before him. His task is to pronounce on the claims to knowledge which are put forward by the scientist, or indeed by the ordinary man in the street. He raises the Socratic question whether we really know all that we think we know. He considers how far and in what manner our most fundamental beliefs are capable of being justified. "Is there anything of which one can be absolutely certain?" was the question which Descartes posed in following his famous method of doubt and it is a question which has haunted Western philosophy to the present day. So empiricists from Locke to Bertrand Russell have started out with the "hard" data of sense-experience and tried to show how much could legitimately be built on this foundation. Kant attempted to fix the boundaries of the possible extent of human knowledge. Since the early work of Wittgenstein, the concern in recent philosophy has been with the boundaries of significant discourse rather than with the boundaries of knowledge, but though they are approached from a different angle the problems are substantially the same.

It is clear that in an inquiry of this sort everything depends upon one's criteria of significance or one's criteria of knowledge. Thus, with regard to the question of what can be known, someone like Descartes (who relies on intellectual intuition) is likely to come up with a different answer from that which would be given by an empiricist like Locke. Therefore, it is necessary for anyone who practices philosophy in this way to try to evaluate the criteria themselves. He is faced at the outset with the questions: What is a legitimate starting point? and What are the legitimate ways of advancing beyond it?

This is something with which to deal in my succeeding lectures, but first I want to examine an argument which puts the whole of this enterprise in doubt. I attribute the argument to the Cambridge philosopher G. E. Moore, though he did not himself explicitly advance it. It does, however, seem to underline his distinctive approach to the problems of philosophy; an approach which has very largely colored the development of contemporary British philosophy and has also had a considerable influence in the United States.

As many of you will know, Moore's chief contribution to philosophy was his defense of common sense. He was concerned to vindicate the common sense view of the world against the attacks which had been made on it by metaphysicians, and his technique was to take the metaphysicians as meaning exactly what they said. The metaphysicians in whom he was mainly interested (for historical reasons) were the English neo-Hegelians who denied the reality of space and time and matter; and his procedure was to reduce their position to absurdity simply by showing what it literally implied. He argued that if time is unreal, it follows that nothing ever happens before or after anything else; nothing grows or changes; no event ever causes another event to happen; and no one ever acquires a belief, including the belief that time is unreal, since the acquisition of a belief is itself something that occurs in time. In the same way, he pointed out that if the proposition that matter is unreal were true, it would follow that nobody maintained it. For if matter is unreal, there are no physical bodies; and if there are no physical bodies, there are no human bodies; and if there are no human bodies, there are no metaphysicians to hold that matter is unreal. This does not strictly refute the proposition, since it could be true even though its truth was inconsistent with anyone's believing it, but it does remove it from serious consideration.

Against these metaphysical extravagancies, Moore simply set his knowledge of the truth of what he called the common sense view of the world. He did not attempt to offer any vindication of this claim to knowledge; he merely insisted on the fact that he did know what he said he knew. Thus, in a famous lecture which he gave for the British Academy, he quoted Kant as saying that it was a scandal to philosophy that nobody had succeeded in proving the existence of the external world, where this is taken to imply the existence of objects in space, outside of our own minds. Moore undertook to put an end to this scandal by offering a proof. It took a very simple form. He held up his two hands and said that both he and his audience knew that these were two human hands. But, he went on, if we know that these are human hands, it follows that two human hands exist, and from this it follows that at least two physical objects exist; and since it is a defining characteristic of a physical object that it exists in space outside of any mind, you have your proof of an external world. For such a proof to be valid it is sufficient that the premises be true, that they should not presuppose the conclusion, and that the conclusion should follow logically from the premises. In this instance, as Moore pointed out, all three conditions are satisfied; consequently, the proof is valid. I shall show later on why one nevertheless feels it to be unsatisfactory.

It is to be remarked that when Moore claimed to know that the common sense view of the world was wholly true he was not committing himself to upholding every proposition accepted by the man in the street. Among contemporary philosophers, common sense has a standing which few of their predecessors have been willing to accord it, but not even its most ardent champion among them would deny that it could sometimes go astray. It was once a mark of common sense to believe that the earth was flat, or that epilepsy was a symptom of possession by demons; it would be rash to assume that none of our common sense beliefs will seem equally misguided to future generations. What Moore had in mind when he spoke of the common sense view of the world was a set of very general beliefs which might be said to underlie all our more specific theories about the way the world works. Such is the belief that there are physical objects which are accessible to different observers and to different senses, so that, for example, the glass which I see on this table is identical with the glass which I touch, and identical with the glass which you see. It is also part of this belief that objects like this glass have a temporal history and occupy positions in a public space. Another belief which Moore took as part of the common sense view of the world is that some—but not all—physical objects have acts of consciousness attached to them, which is a way of expressing the fact that there are mental occurrences, without committing oneself to the postulation of mental substances. For Moore, there can be no doubt that these general propositions are true, since he takes them to follow logically from propositions which he knows to be true; for example, the proposition that I now perceive a glass is understood to entail both that there is at least one physical object—with all that this implies—and that there is an act of consciousness.

I shall now try to show how this championship of common sense can be used to throw doubt upon the conception of philosophy as having a judicial function. As stated earlier, Moore himself did not supply any justification of his claims to knowledge; he merely drew the conclusion that since he knew the common sense view of the world to be true, the metaphysical theories which conflicted with it must be false. It seems to me, however, that he was in fact relying on a form of justification which neither he nor his followers have made fully explicit. If one does insist on asking how we know that this is a glass, the answer is not that we know it by divine revelation or by any form of purely intellectual intuition; we know it on the basis of our current sense experience. We can see the glass; and if this is not thought to be enough one can make sure by handling it. This justifies our assertion that the glass exists, for the very good reason that sentences like "this is a glass" are used in such a way that our having just this sort of experience is the best possible evidence for the truth of what they express. Admittedly, the evidence is not conclusive; one can be deceived—as Moore himself was on a celebrated occasion when he pointed to a dummy skylight and claimed to know that it was a window to the sky. But in all such cases, there are ways to detect one's mistake. Even though the logical possibility of error may always remain, we can make observations which leave us in no serious doubt of the truth. In short, there are recognized criteria for deciding questions of this kind; and whether these criteria are satisfied in any given instance is not a philosophical but a purely empirical question. If someone calls out that the house is on fire, we know how to find out whether he is telling the truth; if our observations bear him out, we are likely to take some sort of action. There is no occasion here for an exercise of philosophical doubt.

But it is not only to statements at the common sense level that this argument applies. It is equally true of the scientific or mathematical statements that there are accredited procedures for deciding whether they are valid. If someone is presented with the evidence which is taken as establishing a scientific theory, and still refuses to accept the theory, then unless he has some special reason for mistrusting the evidence, or supposing that it has been wrongly interpreted, his refusal to accept the theory simply shows that he does not understand it. If someone goes through a mathematical proof (for instance, the proof that there is no greatest prime number), and refuses to accept the conclusion, then unless he can advance some mathematical argument which casts doubt on the proof, he simply shows that he does not understand mathematics. It is a condition of the significance of any type of assertion that there should be criteria for deciding whether it is true or false; and whether the criteria are satisfied is always a question of material or formal fact. Consequently, there is no room for philosophy to intervene; there is no judicial function for it to exert. But in that case what use remains for it?

The next lecture will offer some criticisms of this argument. What I want to do in the remainder of this lecture is to trace the consequence of accepting it. We saw earlier that the philosopher is not in a position to compete with the scientist in giving a description or explanation of the world. If now the function of a judge is also to be denied him, all that appears to be left is some work of clarification. At any rate this is the conclusion to which the followers of Moore and other modern philosophers have come. It is most commonly expressed by saying that the only legitimate contribution that the philosopher can hope to make to the advancement of knowledge is through engaging in philosophical analysis.

Though this is a view which has come to be very widely held (at least in English-speaking countries), there is no general agreement among those who subscribe to it as to what philosophical analysis consists in. In fact, I think it is possible to distinguish at least eight different activities which figure under this general heading. I shall conclude this lecture by saying something about each of them in turn.

The most formal of these activities, and the one most closely allied to science is that in which the analysis consists in the structural description, perhaps even the axiomatization of a scientific theory. This is not very widely practiced because the combination of scientific knowledge and logical skill which is required for it is rare. A good example is to be found in Professor Woodger's axiomatization of a part of biology.

A second and perhaps more fruitful proceeding is to give precision to terms which play an important part in scientific or in everyday discourse. Examples of this are Tarski's semantic definition of truth, Reichenbach's work on the concept of probability, and Carnap's and Hempel's attempts to develop a formal theory of confirmation. The idea is to take a concept which may be used loosely or ambiguously in ordinary speech, if necessary to break it down into a number of different concepts, and then by the use of formal methods to define a term, or a set of terms, which give a sharper rendering to the sense of the concept which you are replacing.

Thirdly, analysis may take the form of showing that certain types of linguistic expressions can be radically transformed or dispensed with altogether. I am thinking here of such things as Russell's theory of descriptions, or Quine's elimination of singular terms, or Goodman's and my own elimination of tenses. The motive for such undertakings may be that of removing some perplexity caused by the use of the expressions on which you are operating. Thus Russell was puzzled by the fact that apparently referential expressions like "the present King of France" could have a meaning, even though they failed to denote anything. And he got rid of the difficulty by proving that the sentences in which such expressions typically occurred could be reformulated in such a way that the misleading show of reference disappeared. Another motive may be the desire to vindicate some general principle, as that everything that is shown in language by the use of demonstrative expressions could be explicitly said. This is one reason for trying to get rid of verbal forms (like tenses) which are tied to contexts. The fulfillment of the program would require that proper nouns, pronouns and demonstratives like 'this' and 'that' be replaced by general descriptions of the person or object referred to, and that all spatio-temporal location be accomplished by specifying the relations of the things described to certain unique landmarks. It is interesting to note that the temporal landmark may be merely postulated. For instance, in the Roman dating system, the point of origin was the founding of the city by Romulus and Remus, most probably a mythical event. Neither does it affect the operation of our own dating system that the evidence points to the birth of Christ as having occurred in the year 4 B.C. The statement that the battle of Waterloo was fought in 1815 A.D. is not held to be falsified by the fact that it was fought not 1815, but 1819 years after the occurrence of the unique event on which the whole system is supposed to be pegged. There is more to be said about the conditions which are required for a dating system to be viable, but it seems clear to me that if we have a viable dating system, we can dispense not only with tenses but with the concepts of past, present, and future. These are devices for indicating the temporal positions of the utterance in which they figure relatively to the event to which it refers; and this information can be made explicit by simply saying whether the event described occurs before or after or simultaneously with the description of it. How important it is to carry out this form of analysis is a debatable question; there are those who would dismiss it as little more than a technical exercise, but I think that in certain cases it can throw a useful light on the way in which our concepts work.

A variant of this procedure, important enough to deserve a place to itself, is what may be called reductive analysis. This is the attempt to eliminate an alleged type of entity in favor of entities of another type which are thought to have a stronger grasp upon reality. For example, it is plausible to hold that nations do not exist independently of the individuals who compose them. The reduction would then consist in showing how everything that we want to say about a nation can be rephrased in the form of statements about its members. A more interesting but also more dubious example is the attempt to reduce mind to matter, or matter to mind. There are philosophers like my colleague Professor Ryle who say that there are no such things as mental processes over and above the fact that people behave or are disposed to behave in such and such ways. On the other hand there are the phenomenalists who claim that physical objects are reducible to sense data. The trouble with reductive analysis is that if the criterion of reducibility is the power to translate statements about the entities which you are treating as logical constructs into statements which refer only to the entities which you are treating as genuine, it never seems to work—except in trivial instances. It is easy to translate statements about the average plumber into statements about plumbers, but it is not easy to find a formula even for translating statements about nations into statements about their members. There is a good deal more to say about this topic in my succeeding lectures.

A fifth type of anlaysis consists in the discrimination of different types of statement, not with respect to the objects to which they refer, but with respect to the function which they fulfill. The question of the nature of moral judgments (whether, for example, they can properly be said to be either true or false) would come under this heading. A notable recent contribution to this form of analysis is Professor Austin's discovery of what he called performative statements. These are statements which do not report activities but help to constitute them. For instance, the judge who sentences you to prison is not predicting that you will go to prison, but helping to bring it about. To say "I promise" under the appropriate conditions, is not to report that one is making a promise but actually to make it.

Professor Austin was also largely responsible for the variety of analysis which consists in a meticulous examination of the ways in which English words, or the words of some other natural language, are actually used. This kind of linguistic philosophy—as it came to be called—is going out of fashion, even in Oxford where it took hold most strongly. But it can be valuable in certain fields, such as the philosophy of law.

A point which the vogue of linguistic philosophy helped to emphasize was that not all explanations of the use of concepts result in definitions. For instance, one might set out to elucidate the concept of memory, not by defining it, but by making such points as that remembering does not necessarily involve the presence of a memory-image; that even when such images do occur the part which they play is logically inessential. A great deal of what is known as the philosophy of mind consists in advancing considerations of this sort. Such informal explanations make up my seventh category.

Finally, there is the approach of Wittgenstein and his followers, who see philosophy as an attempt to free us from the perplexities into which we fall when we misinterpret the workings of our language. By a suitable choice of examples, an attempt is made to expose such naive assumptions as that the things to which a common noun applies necessarily possess a common quality or that words like 'intending' or 'undertaking' stand for mental acts. In Wittgenstein's hands this method can be most illuminating; the same cannot always be said of his imitators.

This classification of the various types of analysis is not intended to be sharp. Neither am I putting forward my eight versions as competitors; different methods may suit different persons or different problems. There has indeed been a certain tension between those who tend to think that only a formal approach can yield anything of cognitive interest and those who believe that the really interesting questions are not of a nature to yield to formal treatment. But I can see no reason a priori why both parties should not achieve significant results. What we do need (especially in the cases where the approach is informal) is a clearer understanding of the purpose for which the analysis is undertaken, and of the ways in which we are to determine whether it has been successful.

Even if we suppose this to have been achieved, the question still remains whether the practice of analysis, in one or other of these different forms, exhausts the legitimate scope of philosophy. To answer this question we shall have to return to Moore's argument. Is there any possibility of escaping from its restrictive implications? And if there is such a possibility, for what kind of critical or even speculative activity does it leave room? These problems will be considered next.

PHILOSOPHY AS CONSTRUCTIVELY CRITICAL
OF CONCEPTUAL SYSTEMS

Let us begin this lecture by taking another look at the argument underlying Moore's defense of common sense. It rests on the premise that every type of statement has its own criteria built into it; if we understand the sentence by which the statement is expressed, we know under what conditions it is to be accepted. It is then pointed out that whether these conditions are satisfied in any given instance is a plain matter of empirical or formal fact. There is, therefore, no place for any philosophical decision.

A version of this argument which has played a leading part in recent philosophical discussions is the so-called argument from paradigm cases, mainly used to rebut skepticism. Suppose, for example, that a skeptic tries to put in question the existence of physical objects, such as a table. It is argued that if the skeptic were right there would at least be some doubt whether the criteria which govern the use of the English word "table" were ever satisfied. But since it is a matter of common experience that the criteria are satisfied (since we constantly do apply words like "table" successfully), it follows that the skeptic must be wrong. Or again, take the vexed question of free will. Surely, it is said, there is a manifest difference between doing something of one's own free will and being constrained to do it. We can easily distinguish between a shotgun wedding and one in which the bridegroom willingly goes to the altar. Distinctions of this kind are provided for in our language, and we know perfectly well how to make them. But from this alone it follows that the skeptic who denies or even queries the existence of free will is simply going against the obvious facts.

This argument is suspect, and in showing you why it is suspect, I hope to be able to throw some more light on our general theme of the nature of philosophical inquiry. The point which Moore and his followers have overlooked is that every word or—if you prefer to talk of concepts—every concept, carries its load of theory. This is obvious in the case of scientific concepts, but the amount of theory which is embodied even in the use of such everyday words as 'table' or 'glass' is much greater than is generally allowed for. As pointed out in the last lecture, the objects to which such words are understood to apply are required to be accessible to different senses and to different persons; they have to occupy positions in public space and to endure through time. They have to be capable of existing unperceived, and it is part of the common sense view of the world to assume that they exist unperceived in very much the same form as they normally appear to us when we do perceive them. This last point is of special interest as it threatens to bring common sense into conflict with science, which tends to draw a distinction between things as they appear to us and things as they really are. For instance, on the scientific level, physical objects are divested of their color. The question whether there is a genuine conflict here (and if so, how it is to be resolved) is a very good example of a serious philosophical problem.

This should clarify what is meant by saying that even the

most ordinary words of our language carry some theoretic load. The point to make now is that the mere fact of our recognizing that a word has application does not commit us to the acceptance of its theoretical background. I will give two illustrations, both of them used before; but as they effectively establish the point, I hope you will not mind.

Suppose there is a tribe whose custom it is to interpret everything in terms of the moods of their deity. When it rains they say that Mumbo-Jumbo is grieving; when the sun shines, they say that Mumbo-Jumbo is happy, and so forth. This is not just a linguistic oddity; their language represents what Wittgenstein called a form of life: it embodies their conception of reality. To make this fully clear, we can develop the story by supposing that their talk of Mumbo-Jumbo is bound up with religious practices, that they attempt to influence his moods in order to bring about whatever they desire. Now consider the position of an anthropologist who is studying this tribe. There is a sense in which he will wish to dismiss everything that they say. Since he does not believe in the existence of Mumbo-Jumbo, he rejects their whole conceptual apparatus. At the same time, the argument from paradigm cases operates against him. There are recognized criteria for deciding whether the statements which are made in this language are true or false; for example, the criterion for the truth of the statement that Mumbo-Jumbo is grieving is that it is raining. It is a matter of empirical fact in any given instance whether or not these criteria are satisfied.

What are we to say in a case of this kind? There are three courses that might be taken. The first would be to apply the verification principle and simply cash these people's statements in terms of the observations by which they were taken to be verified. The conclusion would be that all that these people really meant by saying that Mumbo-Jumbo was grieving was that it was raining. They themselves would deny this, but this would just prove their ignorance of semantics. A second more flexible course would be not to force this reduction on them but to argue, along Moore's lines, that since there are empirical criteria for deciding what mood Mumbo-Jumbo is in, then in the case where these criteria are satisfied, the statements which describe his moods are true. The third course, which seems to me the right one, is to distinguish the core of fact to which the statement corresponds from its questionable theoretical setting. This leaves us free to admit that there is some truth in what these people are saying—there is, after all, a sense in which they do record empirical facts—but also permits us to reject their statements as embodying a false, or even nonsensical conception of the way in which the world works.

This is a fanciful example, but the same point can be illustrated historically. At a time when the belief in evil spirits was a part of common sense, there were recognized criteria for deciding when people were demoniacally possessed. Since these criteria were empirically satisfied in many instances, we should have to conclude (if we rigorously applied the argument from paradigm cases), that the tales of demoniac possession were often true. But this is a conclusion which no rational person nowadays would be willing to accept. We can avoid it quite easily by distinguishing (1) the undoubted fact that certain people displayed the symptoms in question from (2) the erroneous interpretation which was put upon it.

It is in this way, I think, that we should approach the problem of free will. Of course, if we only look at the phenomena, there is a difference between an ordinary wedding and a shotgun wedding. However, it is possible to admit this difference without accepting the interpretations which the concept of free will carries. To put it summarily, free will is a condition of responsibility. It is, in general, only for things which we have done of our own free will (in the sense that we are believed to have been free not to do them), that we are held to deserve praise or blame, punishment or reward. But a philosopher who acknowledges there is a manifest difference between doing something which you have decided you want to do and doing something because you have a gun pointed at your head, may still wish to say that this difference is not sufficient to justify your being held responsible in the one case and not the other. He will argue that so far as responsibility goes, the two are on a level, since causality operates in both. It is only that in the case where you are said to have acted of your own free will, the determining factors are less obvious. This argument may be open to criticism, but it is certainly not refuted by a mere appeal to paradigm cases. Though the question will not be pursued here, there are good grounds for saying that the idea of desert is incoherent, so that if we were rational we should give up our current notions of merit or guilt. We could still continue to praise and blame, reward and punish, on utilitarian grounds; but even so, this would make a considerable difference to our moral outlook and even to the operation of our penal system.

It is already becoming clear that once we distinguish between the extension of a concept and its theoretical background (so that we can admit that a concept has application without being obliged to accept the theory from which it emerges), Moore's argument loses its force. It no longer guarantees the validity of the common sense view of the world. For instance, a disciple of Berkeley's would not have to disagree with anybody else about the application of ordinary words like "glass" and "table." If he followed Berkeley's injunction to think with the learned and speak with the vulgar, his use of common sense expressions would not noticeably differ from that of the man in the street; but what his thinking with the learned would come to would be his rejecting the assumptions which common sense statements are ordinarily understood to carry, beginning with the assumption that things exist unperceived. In current philosophical jargon, he would be adopting a different conceptual system.

I am not going to try to define the rather vague notion of a conceptual system, though I hope that the remainder of this lecture and the following one may help to make it rather more precise. Obviously the most important questions with which we shall have to deal are what is required of a conceptual system, how one discriminates between them, and what grounds there can be for criticizing one or another. But before discussing any of this, I want to pose a more general question to which I do not know the answer. It might be held that there were certain general features which any conceptual system must possess for it to be possible for us to make any use of it at all. This is the position which Kant took; and one of his principal aims in the *Critique of Pure Reason* was to disclose what these general features were. As you know, he represented them as conditions of the possibility of human experience. A similar assumption is made by contemporary philosophers who have been influenced by Kant.

The difficulty here is that I do not see what foundation there can be for this sort of a priori anthropology. I do not see how one could arrive, otherwise than experimentally, at any universal generalization about the way in which the human understanding works. At the same time I am so far in sympathy with Kant that it is difficult to see how any possible world could be other than spatio-temporal. I am inclined to hold, therefore, that any conceptual system which can serve as a framework for an intelligible account of the world must contain the means of ordering things in space and time. But it is not at all clear what sort of necessity this is, or how it could be shown to obtain. As I do not think that I have anything of value to say about this question, I shall not pursue it further.

A less puzzling version of the Kantian approach is to be found in the claim that our conceptual system must have certain features if we are to be able to make certain distinctions that we should naturally wish to make. Thus Strawson has recently argued that if we are to distinguish between an objective world—not necessarily a world of things in themselves in the Kantian sense, but at least an objective world of phenomena—and our subjective experiences of it, then certain objects must be reidentifiable. This is substantially the argument of Kant's first analogy. Or again, there is Wittgenstein's contention that if we are representing a world in which there is communication, then certain objects must be represented as being public, in the sense that they satisfy criteria of identity which allow for the same object to be perceived by different observers. If this contention were valid, it would rule out the most radical form of phenomenalism, in which the world is broken down into a set of mutually exclusive private domains. But it might still allow for a weaker version in which an attempt was made to construct a public world out of neutral data. My difficulty, once again, is in seeing how such conclusions could be established by purely a priori arguments. It seems to be rather a matter of our having to try out possible counter examples and finding, perhaps, that they break down. So if one were unable to devise any form of phenomenalism that met one's requirements, one might give up the whole idea, even in default of an argument that showed it to be contradictory. This takes us back to the problem of what these requirements are.

One way to approach it is to ask what motive there can be for trying to elaborate a conceptual system which is significantly different from the one that we ordinarily employ. It might, indeed, be undertaken for its own sake, simply as a technical exercise. The aim might be to throw light upon the workings of our current system, by showing in what ways and to what extent it is replaceable by a system of a different structure. I think that this motive has been operative, especially in recent times. But what seems to me to have been the most common motive for developing a different system is the belief that our existing system is in some way unsatisfactory.

All this may become a little more clear if we consider examples. I am going now to examine four philosophical positions, each of which I interpret as an attempt to substitute a different conceptual system for the one that we have. In general, this is not what their proponents have thought that they were doing. In most cases, they have thought that they were seeing more clearly into the nature of reality.

The first example is the philosophy of Absolute Idealism; the second an animistic or theological system. You may remember that Professor Quine, at the end of his celebrated paper, "Two Dogmas of Empiricism," maintained that from a cognitive point of view, physical objects were in no better position than the Homeric gods: they are both cultural posits which are brought in to account for our experiences. We will develop this idea by considering a system in which things are supposed to happen by divine agency. This purpose could also be served by the third example, the system of Bishop Berkeley. However, we intend to ignore the theological aspect of Berkeley's philosophy and concentrate solely on his denial of matter or, in other words, his attempt to replace physical objects by collections of sensible qualities which exist only when perceived. Finally, we will go to the other extreme, considering that version of materialism which has come to be known as physicalism, in that it aims at the elimination of states of consciousness, or at any rate their reduction to physical processes. All these systems differ significantly from our present-day system of common sense, and apart from the second example, they are all philosophical in the sense that they result from the kind of speculation in which philosophers typically engage.

The main point to be made about the philosophy of Absolute Idealism, is that its interest is purely negative. On the positive side, the Absolute Idealists are even worse off than our Mumbo-Jumbo people, who at least have a going concern. Though it cannot be supposed that their methods of divination would enable them to understand or control their environment to any very profitable extent, we have represented them as making statements over which there is some empirical control. But what way could there possibly be of controlling such idealist claims as that all that there really can be is the Absolute, self-expressing and self-expressed, or that what masquerades as a system of material bodies in space and time is in reality a collection of immaterial selves timelessly loving one another? We do not know how to handle such statements; we cannot relate them to anything that we actually experience. The philosophers who put them forward were indeed willing to allow that our everyday statements contained some degrees of truth, but they did not have any viable method by which these degrees of truth could be assessed. It seemed almost to come down to vulgar worship of size. Any collection was thought to be more real than its elements, and everything culminated in the grand collection which alone was wholly real. But just because it was so grand one could not say anything significant about it. If you take a book like Bradley's *Appearance and Reality,* you will find that the section on 'reality' is very sad stuff.

By contrast, the section on 'appearance' is of considerable interest. The weakness of the Absolute Idealists is that when they reject the common sense view of the world, they have nothing intelligible to put in its place. Nonetheless, their reasons for rejecting the common sense view are worth looking into. It is not a question of their trying out an alternative to see if it will work; this sophisticated approach is found in some contemporary philosophers like Nelson Goodman, but it is a product of our own times. The philosophers we are speaking of, who flourished at the close of the nineteenth century, sought an alternative to the common sense view because they believed that this view was untenable. Their reasons for saying that space and time and matter were unreal were that they could not find an answer to the intellectual difficulties which they detected in the notion of continuity, or of infinite divisibility, or of things possessing material properties independently of our perceiving them. They certainly went too far in claiming that the assumptions shared by the common sense and scientific views of the world were self-contradictory, but they did call attention to genuine logical difficulties, not all of which have yet been satisfactorily disposed of (as the continuing interest in Zeno's paradoxes shows).

For example, the Cambridge philosopher McTaggart was one of those who denied the reality of time, which made him an easy victim of Moore's literalism. What could be more ridiculous than to suggest that nothing ever happens before anything else; that it is not, for example, true of us that we commonly have our breakfast after we wake up, or that we are all a day older than we were yesterday? But if instead of concentrating on McTaggart's conclusion we look at the arguments which led him to it, we find that they are not ridiculous. He begins by pointing out that the characteristics of being past, present, and future (which every event is supposed to possess) are mutually incompatible. To avoid a contradiction, we therefore have to say that events possess them at different moments. Our position then becomes that every event is past at a present or future moment, present at a present moment, and future at a present or past moment. But then the same difficulty arises with respect to the moments. We either relapse into contradiction or embark upon an infinite regress: This is a perfectly valid argument. What it proves, of course, is not that time is unreal, but rather that the relation of temporal priority has to be taken as fundamental; and past, present and future defined in terms of it by reference to the temporal position of the speaker, this position itself being characterized by its temporal relation to other arbitrarily chosen events. But since the effect of this is to spatialize time in Bergson's sense, since it leads to a "static" picture of the universe as a four dimensional continuum, there is a sense in which McTaggart is vindicated. His conclusion is absurd if you take it literally, but his argument does throw light on the workings of temporal concepts.

Now to the second example. Here again the main difficulty is in seeing how the alternative system could be operated. What criteria would there be for deciding whether Zeus was angry, whether Hera was jealous, and so forth? As in the Mumbo-Jumbo fantasy, you could more or less arbitrarily correlate the moods of the gods with natural phenomena, but in default of anything which enables you to correlate their moods independently of these actual manifestations, the system would have no explanatory value. To be able to make any predictions, we should have to correlate our experiences in some more practical fashion, and the introduction of the Homeric gods, though not entirely nugatory (since there is a sense in which someone who believed in them would see the world differently), would not extend the range of these correlations in any useful way.

The same is true of all religious views of the world. The explanations which they furnish of the course of events are always ex post facto. We are given no criteria for determining what the gods intend other than the observation of what actually happens, and this means that the explanations in question are empty. A theory which accounts for every possible occurrence has no explanatory value; it cannot lead us to expect any one thing to happen rather than any other. This objection would not hold if there were alleged to be reliable methods of receiving communications from the gods. The criticism would then be that these processes of divination did not achieve their purpose; that in comparison, for example, with scientific theories, their yield in terms of true predictions was very small.

It might be argued, however, that this was not a fair test. What it shows is that theological systems come off badly when their results are measured by scientific standards. But why should they not supply their own standards? Why should not their adherents rely on divination not only as a source of predictions but also as a means of determining whether or not the predictions are satisfied? In that event, they might come out very well.

This may seem an absurd suggestion, but it brings out a point of fundamental importance. It is a point to which empiricists pay too little attention and one that I should probably have gone on missing if I had not been engaged in a study of pragmatism. Those of you who have read the works of Peirce will remember that his pragmaticism is based on the principle that the sole object of inquiry is the fixation of belief. His reason for saying this in preference to saying that the object of inquiry is the discovery of truth, is that the attainment of stable beliefs is what the pursuit of truth comes down to in practice. Though truth may not be formally definable in terms of belief, the question of what is true or false—as a question that one puts to oneself—is practically equivalent to asking what propositions one is or is not willing to accept.

I have a favorite illustration to illustrate this point. Consider the following game. You are asked to take two sheets of paper and write down on one of them a list of true propositions and on the other a list of propositions which you firmly believe. The rule of the game is that the lists are to be mutually exclusive; no proposition that is eligible for one list is to appear on the other. Now this is an instruction that you cannot rationally carry out—what you are asked to do is not self-contradictory. It is conceivable, and indeed not improbable, that among the propositions which you firmly believe there are some that are false, and there are certainly a great many true propositions which you do not believe—if only because you have never considered them. So you could fulfill the instructions by accident. What you could not do is to fulfill them by following any rational procedure. If you are asked to give any examples of true propositions, your only honest course is to mention propositions which you firmly believe.

The moral of this is that whatever is put forward as a method for arriving at truth will in fact operate as a method for fixing belief. You may remember that Peirce distinguishes four such methods: the method of tenacity, which consists in holding on to whatever beliefs you happen to have, no matter what evidence may be brought against them; the method of authority, which consists in believing what you are told by those who are placed in authority over you; the a priori method, as practiced by some philosophers who deduce their beliefs from first principles which they find "agreeable to reason"; and finally, the method of science. On various grounds, Peirce himself comes out in favor of the method of science, while still insisting—perhaps a little disingenuously— that it is in the end a matter of choice.

But suppose now that one has decided to operate not with the fourth method—the method of science—but with some variant of the second method, the method of authority. Consider a primitive society in which all beliefs are formed in accordance with the pronouncements of the spirits, which there is some accredited method for ascertaining. So long as they employ the same method for testing their beliefs as they do for arriving at them, they will be able to claim that their theories are in accordance with the facts. The spirits tell them what expectations to form and the spirits assume that these expectations are satisfied.

Obviously these people move in a circle; but, it may be argued, so do we. To a certain extent, at least, we employ scientific method in testing the theories at which we arrive by the use of scientific method. What valid ground can we then have for thinking that our ways are superior? An answer suggested by Peirce is that although our recognition of anything as a fact is always the result of some process of interpretation, nevertheless—at the level of sense perception—the latitude which this allows us is severely limited. The very nature of our sense experience, as it were, forces certain beliefs upon us. The superiority of our method would then consist in its yielding theories which were more closely in accord with these "natural" beliefs. The devotees of the method of authority would try to maintain the same accord by suitably interpreting their observations, but they would not be able to make it work; the data themselves would not permit it. Since I dislike the extreme relativism to which the argument would otherwise commit us, I hope that this answer is correct.

The relevance of this rather crude example to our central theme is that it leads us to face the fundamental problem of the criteria of truth. In another way, however, it has been irrelevant, since we are not supposing that the members of the primitive tribe arrive at their system by a process of philosophical argument. Neither is it suggested that their conceptual scheme (any more than that of the Absolute Idealists) is to be regarded as a serious rival to our own. In this respect, the first two examples differ from the third. For the great interest of Berkeley's system is that it not only puts the common sense view of the physical world into question on philosophical grounds, but also develops what may be a viable alternative to it.

This is not exactly how Berkeley saw it. The idea (found in a book like Nelson Goodman's *Structure of Appearance*) that it is of interest to construct a phenomenal system just to see what can be made of it, is a modern development. Berkeley and those who have followed him (like John Stuart Mill and Bertrand Russell) have taken the position that only a phenomenal system could be legitimate, because it alone sticks to what is observable. As we shall try to show, there is a sense in which Berkeley's denial of the existence of matter is perfectly serious. He rejects the concept of matter, which he attributes to Locke and Newton, on the ground that it does not apply to anything that could possibly be observed. This demand that every concept be put to the touchstone of observation occurs throughout the history of philosophy. It stands at the opposite pole to the Platonic view, in which preeminence is given to the unchanging world of abstract ideas. The difficult question for those who make it is how much of the world of science—or indeed of common sense— they can reconstruct on the basis of what they take to be directly observable.

In recent years, this whole approach has come under severe criticism. Doubt has been thrown upon Berkeley's initial assumption that the data with which we are presented in sense perception are sensible qualities, existing only when they are perceived. The attempt to construct a viable system on the basis of these data is dismissed as an obvious failure; the reasons for which this attempt has been made have themselves been put in question. These criticisms will be examined next.

BERKELEIANISM AND PHYSICALISM AS
CONSTRUCTIVELY CRITICAL

Berkeley's denial of the existence of matter is the kind of statement only a philosopher would make: it impresses but also irritates the plain man. He thinks that he is being told that his world is entirely different from what he takes it to be, and he finds this hard to believe—even though he cannot spot the fallacy. So Boswell, discussing Berkeley's "ingenious sophistry" with Dr. Johnson, remarked that "though we are satisfied his doctrine is not true, it is impossible to refute it." And Johnson answered, "striking his foot with mighty force against a large stone, till he rebounded from it, 'I refute it *thus*'."

If Berkeley's assertion that there are no material things were to be taken literally, then Dr. Johnson's refutation would be valid. For Johnson's procedure exactly foreshadows that which we have seen Moore adopting in his proof of an external world. They both prove that there are material things by indicating examples of them. It is clear, however, that

132

whatever Berkeley was maintaining it was not something that could be refuted by holding up hands, or kicking stones. To this extent, then, his assertion is not to be taken literally. But how then are we to interpret it?

It is tempting to say that what Berkeley was really doing was not to deny the truth of statements which are ordinarily thought to imply the existence of material things, but to give an unfamiliar analysis of them. His own words support this interpretation, insofar as he insisted that he was not depriving the plain man of anything that he believed in. His analysis is not one that it would occur to the plain man to give, but then so long as the plain man can be sure of the truth of the statements that he makes about the things in his environment, he is not concerned with their analysis. That is the province of philosophers.

I am not prepared to say that this is a wholly incorrect description of what Berkeley was doing, but I can no longer regard it as explaining all that needs to be explained, partly because of the obscurity of the notion of analysis. To say that Berkeley was trying to tell us what we really mean when we talk about stones and hands and chairs and tables, etc., is to invite at least two obvious objections. In the first place, if this is Berkeley's concern, he sets about it in a very odd way; he does not engage in any linguistic or sociological investigations. And secondly, if he were giving an account of the meaning which statements of this kind are commonly understood to have, he would appear to be straightforwardly mistaken. It seems quite clear that our ordinary usage of words like 'stone' and 'glass' and 'chair' is such that we conceive of the things to which they apply as being capable of existing without being perceived. But if Berkeley's denial of the existence of matter implies anything, it is that nothing (other than a spiritual substance) exists unperceived. The words which we use to apply to physical objects are used by him to apply to things which have only a strange manner of persistence, as ideas in the mind of God. But it is surely obvious that what we ordinarily mean when we speak of the things in our environment is not anything which entails the existence of God. It would seem, therefore, that whatever Berkeley is doing, he is not giving a faithful account of ordinary usage. It is still open to us to say that he is refining ordinary usage; or, better still, that he is engaging in a form of reductive analysis. But this needs further explanation.

As we saw last time, in cases where a philosopher makes what is obviously an outrageously false statement (as that nothing moves, or that time is unreal, or that there are no material objects), the interest lies not in the statement considered on its own, but in the arguments which lead up to it—in the proof which the philosopher offers. Let us now apply this to Berkeley. The central proposition in his system (from which the denial of the existence of matter follows) is that for anything other than a spiritual substance, to exist is to be perceived. How then is this proposition proved?

The proof which Berkeley offers is very simple. It can most easily be set out in the form of a syllogism. Let us use the general term "things" to refer to what Berkeley took such ordinary words as "table," "chair," "glass," "watch," "stone," to denote. The major premise of the syllogism is that things consist of sensible qualities; the minor premise is that for a sensible quality to exist is for it to be perceived; and the conclusion is that for anything to exist is for it to be perceived.

There is clearly nothing wrong with the logic of this argument. If the premises are true, the conclusion must also be true. But are the premises true? The first point to notice is that they are intended to be necessary propositions. For Berkeley, it does not just happen to be the case that things consist of sensible qualities; for then it would be at least conceivable that we should come across a counter example. He takes the much stronger view that it is only insofar as the things to which we refer do satisfy this condition that it is possible for our reference to them to be successful. In the same way, he does not regard it as a mere matter of empirical fact that sensible qualities exist only when perceived. He treats it rather as a defining characteristic: anything of which this were not true would not be a sensible quality.

Now what Berkeley means by a sensible quality is very much what modern philosophers have meant by a sense-datum. A sensible quality is to be taken, at least in this context, as an instance of a color, or sound, or taste, or smell, existing as a particular entity only as an item in the private experience of the person who senses it, and enduring no longer than the occasion on which it is sensed. All this is a matter of stipulation. But it is one thing to make a stipulative definition and another to show that anything answers to it. It has not been so obvious to all other philosophers, as it was to Berkeley, that these sensible qualities exist. But if there is doubt about the minor premise of Berkeley's syllogism, the major premise is more doubtful still. For even if there are sensible qualities (in the sense here intended), it is a tall order to assume that any collection of them can be an adequate substitute for a physical object—in the sense in which this term is commonly understood. Berkeley assumes it because he is convinced that if we ask what the plain man is referring to when he speaks of the things in his environment, the only possible alternatives are to say that he is referring to collections of sensible qualities or to say that he fails to refer to anything at all. But this again is by no means obvious.

We now see that to get a proper understanding of Berkeley's position, we have to look at the epistemological assumptions underlying it. I propose, therefore, to restate his major premise in a way that will bring this out more clearly. Let us restore to words like "stone" and "watch" and "table" the meaning that they would commonly be understood to have. Then Berkeley's premise may be taken to be that the only evidence we can have for the existence of anything to which such words apply is our perception of sensible qualities.

This is plainly a weaker proposition than the proposition that things consist of sensible qualities. Is it acceptable? If we are to accept it, we have to make a distinction which has recently come under attack. The distinction is between the hard core of observable facts and the interpretation which we put upon them. I am not conceiving of what I called 'hard data' as being altogether uninterpreted; nothing can be called 'datum' unless it is in some way classified. Even a reference to sensible qualities, in Berkeley's usage of the term, allows for some latitude, since there could be other ways of classifying such things as colors and shapes than the ones we actually employ. But even if this is granted, it may still be possible to distinguish between the direct evidence of our senses (in the form of data which involve the minimum of interpretation) and the more far-reaching constructions which we put upon it. A distinction of this kind is, indeed, implicit in the works of classical empiricists from Locke and Berkeley, through Hume and John Stuart Mill, to Russell, Broad, and Price and other sense-datum theorists of our own day. By attacking it, or attacking the use which has been made of it, contemporary philosophers like Austin, Ryle, and Wittgenstein have struck at the roots of this whole philosophical tradition.

Against the trend of current opinion it can be argued that the distinction can be maintained. In order to try to show this, we will reconsider something previously stated. You may remember that I called your attention to the amount of theory that was carried even by so simple a statement as "this is a watch." In claiming to perceive anything of this kind, we were assuming that the thing was tangible as well as visible; that it was accessible to any number of different observers, but also capable of existing unperceived; that it preserved its identity through time, and occupied positions in a public space. I took it to be part of the common sense view of the world that things of this kind persisted unperceived in much the same form as that in which we normally perceived them. There are also special assumptions which are involved in identifying anything as a watch, or a chair, or whatever it may be, but consideration of the more general assumptions which I have listed should be enough for my present purpose.

Now it seems clear (and here I can only state it dogmatically) that there is a very good sense in which to make a statement which carries all these assumptions is to go beyond the immediate sensory evidence. This is not to suggest that the sense experience which I am now having does not justify me in claiming that I perceive a watch on this table. What I am suggesting is that there is more to such a claim than is strictly contained in the experience on which it is based. If I may use the word 'see' in a way in which it might be used by a psychologist who was interested in the quality of my vision rather than in the identification of the objects which come within my view, I am claiming more than I see. This does not mean that it is incorrect for me to say that I see the watch; it means only that in such cases the description of what is seen covers more than what is visually presented. That the watch is tangible, that it is visible to others besides myself, that it persists at times when no one is observing it: all this is a construction which I put upon my present visual data. I confess that I do not see how this can be seriously disputed.

But then the question arises whether it is not possible to devise what might be called a language of minimal commitment. Could we not formulate statements which were designed to do no more than describe what was sensibly given, in the way that I have just been trying to explain? For instance, we could proceed upon some such lines as Nelson Goodman's in his *Structure of Appearance*. Our statements would just record the presence of sense-qualia, without carrying any implication as to the states of these qualia; whether, for example, they are public or private entities, and without containing any reference to what occurs or would occur on any other occasion. One could regard these statements as featuring in a kind of primitive language game (if I may be allowed to pervert a favorite expression of Wittgenstein's) in which the rule is just that when you are confronted with certain sensory patterns, you salute them with the corresponding words. The only element of interpretation is in the selection of the sensory patterns. Though this argument will not be pursued here, it can be shown that such a game is playable.

Since we are speaking in this context of Berkeley's system, it should be made clear that in referring to sense-qualia we are not making the assumption that Berkeley makes when he refers to sensible qualities. The main difference is that

Berkeley takes it for granted that there are entities to which his sensible qualities are given. He assumes the existence of minds as spiritual substances, and speaks of his primitive data as their ideas. But this not only commits him to the objectionable course of starting with what are defined as private objects; it also saddles him at the outset with a heavy and very questionable load of theory. One has no right to take it as a datum that there are minds, in Berkeley's sense, let alone that their experiences are concordant. Neither does he need to make these assumptions in order to obtain an adequate starting point. One advantage which we gain from starting with a very primitive language is that since persons do not figure in it, the question of the privacy or publicity of our hard data does not arise.

Our first step might be described as a refinement of Berkeley's. If you allow it to be taken, how will it help us to understand Berkeley's denial of the existence of matter? The answer is that we can then think of it as imposing a restriction on the possible interpretations of the primitive data. What Berkeley is claiming is that the common sense interpretation is illegitimate. This does not prevent him from attaching a meaning to statements like "this is a watch," which allows them to be true. He simply takes them as being established by the occurrence of the appropriate sensible qualities. What he rejects is the common sense view of the way in which such statements go beyond the data by which they are verified, and the reason why he rejects it is that he thinks it impossible to conceive of material things as existing apart from the data of sense.

The principle which underlies Berkeley's argument is that whereas horizontal extrapolation is permissible, vertical extrapolation is not. What I mean here by horizontal extrapolation is a form of inference in which, starting with entities of a given type, you predict or postulate the existence of further entities of the same type, whether actual or hypothetical. Vertical extrapolation, on the other hand, is a form of inference in which you move from one level to another, concluding with entities which are held to be manifested by (and therefore of a different type from) those with which you start. This is well illustrated by the fourth example, the thesis of physicalism. One motive for taking a physicalistic view of other persons is that it enables us to substitute horizontal for vertical inferences. A horizontal inference, in this context, would be an inference from present to future behavior; a vertical inference would be an inference from observed behavior to a state of mind, conceived as lying behind it.

The reason for preferring horizontal inferences to vertical inferences is that you then avoid having to postulate entities which are relatively inaccessible. So the mental states of other persons, if not subjected to a physicalistic reduction, are inaccessible relatively to their overt behavior. So again, physical objects, if not treated phenomenalistically, are inaccessible relatively to sense-data. Whenever you can substitute a horizontal for a vertical inference you avoid an epistemological problem. This leaves us, however, with the question when this procedure is justified. We have in fact returned by another route to the problem of the criteria of reductive analysis.

An argument which is often brought against these attempts at reduction is that they presuppose what they are designed to eliminate. For instance, if one takes my restatement of Berkeley's starting point, one may perhaps allow oneself to imagine that there are people who play my primitive language game. One might even go so far as to imagine that there are people whose use of language goes no further than this. But in indulging our imagination in this way (even in formulating the rules of the game), we are making use of concepts for which the game itself makes no provision—in this instance, the concepts which are involved in thinking of groups of persons inhabiting a common physical world. This is not objectionable so long as the use of these concepts can eventually be justified on the basis of the elements which they help you to introduce. It would not do if the elements were actually defined by means of these concepts; but I can see no reason why, in giving an explanation of your procedure, you should not make use of all your linguistic resources—the only limitation being that you must not bring in entities which you are not in a position to construct.

But this brings us back to the question: What is to count as a construction? If we continue to follow Berkeley to the extent of dispensing with any vertical extrapolation, we shall be able to admit only what is explicitly definable in terms of our primitive data, or anyhow reducible to them by the process of translation. But this will not give us all that we need. I assume that we want to arrive at some sort of public world containing persistent entities, not necessarily such objects as glasses and watches, but—at any rate—regions of space. Also, we want to be able to distinguish between the objective course of events and their various reflections in the experiences of different persons. The work which has been done on phenomenalism shows that it is not possible to tell so elaborate a story exclusively in terms of sense-qualia. If we adopt the useful distinction which F. P. Ramsay made in his last papers between a secondary theoretical system and a primary system which is treated as factual, relatively to the theory, then we have to say that the secondary system, in this instance, is not translatable into the primary one.

Does it follow then that we cannot represent physical objects as being constructible out of our primary data? Not necessarily. It depends on what we are going to count as a construction. The best procedure will be to see what the relation between the two systems is and then to consider what status we want to assign to the constituents of the secondary one.

The answer to the first question is not at all simple, and can here be dealt with only summarily. It is possible to exhibit the physical world of common sense as a natural projection of our primary data. The empirical fact on which this mainly depends is that qualia form relatively stable clusters. If one considers any fairly elaborate sensory pattern, there will be, as a general rule, only a small number of contexts in which any given observer comes upon it. The consequence is that these patterns are found to be reinstatable, by traversing similar sensory routes. This means that by projecting the spatial and temporal relations which are sensibly presented, one is able to conceive of certain configurations of qualia as being permanently accessible. In this way one arrives at the notion of a phenomenal continuant. Among phenomenal continuants there is one that has the distinctive property of being almost totally pervasive. It is the observer's body, not characterized as such (since we have not yet credited our observer with the notion of himself), but characterizable as the central body. The concept of the central body, since it allows for the observer's movement, assists in the process of fusing visual and tactual space.

By correlating different states of the phenomenal continuants, an observer can now form a rudimentary picture of the way the world works. There are, however, a certain number of presentations which do not fit into the general picture. This leads him to distinguish between those data which fit into his main account, and those which do not. With the arrival on the scene of other observers, characterized in the first instance as continuants which resemble the central body in that they are also producers of signs, he is able to obtain corroboration of his main account of the world and also to acquire the idea of himself not only as a figure in this main account, but also as a maker of signs corresponding to nothing that the others recognize and so as a recorder of worlds existing only for him. This lays the foundation of the public-private distinction from which self-consciousness arises and the attribution of consciousness to others. And so, having proceeded from an entirely neutral basis one is finally able to develop the distinction between mind and matter.

This piece of science fiction—it is only a rough sketch—is intended as a model of the way in which our common sense view of the world is "cashed" at the sensory level. If it is acceptable in this light, one might follow Quine in speaking of the physical objects of common sense as cultural posits. The positing of them would be regarded as a device for linking one's data together and for predicting the course of one's experience. In the same way, the positing of scientific entities, like atoms and electrons, could be regarded as a device for linking together the physical observations that are made at the level of common sense. The positing of unconscious mental states could be regarded as a device for linking together certain sorts of overt behavior. On the other hand, since one arrives at all these entities by processes of vertical extrapolation, one might feel obliged—or at any rate prefer—to treat them realistically. One might think not only of chairs and tables, but also of atoms and electrons, and even of unconscious mental states, as literally existing.

How does one decide this issue? What is actually at stake in the controversy between someone who takes a realistic view of scientific entities and one who conceives of them as operational devices? The dispute is taken seriously by philosophers of science, but it is not at all clear to me what it involves. There may, indeed, be an analytical question about the adequacy of suggested operational definition, but once this is cleared out of the way, it is not easy to see what theoretical issue remains. It comes down to a question of how one chooses to look at the world and what picture one prefers to form of it. There would then be no question of truth or falsehood here, but only of convenience. This is not to say, however, that the issue is trivial; it may have great psychological importance. For instance, it can plausibly be argued that the adoption of a realistic view is necessary for the progress of a science at certain stages of its development.

Let us look at a case in which the realistic view appears to impose itself, although (from a logical point of view) it does not appear to differ in any essential way from those which we have so far been considering. This is the case of propositions about the past. Two illustrations can be used. The first is taken from a book called *Father and Son* by the late nineteenth-century English critic, Edmund Gosse. The elder Mr. Gosse was a member of the sect of Plymouth Brethren, who tended to be fundamentalists. At any rate they accepted the conclusion, which Archbishop Usher had derived from his study of the chronology of the Old Testament, that the world was created in the year 4004 B.C. For such people the development of the science of geology was a great stumbling block, for it appeared to indicate the world had existed for very much longer than was provided for in the Bible, if the archbishop's calculations were correct. However, the elder Mr. Gosse found a very ingenious way of getting round the difficulty. He maintained that God had indeed created the world in 4004 B.C., but filled it with delusive signs of greater antiquity in order to test men's faith. The stronger the geological evidence appeared to be, the farther it showed that the Deity was prepared to go in carrying out this test.

The point of this illustration is that if we allow Mr. Gosse his notion of a Creator, if we allow even that the world had a beginning in time, there is no way of refuting his position. Any evidence which the geologists interpret in their way, he can interpret in his; it is simply a multiplication of the deceptive signs. Of course if we put it to the vote, hardly anyone would be found to side with Mr. Gosse, but that would not have worried him, except as a proof of human weakness. The only argument that we can think of is that if you are going to accept the findings of science in other fields, it is hardly consistent to assume that its laws break down at just this point. It would seem extraordinary that a generalization concerning the rate at which radio-atoms disintegrate should fail only when we draw inferences from it which apply to time earlier than 4004 B.C. But all that this shows is that Mr. Gosse's system is uneconomical; it does not show that it comes into conflict with any observed facts. In the end we deal with Mr. Gosse in the same sort of way as we would deal with the Mumbo-Jumbo people. His conception of the way the world works is one that we simply refuse to accept.

The second illustration is taken from my own work, *Language, Truth and Logic*, where I maintained that statements about the past were equivalent to statements which described the present or future observations which would be counted as establishing them. So, to assert (for example) that Julius

Caesar crossed the Rubicon was to make an assertion about what you would see if you looked into history books. My reasons for taking this implausible view were the same as those which led Peirce to the same conclusion, though I did not discover this until quite recently. The past events themselves being inaccessible, the only grounds that one could have for asserting their existence must lie in the nature of the present evidence; to deny that some received opinion about the past was true would be a completely idle performance unless one were either setting out the existing evidence in a new light or predicting that further evidence would favor a different view. This is in line with Peirce's saying that practically speaking the meaning of every factual proposition lies in the future.

I have long given up this view. For one thing, it is inconsistent with the view that tenses are eliminable; for another, I cannot accept the consequence that the meaning of every sentence which expresses a statement about the past is constantly subject to change, as further evidence comes to light. But mainly it now seems obvious that a statement like "Caesar crossed the Rubicon" can neither entail nor be entailed by any description of what is to be found in history books. It is logically possible that the event should have occurred without its being subsequently recorded, and it is logically possible that the historians should all be giving a false account. I am bound to acknowledge, however, that the significance of these possibilities is purely formal. If there is no record of a past event, one is not in a position to say anything about it; if all the records go to show that a given event occurred, one can have no reason to assert that it did not. In postulating the existence of the past, independently of any record, one is therefore making a formal concession to realism.

This is in accordance with common sense. It is to be noted, however, that the common sense view of the world is not consistent in its treatment of time. The past, but not the future, is treated realistically. Yet logically there is no difference between them. In either case, the objective fact is that an event of such and such a kind is located at such and such a date. From this point of view, the question whether this date precedes or succeeds the date of our reference to the event, is irrelevant.

The fourth example is the thesis of physicalism. This is again a question about the existence of a certain class of entities, in this case mental states and processes. The thesis of physicalism is that there is no need to postulate such entities, in addition to physical processes. Another way of putting it would be to say that statements about mental entities are reducible to statements about physical ones. If one starts with qualia, this is a question that arises only at the secondary level; and here I am inclined to think that this applies to ontological questions as a whole. I am inclined to think that the question what there is, at any rate as it figures in discussions of this kind, is a question of what we want to put into our picture of the world, and therefore that it does not relate to our primitive data, but only to the construction which we put upon them. Once again, this brings me close to Peirce, who assigns existence to the category of Secondness (the category of relation), and not to that of Firstness (the category of quality). It is to be assumed that our secondary system provides for the existence of physical objects. Whether it can admit the reality both of the physical world as it is represented in science, and of the physical objects of common sense, is an interesting and difficult question, not entered into here. In whatever way it is answered, the thesis of physicalism will not be affected.

What are the motives for adopting this thesis? The main motive is epistemological. We constantly make judgements about other people's states of mind, and in many cases are confident of their truth. We do not believe that these judgements are infallible, but we do believe that they are well-grounded. Very often we should say that we knew what another person was thinking or feeling; whether, for example, he was angry or in pain. But now if we have to conceive of the mental states of others as being hidden from us, in the sense that all that we can ever hope to observe is their physical effects, it is not clear how we can be justified in claiming any such knowledge. It is not clear what warrant we can have for making a vertical inference from people's overt behavior to the mental processes which are believed to underlie it. On the other hand, if mental processes can be identified with physical ones, this difficulty is removed. It will then be only a matter of our having to justify horizontal inferences, from one piece of behavior to another or from the agent's behavior to his physical condition.

Another motive is a semiscientific one. If you believe that everything that happens in the world can be explained in terms of the laws of physics, you will be driven to conclude that the postulation of mental occurrences serves no scientific purpose. As Professor Feigl puts it, they are in the position of 'nomological danglers,' and in the interest of economy one should try to shave them off. Against this, it may be said that the fact that a class of entities was scientifically superfluous would not be a sufficient reason for ruling them out of existence, if there were other grounds for taking them to exist. In any case, it has yet to be shown that the laws of physics are capable of accounting for everything that happens.

The scientific motive, for what it is worth, applies to the existence of any mental state; the epistemological motive applies, in the first instance, only to the attribution of mental states to persons other than oneself. There are, however, very good grounds for holding that the meaning of a statement in which a mental state or process is attributed to a given person must be essentially the same, whether the attribution is made by the person himself or by others; and in that case if you accept a physicalistic account of other people's mental states you will have to extend it to your own.

This consideration also goes the other way. The strongest objection to physicalism is that one seems clearly able to distinguish between one's own mental state and any physical event; and if one acknowledges this distinction in one's own case, it will follow by the foregoing argument that one must also acknowledge it in the case of other people.

This objection tells most strongly against the thesis which Carnap has put forward, that statements which apparently refer to mental states or processes are logically equivalent to statements about physical events. The difficulty here is that there is no sure method of determining logical equivalences when they are not governed by the rules of a formal system. One may adduce what seem to be obvious counter examples, but the proponent of the thesis may refuse to acknowledge them. At the same time, it can safely be said that this interpretation of the meaning of statements about mental occurrences would not be likely to result from any dispassionate examination of the way in which these statements are actually used. The reason why some philosophers have accepted it is that their epistemological or metaphysical presuppositions appeared to leave them no alternative.

This objection does not apply, or anyhow not with the same force, to the thesis (which for some reason appears to be especially attractive to Australian philosophers) that mental states are not logically but factually identical with states of the central nervous system. This thesis depends on the assumption that all our experiences are causally determined by the condition of our brains. Its proponents recognize that this is an empirical and not a logical assumption, and are therefore careful not to claim that the identity for which they are arguing is a logical identity. They do believe, however, that there are strong empirical grounds for taking their assumption to be true. If it is true, they think that one would be entitled to regard mental states as being identical with states of the central nervous system in the factual sense in which, for example, the Morning Star is identical with the Evening Star, or lightning is identical with a discharge of electricity. But since they put forward no criterion of identity, apart from the assumed causal dependence of mental upon physical states, it is doubtful if their thesis amounts to anything more than a recommendation to adopt a certain way of speaking. Even if their causal hypothesis is granted, it is still open to anyone to regard mental states as existing concurrently with physical states, without being identical with them. In the absence of any further criteria, this is not a question that can be decided empirically. The choice is between two different ways of conceiving what there really is.

One advantage of physicalism is that it simplifies the problem of personal identity. Though I think that this price is too high to pay, I must also confess that I have never yet found an analysis of personal identity with which I could be satisfied. In these circumstances, one may be tempted to take the lazy course of postulating a soul, or spiritual substance. But since this supplies us with no criterion for determining when two different mental states are states of the same soul, it hardly deserves to be considered as a genuine theory; it is rather an admission that the notion of personal identity is not able to be analyzed. We may in the end be driven to this, but it is not a position that we should allow ourselves to adopt until we have thoroughly explored all the forms of analysis that seem to have any chance of succeeding, and we have found decisive objections to them.

The point of these examples has been to show how philosophers can legitimately engage not only in the work of elucidating concepts but also in that of constructive criticism. I doubt if my treatment of them has provided you with a sufficiently clear answer to the question what philosophy is; but I hope that I have succeeded in doing some philosophy along the way.

STEPHEN COBURN PEPPER

was born on April 21, 1891, in Newark, New Jersey. He was educated in the public schools of Concord, Massachusetts, and at Browne and Nichols School, Cambridge. He attended Harvard, where he took the A.B. in 1913, M.A. in 1914, and Ph.D. in philosophy in 1916. Having taught at Wellesley College in 1917–18, and having spent some months in the army until World War I ended, he went to the University of California, Berkeley, in 1919, where he held many and varied posts, became full professor in due time, and emeritus in 1958. He was appointed Carus lecturer in 1960. He received honorary degrees of L.H.D. from Colby College in 1950, and from Tulane University in 1961; and L.L.D. from the University of California in 1960.

He is a member of the American Philosophical Association, American Society for Aesthetics, College Art Association, Academy of Arts and Sciences, and International Institute of Philosophy. He has traveled extensively at various points in his long life, and continues to do so even now.

His principal books are Aesthetic Quality *(1938); the now classic* World Hypotheses *(1942) in which he put forth his root-metaphor theory of the origins of philosophizing, a theory which is now almost automatically associated with his name;* The Basis of Criticism in the Arts *(1945);* A Digest of Purposive Values *(1947);* Principles of Art Appreciation *(1950);* The Work of Art *(1956);* The Sources of Value *(1958);* Ethics *(1960); and* Concept and Quality *(1967) based on the Carus lectures. In addition to this impressive list of books, he has published over 125 articles and reviews in various journals, anthologies, and commemorative volumes.*

THE SEARCH FOR COMPREHENSION, OR
WORLD HYPOTHESES

I hold to a certain ancient tradition of philosophy preserved over the years from the Greeks—philosophy as the love of knowledge, as the pursuit of knowledge for its own sake, the desire for an understanding of the nature of things—in a word, for the truth. And the truth sought by this impulse is for comprehension not to be satisfied by competence in limited fields. I hold also that this aim has a highly practical side, for it issues in philosophies of life offering rational guidance to individual action and social policy. In short, it is the source of well-grounded ethical and political ideals.

I also find it useful to note that among the Greeks and until well into modern times, there was no distinction between philosophy and science. Anyone in pursuit of knowledge was a philosopher. Then rather suddenly, only three or four centuries ago, extraordinarily effective methods of observation and experiment were developed which so augmented the mass of knowledge and the skills of obtaining it that no man could encompass it all. The age of the savant passed, and the age of the scientific specialist came in. And now a contrast emerged between the philosopher still bent on comprehension and the scientist bent on precision of knowledge within a special field. The philosopher then became primarily a specialist in nonspecialization.

Growing out of this situation, with the scientists as a body outnumbering the philosophers by huge and increasing proportions, suggestions began to be heard that philosophers could perhaps be dispensed with. At such moments it is pertinent to recall the history of philosophy and to be reminded that the special sciences directly or indirectly all came out of philosophy, and none of them retains the central interest in comprehensive understanding. This interest by its very nature will never turn into a field of special subject matter. It will necessarily have all things within its scope including the special sciences and everything else. This domain is what I call *world hypotheses,* though some call it the domain of *speculative philosophy,* or *metaphysics,* or *ontology.* These terms are all applicable, and have only minor differences of connotation.

Actually, philosophy now performs some tasks outside this central one of comprehensive understanding. These other tasks are, in a way, mostly leftovers from the special sciences after they broke away from philosophy. Thus there is the philosophy of science or scientific method (a subject in which the special scientists themselves are too busy to take any great interest), the philosophy of history, the philosophy of the state, and the philosophy of mind. There is also of a slightly different cast, the philosophy of religion, and the philosophy of meaning (semantics), and so on. Then there are what might be called embryo sciences—ethics, aesthetics, theory of value, and logic. Until the 1920s, psychology was one of these. Symbolic logic shows symptoms of leaving philosophy, too, very soon. Then there is always an interest in conceptual analysis, or the clarification of meanings bearing on important concepts such as space, time, event, causality, law, responsibility, freedom, etc., many of these also leftovers from the special sciences. But the heart of philosophy is and, I am sure, will always continue to be, comprehensive understanding or what I call world hypotheses. From now on let us concentrate on this aim.

In the thirties I summarized for myself the achievement of comprehensive philosophy up to that time, and called the book *World Hypotheses.* Questions of method for constructing world hypotheses inevitably came up. I found I could not accept one of the commonest traditional methods—the method of certainty, a most attractive and natural method to be drawn into. If we really want to know something, we want to know it as completely as possible, and the ultimate terminus of complete knowing would be knowing for certain. In fact, "knowing" is frequently defined that way. If you are not certain about something, then you should not say you know it. But, of course, lesser degrees of knowing are also admissible in our usage, and I shall assume this wider sense of the term in what follows. That is, I shall assume that a person's knowledge may contain some error, and that there are degrees of knowledge.

But if one is in pursuit of certainty, it is natural that he should scour the universe for bases of certainty from which to build a firm conceptual (or perhaps even an intuitive) view of the world. So in the past (and even the present) philosophers have claimed certainty for the fundamental concepts and intuitions of their systems. Thus we find claims of certainty for sense experience, sense data, impressions, awareness, a self, a God, gross immediate experience, Gestalts, universals, axioms, laws, and even an intuitive vision of the totality of the universe itself. I found the copiousness of these deliverances and their mutual contrariety overwhelming— and these examples are only a sampling. I decided the only reasonable thing to do was to throw the whole batch out. I shall not go here into a more detailed justification for this rejection. There will be occasion to consider the matter of the futility of the appeal to certainty in a concrete instance at a later lecture, namely, that on existentialism as developed by Sartre.

Once the method of certainty is set aside, the method of hypothesis comes forward clear and untrammeled. A comprehensive philosophy now appears as a world hypothesis. And a clear definition can now be made, distinguishing a world hypothesis from scientific and other less comprehensive hypotheses. A world hypothesis is an unrestricted hypothesis. Scientific hypotheses are limited to certain areas of subject matter, the areas of their specialties. In scientific investigations, types of evidence can be thrown out or ignored as irrelevant and not within their area of concern. Such hypotheses can legitimately restrict their field of evidence, but a world hypothesis must accept all evidence presented: there are no restrictions. Its problem is to adjust the totality of the world's evidence to a comprehensive system.

The way this has been done is through selecting a set of guiding concepts whose degree of success in attaining a comprehensive system of interpretations determines the adequacy of the world hypothesis. This, in turn, is relative to the scope and precision of the interpretations. It is perhaps not surprising (in view of the nature of the task) that though many world hypotheses have been developed, none of them seems to be fully adequate. The great sources of inadequacy are, of course, either lack of scope or lack of precision.

Lack of scope happens whenever certain areas of evidence do not submit to consistent interpretation in terms of the guiding concepts. This is rarely openly admitted by the exponents of the philosophy. One of the commonest devices for concealing the deficiency is to classify recalcitrant evidence as "unreal." When a world hypothesis is found interpreting any presented material as absolute unreality, this is tantamount to admitting it cannot find any interpretation for it consistent with its guiding principles, and consequently that it lacks scope. For within an unrestricted hypothesis, everything presented for interpretation must be accepted as a kind of reality. How else can it be presented? Dreams are real in their own way; and so is a falsehood, an error, and a vacuum. They can be interpreted legitimately as relative 'unrealities'—that is, as realities that are 'unreal' relative to other realities. So a dream may be considered 'unreal' relative to waking life, an error relative to an intended act, a vacuum relative to filled space. But as items of the universe, dreams are realities of some sort not to be rejected by an unrestricted world hypothesis.

Lack of precision—the other big source of inadequacy—occurs when more than one interpretation is consistent with (or worse, demanded by) the guiding concepts. Absolute precision is undoubtedly unattainable, and a demand for it is perfectionistic. Like precision of measurement in the technical sciences, a certain range of discrepancy is permissible if this range is clearly noted. It is gross differences of interpretation that are disturbing for the adequacy of a world hypothesis.

It has become customary to call the guiding concepts of a world hypothesis its categories. The question forces itself upon us as to where these sets of categories come from. It has long been noticed that in spite of the many philosophers teaching and publishing through the centuries, there have been relatively few types of philosophy. The men work in schools. It becomes obvious that these schools fundamentally differ from each other in their modes of interpretation—that is, in their sets of categories. The conclusion is drawn that the men of a school are all working with essentially the same set of categories, developing one world hypothesis. Examination of the works of a school bear this out (though this conclusion greatly simplifies the situation). We then have relatively few world hypotheses to deal with, and the question of the origin of a set of categories is open to investigation by studying the history of a school and seeing how its categories developed.

Starting from this conclusion, I conceived that the source of a set of categories would probably be some striking experience that could act as a model for speculation on the structure of the universe. This conception seemed to be borne out in tracing the development of the schools. I called it the root metaphor theory.

I found later that Francis Bacon had the same hunch but used it to disparage metaphysics and hypotheses in general, in contrast to the simple inductive method he advocated of collecting observations and summarizing their similarities. Of course, these summaries were themselves hypotheses; he even called them "anticipations" of nature. Since his time, hypotheses have become respectable in scientific method, whatever name is given them. (A recent name is axiomatization.) Cognition cannot rest on collections of observations alone; it must reach outside them, or be condemned to stagnation. The principal function of memory is to stimulate and control recognitions and anticipations; it is a storehouse of hypotheses with dynamic references not only to the past but to the environing present and the future.

An unrestricted world hypothesis is simply the extension of the cognitive function of recognition and anticipation to the furthest limit. For a man with a deep desire to know what the world is like through and through, what more natural way of proceeding than that by which he approaches any particularly puzzling problem? He looks back over his past experience for a promising analogy, he analyzes the structure of his analogy and applies it to the problem at hand. For the problem of understanding the structure of the world without restriction, the selection of such a promising sample of experience as a model to work from, I call a root metaphor.

This is not the only method conceivable. There was the method of certainty, of course, which I have found dogmatic (that is, inhibitive of critical thought) and undependable. There is the method of the positivists who optimistically suggest that a combination of the scientific techniques of experiment with mathematics may ultimately yield a universal postulational deductive system which will have unrestricted application to the world. Some are suggesting that the computers might bring this about—perhaps even presenting us with a variety of such systems all equally applicable, with transformation equations provided by which you can pass smoothly from one to another. There is also at the opposite pole the logical possibility of a comprehensive intuition in immediate experience of the totality of the world.

The mystics have made this last method familiar to us and have often claimed to have had the experience, but their claim of certainty makes it suspect at once to me, as I pointed out earlier. Also, the reports of the mystics regarding the content of the experience entail interpreting as 'unreality' so much of human experience familiar to us that I do not find it a serious competitor with a number of relatively adequate world hypotheses already at our disposal.

Regarding the positivistic and the computer proposals, I would make a similar (though somewhat more reserved) comment. What mathematical symbolism may ultimately be capable of achieving is not to be prejudged. However, what I suspect might happen (on the most sanguine supposition) is that a relatively adequate world hypothesis of root metaphor origin could be mathematically symbolized and axiomatized. The critical point I want to make, though, is that this mathematical symbolization must be able to lead into and fully characterize the concrete qualitative experiences and durations and transactions of human immediacy. I don't see this sort of connection between mathematics and qualitative immediacy rising on the horizon among either the positivists or the computers. Until that happens such symbolic systems will have nowhere near the scope of several relatively adequate world hypotheses of the root metaphor type. And anyway, if a mathematical symbolization of a root metaphor world hypothesis were achieved, the mathematical system could make its contact with actual experience only by way of the more concrete conceptualization of the root metaphor system. Lastly, there is a suspicion that logic and mathematics themselves are not conceptually innocent, not free from certain far-reaching presuppositions in their structures and procedures. To symbolize things in logical or mathematical terms may be to atomize them into interpretations sometimes foreign and distortive of their intrinsic nature.

So, I maintain that the root metaphor method of generating world hypotheses is the most promising one at our present disposal. The method consists of a number of steps. The first step is selecting the sort of experience to be used as the model. When the choice is a fruitful one, this, by the way, is an act of creative imagination comparable to that of a novelist or a painter in selecting a subject capable of fruitful artistic development. But in philosophy the insight can rarely be traced to one man. It usually rises out of common sense, often prompted by a cultural confusion, and often from the midst of a hostile context. It gradually separates itself from its dross and finally stands out as a novel idea. After the selection, and proceeding along with it, is the second step—that of lifting out the conceptual structure of the root metaphor. This is the generation of a set of categories. The third step is the application of the categories to the whole breadth of human experience. This would seem a gigantic task, but it is simplified by the discovery over the centuries of the location of the most troublesome philosophical problems of interpretation and synthesis—the perennial problems. A set of categories that can handle these without resort to the devices of dogmatism or to the emptiness of 'unreality' are well on their way to adequacy. In the course of application the categories themselves are modified and refined so that the end result may appear quite different from the original crude model.

Of the numerous attempts in the history of human thought, I have found only four that have proved relatively adequate: formism, based on the root metaphor of similarity, associated with Platonic and Aristotelian developments; mechanism, based on the root metaphor of bodies in interaction, or the machine initiated by Leucippus and Democritus and developed later by Galileo, Descartes, Hobbes, Locke and others; organicism, based on the root metaphor of a dynamic organic whole, associated with Hegel and his followers; and contextualism (or pragmatism) based on the root metaphor of the transitory historical event in its biological and cultural context, associated with Dewey and his school.

None of these categorial systems is fully adequate, though all of them seek and approximate worldwide scope; that is, they have interpretations for everything presented. But some of these interpretations seem strained and there are gaps of discontinuity and imprecision. The location of their inadequacies have been fairly well spotted, and seem to lie in the sets of categories themselves and not in errors of application.

The tempting idea of obtaining a more adequate theory by picking out the best features from each of the most adequate theories and combining them in one synthesis is not workable. No coherent synthesis can be gained that way—just an incoherent agglomeration in which each categorical interpretation presses for completion upon each other one in total confusion. And this is the fallacy of eclecticism.

Yet each of these relatively adequate world hypotheses offers a wide range of insight into the nature of our world. To throw them all out because none is fully adequate would be foolish; there is nothing that takes the place of a world hypothesis. Let me dwell on this statement for a moment, because positivists and many specialized scientists are prone to question it. For these critics the utility of an hypothesis is likely to be identified with its predictive power, and they notice that world hypotheses are not notable for their predictive powers. Then what is their use? For insight.

Something more than an analogy can be drawn at this point. I shall refer to an article by W. W. Meissner on "The Operational Principle and Meaning in Psychoanalysis."[1] In this article Meissner is concerned with the demand of specialized psychologists with a behaviorist and operationalist bias that psychoanalytical theory and practice be brought into line with these specialists' norms of objective control and predictive power for hypotheses. The implication is that failure to comply with these norms would render psychoanalytic interpretations unscientific, uncorroborative, subjective, and use-

less. Meissner argues that these special norms derived mainly
from the physical sciences are of limited application and to
universalize them is dogmatic. He draws a parallel: "It is
unscientific," he says, "to insist on the norms of mathematics
when one is dealing with physics. Physics certainly uses mathematics, but if the theorist used only norms of mathematics
he would clearly be doing mathematics and not physics."[2]
With this comment in mind, I now present Meissner's illustration of the use of hypothesis and interpretation in the
domain of psychoanalysis.

Let us take the example of a dream analysis. A patient
reports a dream; to him it seems utterly devoid of meaning.
As the analyst listens, he fits it into a context which he has
been assembling from the beginning of his association with
the patient. He may ask for the patient to free associate to
the content of the dream to help him find connections between portions of the dream fragment and the developing
context. The context is provided not merely by the mass of
evidence that the therapist has gained through his contact
with this patient, but also through all the experience and
clinical awareness developed in his work with other patients.
The more experienced the analyst is, particularly with the
type of patient he is now dealing with, the better developed
will be his context of meaning. The context is also determined by the collective experience of other psychoanalysts,
psychiatrists, and psychologists, transferred to the therapist
through his formal training and study and constant professional exchange with his colleagues. In discussing the dream
with his patient, the analyst brings this context of meaning
to bear on the dream so that certain parts of what the patient
has said begin to take on meaning for him. He begins to perceive the possibilities for understanding the context of the
dream and he receives clues that begin to open up the meaning of the dream. But his penetration of the mystery of the
dream is only partial, leaving the analyst still wondering
what it all means. For several days he mulls the matter over
until suddenly he sees a whole pattern of significant relationships in the dream that he had not seen before. In his next

session, the patient reveals his insight to the therapist and the process is thus extended. The therapist combines his previous interpretations with the patient's new insight and fits this new level of meaning into the general context of meaning; thus he begins to probe more deeply into the meaning of the dream, to fit it into the general pattern of the patient's life, to draw the dream and other things revealed in the process of therapy into a consistent and intelligible pattern that makes sense to the patient and gives him the opportunity for increasingly effective and penetrating insight into himself and his problem.[3]

In summary, he continues: "In so far as the interpretation fits the pattern of the patient's life and is recognized by him as doing so, the validity of the interpretation is bolstered. In so far as the interpretation is consistent with the body of analytic thinking, it serves as substantiating confirmation of the theory itself."[4]

The joke is that though Meissner here makes no claims of predictive power for psychoanalytic hypotheses, actually this power also does inhere in them. Insofar as these hypotheses are confirmed in analysis, predictions can be reliably made about the future health and conduct of the patient.

On a worldwide scale this is the sort of thing a world hypothesis does: it synthesizes the enormous diversity of evidence the world offers, and the hypothesis is tested against this evidence. Insofar as the hypothesis is confirmed, it explains the interrelationships of the evidence and gives insight as to its meaning for man—thus furnishing an enveloping evaluative system for human action and decision. In performing these functions it has predictive powers, for an adequate world hypothesis covers the predictive evidence of the natural sciences and offers an explanation for their predictive powers. But its main function is insight.

Since writing *World Hypotheses* and describing the categories and modes of interpretation of the four relatively adequate theories that appear to have emerged from our cultural past, I have been interested in carrying forward what seems to be a promising fifth type of world hypothesis based on a fresh root metaphor. As a concrete illustration of the action of the root metaphor theory in the construction of a world hypothesis, a brief sketch of my experiences in this process may be revealing.

I did not set out with any notion that I should find myself working into a new world hypothesis; this would have been arrogant and absurd. What I set out to do was to make a full and careful study of the field of value. Being keenly aware (through the study of world hypotheses) that sets of categories can deeply affect one's conceptions of values and one's descriptive interpretations, I planned to study the field from the point of view of each of the four relatively adequate hypotheses. I had already done this sort of thing in *The Basis of Criticism in the Arts* describing the types of aesthetic criticism generated by mechanism, contextualism, organicism, and formism, recommending that the insights of each of these views be considered for the soundest judgment of a work of art.

I began with what I thought would be an intensive descriptive interpretation of value in mechanistic terms and a basically behavioristic treatment was the obvious approach for this sort of interpretation. Two highly systematized studies of this sort were recently completed—R. B. Perry's *General Theory of Value* and E. C. Tolman's *Purposive Behavior in Animals and Men,* two books in close sympathy with each other. As I had done my graduate work largely under Perry, and Tolman was a colleague of mine in California, I had available for my study a range of descriptive material and theoretical conjecture far in excess of the contents of either book.

There was no question in my mind that purposive activity was at least one of the principal sources of value. So I knew an intensive study of purposive structure would be relevant throughout, but I did not exclude qualitative introspective data as the strict behaviorists would have done. Both types of data were relevant to the categories of mechanism, and for the fullness of description, both types should be developed. I came out with parallel descriptions of purposive activity. Each type of data (the behavioristic and the introspective) was helpful to the other in filling out the detailed structural descriptions of the various types of purposive actions.

When this part of the work was through, I discovered that all the typical value concepts associated with individual action had found their place—desire, conation, achievement, frustration, satisfaction, pleasure, pain, etc. And their interconnectedness within the various structures was revealed in a manner never so clear before. From single purposes, I was drawn on to study conflicts and cooperations of purposes as these emerged in personal situations, and became established as dispositions of personality structures, and thence out into social situations and the dispositional structures of cultural patterns.

Meanwhile a brand new concept emerged—the concept of a natural norm imbedded in purposive structure. I called it a 'selective system,' most easily explained in terms of what we commonly call the means-end relation. But viewed as a mere relational concept, the dynamics of the structure does not show up. Means and ends are not just external objects, they are goals within purposive structures. A means or instrumental object is the goal of a subordinate act, and this subordinate act has a drive or impulse for its subordinate goal derived from the drive of a superordinate act for which the goal is the end object. If I want a glass for a drink of water, the dynamic desire for the glass is derived from that for the water. Let my thirst be slaked, and I no longer want the glass. But there is another way in which I may no longer want the glass even though the desire for the water continues. If I learn that the glass is a trick glass and that no water reaches my lips, I cease to want that glass; that is, all the dynamics goes out of that subordinate act. My thirst drive then motivates me to seek another glass that will function.

What we notice here is that the superordinate act of desire for water dynamically functions as a norm for the selection of the subordinate act for a goal object as a means of conveying the water to the mouth. The critical relation here is not the potential causal relation of the means object to the end object (though this is an important secondary requirement); it is the dynamic one of the drive for the end charging the drive for the means. If the drive for the means fails to yield satisfaction to the drive for the end, the former drive is eliminated. In short, the dynamic structure of the superordinate act spontaneously selects *against* incorrect subordinate acts and *for* the correct ones; that is, it selects the right from the wrong. This is the sort of structure I call a selective system.

I found this sort of structure repeated in the integrative action of the nervous system and of the personality structure. It was also repeated in the social situation, the controlling action of social institutions and social patterns, in the biological process of natural selection, and even further in the emergence and maintenance of steady states through the various levels of organic and inorganic nature.

My value studies carried me through the action of selective systems to and including that of natural selection in its operation upon man and his social systems. And a strange outcome (for me) was that I never found myself brought to a stop in applying this set of categories from which I started—the set gained from the analysis of purposive structures. I was not blocked at one point or another (as I had been in working with the limited range of aesthetic values in *The Basis of Criticism in the Arts*) from an inability to do justice to the insights of other world hypotheses than whatever one I was working on. These categories for a selective system went unchallenged through all the empirical insights of the traditional world hypotheses on the subject. It dawned on me that I might have stumbled upon a new fruitful root metaphor for a novel world hypothesis which might be called *selectivism*.

Now remember, I started out with an analysis of purpose in terms of what I thought was a conventional application of mechanistic categories to the subject. I took behavioristic concepts and a parallel set of introspective concepts—a typical mechanistic procedure in terms of psycho-physical parallelism. They were mutually helpful in this field of subject matter, but it was true that the qualitative introspective material acquired greater and greater weight as the analysis proceeded. Particularly it gave a nonmechanistic emphasis to the qualitative immediacy of the specific area of actual purposive selection and choice within the living duration of the specious present.

The typical mechanistic treatment of space-time as a cosmic container lost its authority as a primary category, taking on the interpretation of a systematizing scheme for the scientific localization of cosmic events. But it remained more than a merely operational scheme (as the contextualists would interpret it), for the locations designated were verifiable and also the articulations of qualitative purposive events in their full intrinsic immediacy.

For instance, when a purposive process entered the field of an anticipated goal object localized on a well-conceived space-time schedule, the event anticipated was verified in the full qualitative immediacy of a lived-through duration at that location. If the anticipation was correct, there was a verified correspondence not only of the qualitative anticipations of the perceptual features of the event but also of its space-time location. A correspondence theory of truth—in some sense more qualitatively filled than a pragmatic operational theory can offer—is called for to interpret the situation. The space-time scheme must be treated as representative of the cosmic disposition of events in some more literal manner than a typical contextualist can offer in terms of a pure operationalism.

I have already expanded here upon the metaphysical implications of my study of value beyond anything that appears in *The Sources of Value*. But such expansions resulting from the unexpected discovery that the categorial analysis I had made for the study of purpose proved adequate to carry me through the whole accumulation of empirical insights of the relatively adequate world theories on the subject. Just how these insights find their place under the selectivistic categories, is described in *Ethics,* a kind of supplement to *The Sources of Value.*

The next step was to work seriously to develop the new root metaphor into the full-fledged world theory it seemed to have potentially in it. The root metaphor in its more refined development—it should be noticed—is not any longer literally simply that of a human purpose in action. It is the structure and content of a dynamic selective system. One might draw the categories equally well from the integrative action of personality structure, or from the normative action of a social structure. The only practical restriction is that the sample taken should contain not only the data for a so-called "objective" description but also its qualitative content available to immediate human inspection, otherwise the qualitative categories will be neglected.

Having caught this idea of a new root metaphor—or, better perhaps, having been caught by it—I suddenly found I appreciated and understood Whitehead's philosophy in a new way. He is, I should still maintain, eclectic. His 'eternal objects' seem to call for formistic categories, and his interpretation of God seems to bring in organistic categories. But his treatment of the central dynamic agency, his "actual entity," with its process of "concrescence" in the context of other actual entities, drawing upon the determinate past and projecting itself through its living duration into a partially indeterminate future, all described in terms of immediately felt qualities—all this material is through and through purposive and normatively selective. It is the action of a natural norm, a selective system, and conceived by him as cosmically pervasive.

If one man can be credited as the creative discoverer of dynamic purposive structure as a fruitful root metaphor for a new world theory, it was Whitehead. And with him (as so often in the development of root metaphors) this novel conception emerges in the midst of an eclectic background. I have attempted to free the root metaphor from the confusions of this background, developing it on the dynamics of its own potentialities for cosmic interpretation. But often in wondering if perhaps here or there the momentum of interpretation by these categories might be leading to an extravagant conclusion, I have found reassuring support from Whitehead. An outstanding instance is the demand of these categories that feeling qualities be not limited to the islands of so-called human consciousness, but shown to pervade natural processes through all levels—not only the biological but also the inorganic. Whitehead proposes this on the same grounds.

Other intimations of metaphysical reflection among contemporary philosophers are centered on dynamic purposive and social structures. Many Whiteheadians of various sorts are active; some also may hold that this root metaphor is implicit in the pragmatic or contextualistic movement. It may be held that what I call selectivism is just a species—or possibly a culmination—of the contextualistic world hypothesis. There are broad areas of congruence which are suggestive, but there are also several wide departures—such as the unacceptability of a purely operational theory of truth and of scientific method.

Many writers in the existential movement also take as their point of departure the dynamic structure of purposive activity, as if they, too, felt the breath of a new inspiration there. We shall have a chance to look into this later.

I have recently put together a systematic treatment of selectivism as a world hypothesis under the title *Concept and Quality*. In this lecture, however, I have been referring to the working out of this theory only as a personal illustration of a way by which philosophy can be profitably developed to offer men a well-grounded comprehensive view of things. And such comprehension I regard as an important human need which only philosophers are competent to supply.

THE ORDINARY LANGUAGE MOVEMENT

Since *World Hypotheses* was published early in 1942, two philosophical movements have grown into prominence—linguistic analysis and existentialism. These were already stirring in the thirties, but many of us did not regard them as likely to be serious rivals of traditional systematic philosophy. They have nonetheless proved to be this to such an extent that systematic philosophy in the sixties has been rather on the defensive. In this and the following lecture I wish to examine these two movements, relating them to the standpoint of *World Hypotheses*.

The movement of linguistic analysis has several phases, but I shall concentrate on its vital core, the "ordinary language" school, spoken of here as the "ordinary language movement."

The history of its origin is not irrelevant to its tenets and procedures. It is in large degree an inheritance from logical positivism which was at its peak in the thirties and forties but dwindled with surprising rapidity in the next decades.

In terms of *World Hypotheses,* logical positivism is essentially an extreme form of the mechanistic world theory. It tried, however, to conceal its mechanistic presuppositions behind a mask of scientific positivism. This mask was quickly penetrated by its critics chiefly through an analysis of its theory of meaning.

Positively it identified significant meaning with the possibility of verifying scientific statements with ultimate sensory data. The ultimate verificatory statements were often called protocol sentences, and statements that could not be reduced to such protocol sentences were dubbed meaningless. The latter conclusion, of course, was contrary to common sense and a long intellectual tradition. This extremely narrow theory of meaning led to an intensive analysis of meaning and especially of common sense meanings and their reflection in common speech or ordinary language. The latter emphasis was accentuated by the great influence of the later Wittgenstein, who earlier in his *Tractatus* had offered a systematization of logical atomism which was a phase of logical positivism, and with which he subsequently became disillusioned.

In his *Blue and Brown Books* and his posthumous *Investigations,* he identified philosophy with the analysis of concepts, which was already a thesis of the logical positivists. If all meaningful statements were scientific statements, what function was left for philosophy? The answer was the clarification of meanings and the analysis of concepts. The positivists seem to have had in mind the positive clarification of scientific concepts; they already had dubbed all metaphysical statements meaningless. I vividly remember one of the founders of logical positivism, Moritz Schlick, sitting in the Berkeley department's seminar room lined with the philosophical classics. With a sweeping gesture around the room, he asserted, "All these are nonsense." Wittgenstein went a step further and pronounced it the function of philosophy to analyze out all this "nonsense" in terms of ordinary language. This procedure was presented as a therapeutic undertaking (a sort of linguistic psychoanalysis), to cure philosophy of its diseases and ultimately to dispense with such pseudo-intellectualism altogether. This undertaking, you can see, was an inheritance from logical positivism. The ordinary language school thus initiated, then carried over—it will be found—a good many other such inheritances from logical positivism, most of them concealed under ordinary language procedures.

This point is important because it indicates the concealed presence in much ordinary language analysis of some of the typical metaphysical categories of a traditional world hypothesis—namely mechanism. For the mechanistic categories clearly underlie the procedures and system of logical positivism. The orginary language school could, of course, partially justify these mechanistic inheritances by regarding them as meanings imbedded in contemporary ordinary language. But this in itself would be illuminating of the nature of ordinary language.

One more important influence upon the ordinary language school must be mentioned—that of G. E. Moore. At least in all his earlier work, G. E. Moore was a typical British realist using the formistic categories of subsistent universals and existent particulars. But he attached to this realism (or followed it with) a common sense view setting up common sense disclosures as ultimate criteria of cognitive significance and factuality. For instance, to the question of the existence of material objects, his answer was to raise one hand and then the other saying, "Here is one material object and here is another." There they were, by ostensive common sense demonstration. It was much the same as Dr. Johnson's famous refutation of Berkeleyan idealism, which he declared refuted by kicking a stone. The ordinary language school picked up this side of Moore's philosophy, dropping, however, his subsistent theory of universals.

They were also deeply impressed with Moore's linguistic analysis of "good," leading to his doctrine of the naturalistic fallacy. To a man, they accepted some form of A. J. Ayer's interpretation of this fallacy, rejecting Moore's solution that the fallacy indicated that "good" was an intellectually intuited unique formistic universal, and substituting the doctrine that all expressions of value are emotive expressions, or like them, in not being true or false statements. They are not necessarily meaningless (Ayer, it is generally agreed, went too far in originally asserting this); but their significance, important as it may be, is not like that of scientific statements open to factual verification.

From the foregoing introduction it can be seen that the natural language school in one way or another sets up the disclosures of common sense and the meanings of ordinary language as ultimate philosophical criteria over a wide range of experience. This is clearly quite contrary to the treatment of common sense in *World Hypotheses,* where common sense is described as a rich source of cognitive insight, the source of most root metaphors, but in itself a sphere of confusion, vagueness, contradictions and cognitive irritation—something to be cognitively refined by multiplicative or structural corroboration, but never to be depended upon as an ultimate cognitive criterion.

The usual procedure recommended by *World Hypotheses* for overcoming the vagueness and ambiguities of common sense concepts is to submit them to refinement by successive definition, through confronting them with empirical experience and such knowledge as has already been found relatively adequate in respect to scope and precision. In the course of this procedure, consistency comes also to be empirically demanded to avoid imprecision; and as the refinement proceeds, the concepts usually become much more detailed and articulated than they were in their first emergence from common sense. Consequently, they no longer look just the same.

In this way the concepts of science and philosophy are contrasted with those of common sense, which remains with us, however technical our science and philosophy may grow. There is, to be sure, something of a counter movement too, insofar as scientific and philosophical refinements get incorporated into common sense—sometimes to the added confusion of common sense. To the ordinary man today, water is

H_2O, as well as a colorless, thirst satisfying liquid, and quite likely (at the same time), one of four cosmic elements of the ancient Greeks—earth, air, fire, and water. For *World Hypotheses* the ultimate cognitive criteria are to be sought in the highest refinements of science, mathematics, and philosophy, including those most nearly adequate comprehensive syntheses which are world hypotheses.

Opposed to this approach in *World Hypotheses* we meet such downright statements as Norman Malcolm's in his article on "Moore and Ordinary Language" asserting that "Ordinary language is correct language."[5] He made this pronouncement in preparation for a criticism of the sense-datum theory of perception, and by implication of any other theory of perception, presented as a refined analysis of such ordinary language expressions as "seeing a cat." The idea is that any philosophical or psychological analysis of distal visual perception which does not conform to the simple ordinary statement "X sees O" (generalizing "a man sees a cat"), is—insofar as it fails to conform to common sense—*incorrect*.

There is just a modicum of agreement with the approach of *World Hypotheses* in this matter. There, a common sense ostensive or descriptive definition of any topic is accepted as a test definition of the relative identity of that topic among the diverse analyses given by different world hypotheses of the same topic. But a test definition is never regarded as an ultimate cognitive criterion; it might be rejected altogether, if the topic turned out to be so vague or ambiguous or lacking in corroborative evidence as to be cognitively useless.

Statements like Malcolm's (though rarely so sweeping) can be found throughout the literature of the ordinary language school. In fact, even Malcolm may not intend the criterion of ordinary language to cover either the physical sciences or mathematics. If so, this qualification would be an inheritance from the logical positivists.

Let us then turn for a less doctrinaire writer to some of the statements of J. L. Austin, who seems to have been one of the most constructive and penetrating exponents of the ordinary language school. He is also one of the least dogmatic. His essay, "A Plea for Excuses," outlines the program of ordinary language philosophy.

He begins with the following: "Perhaps this method, at least as *one* philosophical method, scarcely requires justification at present—too evidently, there is gold in them thar hills: more opportune would be a warning about the care and thoroughness needed if it is not to fall into disrepute. I will, however, justify it very briefly."

Three partly factual, partly normative generalizations follow. "First, words are our tools, and, as a minimum, we should use clean tools; we should know what we mean and what we do not, and we must forearm ourselves against the traps that language sets us. Secondly, words are not (except in their own little corner) facts or things; we need therefore to prize them off the world, to hold them apart from and against it, so that we can realize their inadequacies and arbitrariness, and can relook at the world without blinkers."

Then comes his most revealing statement: "Thirdly, and more hopefully, our common stock of words embodies all the distinctions men have found worth drawing, and the connexions they have found worth marking, in the lifetimes of many generations: these surely are likely to be more numerous, more sound, since they have stood up to the long test of the survival of the fittest, and more subtle, at least in all ordinary and reasonably practical matters, than any that you or I are likely to think up in our arm-chairs of an afternoon—the most favored alternative method."[6]

This is a revealing statement with an insight about ordinary language which, however exaggerated, gives at least the first inkling of something positive of fairly massive proportions to be found in the ordinary language program. So much of their program (nearly all of Wittgenstein's, it would seem) has been negative and destructive—and much of that far beyond justification. This strong positive affirmation of Austin's is a relief and an augury of greater maturity and trustworthiness in the method. Notice, for instance, that Austin speaks of "this method, at least as *one* philosophical method," leaving an opening for other fruitful philosophical methods; and that the usefulness of this method "at least in all ordinary and reasonably practical matters" leaves open the usefulness of other methods outside the range of "ordinary practical matters." But the modesty and tolerance of these concessions is almost spoiled by his final impetuous phrase about "the most favored alternative method" consisting of "distinctions . . . that you or I are likely to think up in our arm-chairs of an afternoon." No world hypothesis was ever developed that fast or in that way.

We must also protest Austin's idea that ordinary language "contains all the distinctions men have found worth drawing . . . in the lifetimes of many generations." It is too obvious that the structures of different cultures differ and that their languages reflect their cultures, whether separated by time or geography. Austin immediately takes this objection up as a "bogey." He admits that "people's usages do vary, and we do talk loosely," but replies "not nearly as much as one would think."[7] This is clearly an empirical matter for the linguists to demonstrate, but I will admit to "not quite as much as *I* had thought" previous to the constructive work of the ordinary language school. And a rough estimate of the school's new contribution is what should be presently considered.

Austin also takes up the objection that the results of ordinary language are not the last word—what I have been calling the ultimate cognitive criterion. He admits that "certainly ordinary language has no claim to be the last word,"[8] and "that superstition and error and fantasy of all kinds do get incorporated into ordinary language."[9] He says that it "will often have become infected with the jargon of extinct theories, and our own prejudices too,"[10] but he concludes "only remember it *is* the *first* word."[11] With all of this, the conception of common sense in *World Hypotheses* could well agree. But I am sure that Austin meant more by "the first word" than that, though I really cannot be precisely sure what he does mean. For "first" is an ambiguous word, and in this context we might suspect it retains a little of the connotation of what Austin meant by "the last word."

After these preliminary remarks, Austin proceeds to outline his method of digging out the meanings of words in ordinary language, with the word *excuses* as his example. He remarks on his reason for selecting just this word: he has a hunch that it will be fruitful in bringing out hidden discriminations in human conduct. It has the advantage of not being a term customarily worried over in traditional ethics or other specialized social studies, as "justice" and "obligation" and "conscience" have been.

He then lists the sources of his data. First comes the dictionary. One might go systematically through an English dictionary picking out relevant words, but he seems to prefer another less mechanical method: "to start with a widish selection of obviously relevant terms and to consult the dictionary under each; it will be found that, in the explanations of the various meanings of each, a surprising number of other terms occur, which are germane though of course not often synonymous. We then look up each of *these,* bringing in more for our bag from the 'definitions' given in each case; and when we have continued for a little, it will generally be found that the family circle begins to close, until ultimately it is complete and we come only upon repetitions. This method has the advantage of grouping the terms into convenient clusters."[12]

This detailed and compendious use of the dictionary prompts me to make a curious comment. The results from this method are bound to exceed the limits of any plain man's vocabulary, and what Austin will get will resemble much more closely the large vocabulary and sensitive discriminations of a highly experienced author like Henry James. Just as Henry James can make a little word like "the" or "any" ring (in a certain context) with a meaning never quite sensed before, and yet exactly right in the genius of the English language of today, so can Austin.

But in their writings, Henry James and Austin are not

speaking like any ordinary plain man on the street. One has only to talk a little while with a store clerk or a truck driver or a lumberman to observe the difference. Go no further than the size of vocabulary. James and Austin have command of many thousand words; the clerk and lumberman only of some hundreds. The scarcity of expressive adjectives for many of these plain men is astonishing. To be sure, the variety of shadings the plain man can give to his few words in the various contexts of the day can also be astonishing, but these come from the behavioral environment like a dog's bark. Still the vocabulary is very small. The fine discriminating choice of words we so admire in Henry James and Austin would be completely lost on these plain, ordinary men.

Consider a particular point Austin makes about his ordinary language in this very article on excuses. He says "a word never—well, hardly ever—shakes off its etymology."[13] I think it was Pater, of whom it was said that he never used a word without thinking of its etymological origin. Such scruples are the mark of the highest sophistication; they are not characteristic of the clerk or lumberman. The latter would just stare at you if you told him that "accident" trails the etymology of "befalls," or "error" that of "straying."[14]

Austin's ordinary language is thus not ordinary at all: it is quite extraordinary. It is used and fully discriminated only by the most highly cultured English speaking persons, but it is the standard English all the same, just as it has been written and spoken. It has a cultural authority behind it, and (as Austin truly says), it is the repository of many subtle discriminations out of past human experience. I do not in any way wish to demean the positive results of Austin's careful analyses of these subtle discriminations, but these do not get their authority from the talk of the plain ordinary man in the street. The authority is that of literary usage, which is only vaguely reflected, if at all, by the man in the street. Let any plain man see what he could get out of Austin's penetrating article on "Ifs and Cans." Would he have any feeling for the crucial shades of meaning for "shall" and "will" and "should" and "would" and "could" and "can"? We suddenly discover it is not literally ordinary language that Austin is exploring but rather a natural language. This discovery prompts in me a number of other qualifying reflections, but they are not essential to our present purpose—which is to find out what Austin and his school have positively contributed to philosophy. There is no question that we are much more informed about the meanings of "Ifs and cans" and "Excuses" through Austin's presentations than we ever were before.

So Austin mentions the dictionary as his first source. His second is the law. "This will provide us," he says, "with an immense miscellany of untoward cases, and also a useful list of recognized pleas [remember the subject is "Excuses"], together with a good deal of acute analysis of both."[15] At the same time Austin warns us that we must not take it entirely on its own terms. It needs sifting for Austin's purposes, for he says "practising lawyers and jurists are by no means so careful as they might be to give to our ordinary expressions their ordinary meanings and applications. There is special pleading and evasion, stretching and strait jacketing, besides the invention of technical terms, or technical senses for common terms."[16]

This passage is also illuminating. Clearly the sifting to be done is to be done under the guidance, the criteria, of the authoritative meanings of the dictionary. Notice particularly the elimination of legal technical terms, and technical senses for common terms. This would have the effect of eliminating expert legal refinements of common sense concepts. This restriction should be emphatically noted, for it would seem to have the effect of excluding the expert treatment of a considerable quantity of Austin's subject of "Excuses." Is Austin implying that he is not interested in the *subject* of "Excuses" but only in the common and dictionary *meanings* of the word? The results obtained from other than linguistic experts in analyzing this subject of 'pleas' and 'excuses' are then to be discarded as irrelevant. Does Austin want to say this?

This would be equivalent to adopting Malcolm's dictum that "ordinary language *is* correct language." It would come near to setting up lexicography as the dictator of cognition. This is what the critics of the ordinary language school often suspect and find absurd. But I do not believe Austin means this. We have already quoted him speaking of his linguistic method as "*one* philosophical method." The legal profession in its technical refinements can have another and the subject of "Excuses" can profit from the contributions of both lawyers and linguistic philosophers. Systematic philosophers would be just the ones to bring these and other contributions together for the fullest understanding of the subject.

Austin, nevertheless, deserves commendation for his willingness to consult specialists outside his group of linguistic analysts. He does it again in regard to psychology for he accepts this along with anthropology and animal psychology as his third source of data for the analysis of "Excuses." And here he explicitly makes the concession of accepting some psychological data relevant to this subject that have not found their way into ordinary language. This is such an important concession in view of a widely prevalent attitude in the linguistic school that Austin's words should be quoted: "Some varieties of behavior," he says, "some ways of acting or explanations of the doing of actions, are here noticed and classified which have not been observed or named by ordinary men and hallowed by ordinary language."[17] Specialists and experts in other fields are hereby given recognition—even though a rather restrained recognition—for Austin adds after the quotation above the clause "though perhaps they [the unnoticed acts] might have been so [noticed] if they had been of more practical importance." And he ends the paragraph with another ambivalent sentence. "There is real danger in contempt for the 'jargon' of psychology, at least when it sets out to supplement, and at least sometimes when it sets out to supplant, the language of ordinary life."[18]

According to *World Hypotheses* all this trepidation on Austin's part (over the analyses of experts in fields other than his, and their coining of precise technical terms to summarize their results) is unnecessary, and if heeded could actually hinder or obstruct the progress of knowledge in those fields— be it "excuses," "freedom," "perception," "similarity," "causality," "induction," "physical object," or what not. There is nothing intrinsically fallacious or confusing in redefinition in pursuit of precision and the giving of a technical term to the resulting concept to mark the step attained. Quite the contrary; to block this typical cognitive procedure would be one way of holding knowledge back. But at least Austin has made the important gesture of accepting data from special sciences and other institutions of experts even when these data have not as yet been hallowed by ordinary language.

There is another source of data (or rather a procedure yielding data) used by Austin. It might be called the 'job principle.' It consists in trying out words in a variety of verbal and situational contexts to find out where they work naturally in the feel of the language and where they do not. So a linguist will say, "It makes (or it does not make) good sense" to use such and such a word in such a context, or most characteristically "It is *odd*" to use the word in such a context. As Austin writes in the present essay: "I sit in my chair, in the usual way—I am not in a daze or influenced by threats or the like: here, it will not do to say either that I sat in it intentionally or that I did not sit in it intentionally, nor yet that I sat in it automatically or from habit or what you will. It is bedtime, I am alone, I yawn; but I do not yawn involuntarily (or voluntarily!), nor yet deliberately. To yawn in any such peculiar way is just not to just yawn."[19]

Trying a word out in a variety of such contexts brings out the particular job it does in the language. It traces the path of its normal functioning through the maze of human experiencing and reveals a subtle discrimination, a mode of behavior or of social conduct that has often escaped notice. This sort of procedure with words is not entirely novel; philosophers through the centuries have made use of it. Think of the classic analyses of the meaning of "beauty," "sublime," "grotesque," "wit," "humor," etc. But never has the procedure been carried to such lengths or regarded as so central to the philosophical enterprise. It strikes me as the basic methodological and normative principle of linguistic philosophy —at least in its constructive phase.

There are two or three other matters closely allied to method characteristic of linguistic analysis that should be mentioned. First there is the emphasis on the open texture concept and what is closely related to it, the family resemblance concept. Both, and especially the latter, owe their prominence to Wittgenstein's work. These concepts are opposed to the sharply bounded definitional concepts associated with the pursuit of rigor of thought. Many common sense concepts are not susceptible to rigorous boundary determination, and yet are useful instruments of ordinary practical communication. Wittgenstein's prime illustration is the concept of "game." There is no obvious set of common characteristics that can rigorously define the boundaries of this concept—to include such diverse activities as chess, card games, cricket, football, field sports, gambling, child play, etc., etc. They overlap one another, and new activities can be added to the group without misunderstanding. They have a family resemblance.

Then there are concepts that shade off from a central model, where the outer boundary lines are hazy. These are held in place by the notion of the "paradigm case." This notion has been so strenuously used by some ordinary language philosophers that some critics have plausibly identified it with the philosophy itself, so persuasively so that Antony Flew offered a rebuttal in a key article in a recent publication.[20]

In this article Flew refers with particular irritation to Ernest Gellner's *Words and Things,* containing a commendatory introduction by Bertrand Russell.[21] Gellner refers to the Paradigm Case Argument (PCA) as a central pillar of the ordinary language philosophy. "The argument from the Paradigm Case is this," he writes. "Stress that, after all, words mean what they normally mean (unless and until refined). Their meaning is their use. We often have occasion to use the word 'table.' It means whatever it is used to refer to, and, as we often do use it, that to which it refers to *is* a 'table.' Therefore, tables exist."[22]

He continues:

> The argument may also be applied to more controversial cases. . . . For instance, it may be used to establish the—most controversial—reality of free will. What do expressions such as "of one's own free will" mean? Why, let us look at their paradigmatic use. Should we not use it of a smiling bride-groom marrying the girl of his choice? Well then, *that* is the kind of thing the expression means. What else could it mean? Ergo, free will is vindicated. The proof is breathtakingly brief. All the worry about how to square human responsibility with what is known of nature, of human physiology, with what appears to be the case in psychology, with what may be the case about the march of history . . . all that was, it appears, quite unnecessary. The Argument from Smiling Bridegrooms solves it all."[23]

It is easy to understand why Flew was irritated and Ryle was angry. Yet though this description is something of a travesty, it is a mode of argument frequently used—or, worse, insinuated. It is imbedded in Malcolm's phrase earlier quoted: "Ordinary language is correct language." Even Austin has difficulty restraining himself from saying it "is the last word," as we have just seen. In his rebuttal article, Flew spends most of his time making qualifications of Malcolm's famous phrase. But he never gives up the principle of a primacy of ordinary language.

It cannot be denied that the ordinary language school generally exhibits a rather dogmatic attitude. And insofar as they use the PCA, their dogmatism consists in a covert appeal to certainty, differing from G. E. Moore's direct use of this device of dogmatism only by its being an indirect use. Where

G. E. Moore simply raises his two hands in front of his eyes and declares in the name of common sense that there *certainly* are two material objects, the ordinary language men make a circuit by way of ordinary (common sense) language, pick out a phrase with its common sense meaning, set this up as a paradigm case for the concept (material object), and affirm thereby the justification for belief in the meaning of the concept (namely, the existence of material objects as they appear before your eyes).

Though the ordinary language school frequently employs this maneuver, I have made no reference to it here. I have treated them as empiricists with an excessive confidence in the evidences furnished by common sense and natural language, and have overlooked any overt or covert appeals to certainty mingled with their procedures. The paradigm case has been regarded simply as a way of developing a special sort of concept, useful for particular kinds of analysis.

It is an important notion in this philosophy, but hardly to be made out the whole of it. It is not even original with the ordinary language school. It is employed, for instance, in the Aristotelian conception of a natural species defined in terms of the 'perfect specimen,' or as the form for the species which existing individuals fulfil in various degrees. But, of course, for the ordinary language philosophers the paradigm case would not be ascribed to a formistic category but would be firmly deposited in common sense or in ordinary linguistic usage.

With the foregoing principles of linguistic method in mind (and these must not be taken as exhaustive but only as representative) let us consider the results of this philosophy in relation to those of synthetic philosophy as outlined in *World Hypotheses*. For this purpose I have sought for a fair sampling of the vast literature of articles regarded as representative of this school. Antony Flew's two series of selections in *Logic and Language*—the first published in 1951, and the second in 1953—could serve properly for this aim.[24] They were assembled at what might be considered the peak of optimistic enthusiasm within the school as an example of what it could do.

There are twenty-one articles altogether and they can be classified in two groups—those that conspicuously employ the ordinary language procedures, and those which though analytical could just as well have been written before the advent of G. E. Moore and Wittgenstein. That is, the latter are more concerned with the clarification or evidential justification of concepts than with the subtleties of linguistic usage. They could further be classified as to whether they were primarily destructive in their results or constructive. So there were in all three groups: (1) the destructive ordinary language analyses; (2) the constructive ordinary language analyses; and (3) the straightforward conceptual analyses all of which in these essays I found constructive.

Rather than carry you through my own analyses in the above terms of each of the twenty-one articles in the two series, I will just give two or three examples. Rarely do I find the destructive articles very convincing. If I were to rely upon them alone as representative of the movement, I should say that they tended to be more destructive of their own procedures than of those attacked. They consist mainly in pointing out discrepancies between the doctrinal assumptions of the school and the cognitively refined work of other philosophers. The constructive work of these other philosophers under attack remains largely intact, only sometimes calling for further refinement or more extensive synthetic treatment.

Ryle's opening article of the first series is an example of such destructive analysis. The title, "Systematically Misleading Expressions," sets the theme. He offers four groups of such expressions, the first dealing with quasi-ontological statements, and he starts off with 'exists' as a predicate as in "God exists." There is a point to be made here, but treating it as systematically misleading is unconvincing. Ironically, G. E. Moore has an article in the second series, "Is Existence a Predicate," which makes a plausible case for occasions when 'exists' can legitimately be a predicate. Apparently, ordinary language experts can disagree about ordinary correct usage. The same is to be noted in respect to "is real or a reality." Waismann in a later essay in the first series writes, "Not that I deny for a minute that a word like 'reality' is a blessing; it definitely is."[25] It would look as if it were Ryle who is misleading. Parenthetically, how would we compare alternative ontological theories, such as world hypotheses, without the use of these ontological predicates?

Ryle's second group of systematically misleading expressions is those "seemingly about universals." He frames a number of verbal combinations to suggest the absurdity of referring to universals as 'objects.' "So 'universals' are not objects," he concludes—"in the way in which Mt. Everest is one, and therefore the age-old question what *sort* of objects they are is a bogus question."[26] Nevertheless the age-old question does remain. It is not dismissed by arguments from verbal usage, or from verbal references. It happens to be based on a pervasive empirical datum—that of observed similarity and regularity in natural events. The handling of this problem depends on one's total empirical outlook, on the categorical presuppositions of a world hypothesis. Common sense itself is vague and disturbed on the subject—for instance, about the status of laws of nature. Ryle here is simply exhibiting his presuppositions for a naturalistic, nominalistic, metaphysics in which only particulars exist. His linguistic attempt to destroy the doctrine of universals thus comes to nothing. The same could be said of all his other destructive attempts in this article.

For the nature of the constructive essays I shall here first of all refer back to the sort of discriminations we found in Austin's analysis just reviewed. Similarly constructive is Austin's essay on "Other Minds" in the Second Series. Also I would say is Urmson's essay "On Grading"[27] and H. L. A. Hart's essay, analyzing the concept of defeasibility, adds a major contribution to the understanding of legal and other conceptions of 'responsibility' and 'rights.' And Ryle's essay in the second series brings out the useful concept (useful up to a point) of 'category mistake.'[28] And so with numerous others.

As a fine example of an analysis that has no dependence on natural language procedures, I call attention to Fred Will's article with the title "Will the Future Resemble the Past?" It is a constructive treatment of the problem of inductive inference and the confirmation of predictions. It justifies such inferences in opposition to Hume's famous analysis which denies a justification. The refutation of Hume's position is based upon an ambiguity in the meaning of 'future' in the sense of (1) unexperienced events that always lie in advance of any given present, and in the sense of (2) references to unexperienced events that are progressively actualized within experience in successive presents. The future in the first sense by definition can never be experienced for confirmation of predictions. But future in sense number two is always open to confirmation whenever the dated future event becomes actualized as an experienced present at the predicted date. The argument as against Hume does make use of a verbal ambiguity; this is the only linguistic element in the analysis. But the basis of the argument is not at all on questions of linguistic usage but entirely on an empirical analysis of the sequence of events in observed human experience and in the observed procedures of scientific prediction.

It is illuminating to contrast Will's article in the second series with Paul Edwards' article on "Bertrand Russell's Doubts About Induction" in the first series: the two men come to the same conclusion. But Edward's article depends entirely on the evidences of the ordinary usage of "reason for an inductive conclusion."[29] Will's article makes no particular reference to common sense or ordinary usage. He cuts right through language, however it may be used by men on the street or by philosophers like Hume and Russell, and goes to the observed evidences in the making and confirming of predictions. His argument is convincing; Edward's is no more than persuasive. And what persuasion it has comes from our sensing the possibility of Will's empirical analysis underlying Edward's linguistic one.

Leaving such examples, let me now offer a summary of my reactions to this set of articles. According to my statistics, sixteen of the twenty-one articles are ordinary language analyses. Of these, six are destructive in their conclusions, and ten wholly or in part constructive. The remaining five are direct factual analyses having nothing—or only incidentally—to do with language. They are such as could have been written quite outside the ordinary language school.[30] It is interesting to notice that all the articles of the first series are analyses in ordinary language, while in the second series only seven are in ordinary language and five are analyses not dependent on ordinary language. Furthermore, in the first series five out of the nine articles were destructive, and only four constructive, while in the second series only one of the seven ordinary language analyses was destructive, the remaining six all constructive. There seems to have been a movement even as early as 1953 away from the destructive activity of the ordinary language school (aimed at annihilating metaphysics), toward more constructive uses of their modes of analysis; and more enlightening still, a movement towards recognition of the value of analyses outside the ordinary language techniques. Incidentally, some philosophers raised in the ordinary language school have lately even ventured into the field of synthetic philosophy, notably P. F. Strawson, with his *Individuals*, "an essay in descriptive metaphysics," (the author's subtitle); and J. J. C. Smart, with his *Philosophy and Scientific Realism*.[31]

In reviewing this set of essays I am more than ever persuaded of what was said earlier: that the destructive phase of the ordinary language movement is its weakest phase. The destructive analyses are challenging but rarely decisive. The perennial problems of philosophy are still with us—the problem of similarity or universals; the problems of time, space, and change in immediate experience and in history and in science, and the relation of these to each other; the problem of visual perception, of objects, and especially of so-called "material or external objects," and of the structure of mind and immediacy; and, of course, of values. These problems have neither been solved nor dissolved by the ordinary language analyses; the most that can be said is that the issues have often been outlined more vividly.

My interest is aroused rather by the constructive phase of the movement. Analyses like Waismann's and Hart's and Austin's have opened my eyes to the presence in common sense of a much deeper rootage and interconnectedness of concepts and meanings than first suspected when *World Hypotheses* was written. The fruitfulness of the ordinary language techniques has been enlightening—that of tracking down the jobs words do, of uncovering the open texture concept, the family-resemblance concept, and the paradigm case device, etc. I would now have to qualify what was said earlier about the vagueness and contrarieties of common sense in terms of the considerable positive contributions of the ordinary language school. Clearly, the techniques of the ordinary language school will never be powerful enough to displace direct factual analyses like Will's and MacIver's nor the need of synthetic philosophy and world hypotheses. Despite all that the ordinary language school has contributed, the area of common sense—including the language and persuasions of ordinary men—is still a cognitively irritating area to be confined in. We have to get out of it to make the most of our cognitive abilities. The special techniques of the sciences and of mathematics and logic and conceptual analysis will take us out in a number of directions, but those of synthetic philosophy are the only ones we can expect to offer us what J. J. C. Smart calls an "adumbration of a world view."

EXISTENTIALISM

For existentialism I am going to concentrate on one man, Jean-Paul Sartre (who I believe is most responsible for the initiating impulse of the movement) and on the one central philosophical book of his, *Being and Nothingness*.[32] I realize that the movement has extended far beyond him and now has many orthodoxes and heterodoxes, but for our purpose of comparing the approach of existentialism with that of *World Hypotheses,* we cannot do better than to concentrate upon this one book.

In regard to one basic doctrine of method, Sartre is in flat opposition to the approach of *World Hypotheses*. His work is founded throughout on the appeal to certainty, on an appeal at every critical juncture to the indubitability of what is offered as given. In *World Hypotheses* any appeal to certainty as an ultimate cognitive or ontological criterion is immediately suspect. The aim of such an appeal, it is there said, is to silence criticism of the item offered. For

World Hypotheses any ultimate appeal to certainty, whether by way of self-evidence, indubitability, incorrigibility, or what else, is a red signal to stop, to consider, to question, and ask for corroboration. The basis for this questioning is the many times confirmed insecurity of this appeal in the long history of philosophy. In view of that long history of previous failures, one can only wonder how philosophers can bring themselves to offer up this same old criterion seriously again, particularly as it is a criterion that claims to be intrinsically infallible.

However, it is also a point of method brought out in *World Hypotheses* that the appeal to certainty need not totally vitiate a philosophical system. The appeal may be set aside by the critical reader, and the philosophical system viewed as a world hypothesis examined for its adequacy in the scope and precision of its statements. Nearly all classical philosophers representing the various schools with their contrary sets of categories have appealed in one form or another to certainty for the acceptance of their basic concepts. Of course, these appeals are nearly all contrary to one another. They cannot, consequently, all be genuine certainties; the most plausible conclusion is that not any are. But the relative adequacy of these various men's philosophical theories remains unaffected by the conversion of their certainties into corrigible convictions.

So we shall, in the end, set aside Sartre's frequent appeals to the indubitability of his numerous 'givens,' directing our attention to the adequacy of his system as a world hypothesis.

Sartre's appeal to certainty is comparable to the ordinary language school's appeal to common sense as a philosophical ultimate. If either could be unconditionally established, it would seriously affect the philosophical method, the attitude, and some of the conclusions of *World Hypotheses*. For our hypothetical mode of approach, however, it is encouraging that neither of these modern attempts to reinstate the ultimacy of these 'devices of dogmatism,' brought up any new evidences for their claims of reliability. In fact, these two schools seem to oppose each other regarding their respective ultimate claims. For over and over again, Sartre challenges the deliverances of ordinary language, and either abandons them for his own insights and coins new terms, or else redefines common terms to fit his concepts and intuitions. And the ordinary language people (particularly Austin) have generally been extremely critical of the claims for indubitable givens.

In fact, the contrast between these two modern schools is in itself philosophically illuminating. The transition from the logical and verbalistic atmosphere of the British linguistic analysts to the luxuriant expanse of qualitative dramatic experience (with its personal frustrations, and its entanglements, and the 'anguish' of the continental existentialists) is like coming down from the Arctic Circle to the jungles of the Amazon: they complement each other. Each, to an uncompromised observer, seems to need the other, and a synthesis of some sort clamors for achievement.

The linguistic movement, so far as I can see, evolves no system.[33] It is a method of sporadic analyses solely. But the existential movement does evolve a system. The subtitle of *Being and Nothingness* is "An Essay on Phenomenological Ontology." It reaches out towards an unrestricted hypothesis, a complete ontological system, but like mysticism, it lacks scope. And also, like mysticism, the main reason it fails to see its own gaps of inadequacy is its self-imposed blindness of dogmatic certainty. Once the curtain of dogmatic certainty is removed, its descriptions of human drama are capable of extension into a new and exciting and possibly more adequate world hypothesis than any of the traditional four outlined in *World Hypotheses*. We may have here one of several tentative approaches converging toward a new world synthesis.

I now proceed to an outline of Sartre's view. His point of departure is what I would call a conscious center. He calls it a 'for-itself.' Indeed it is, to begin with, his own 'for-itself,' or—for you and me—our own 'for-itselves.' He calls it conscious and refers deliberately to Descartes' *cogito ergo sum* to give his reader a point of vantage. The consciousness of the for-itself is as indubitable as Descartes' was. But Descartes apparently made a mistake in arguing for a separation be- tween the consciousness and something that is the object of consciousness—i.e., between the *cogito* and the *sum*—in this act of ultimate immediacy. The inescapable grammatical ex- pressions of our language—"awareness of something," "con- sciousness of something"—lead us astray. So Berkeley mistak- enly set up a 'spirit' outside of ideas to be aware of ideas. Hume, as William James much later, dropped out this super- fluous entity. What we have is conscious perception, not a consciousness *of* a perception. Sartre suggests "we shall put the 'of' inside parentheses to show that it merely satisfies a grammatical requirement."[34] For the original conscious im- mediacy is not an instance of 'knowledge' with a reference to an object. This would lead us, as he writes, "to fall back into the illusion of the theoretical primacy of knowledge. . . . This would be to make the psychic event a thing and to *qual- ify* it with 'conscious' just as I can qualify this blotter as 'red.' Pleasure cannot be distinguished—even logically—from consciousness of pleasure. Consciousness (of) pleasure is con- stitutive of the pleasure as the very mode of its own existence. . . . Pleasure does not disappear behind its own self-conscious- ness; it is not a representation, it is a concrete event, full and absolute . . . an indivisible, indissoluble being . . . a being which is existence through and through."[35]

What Sartre is describing here is clearly an actual ongoing event as qualitatively felt in full immediacy—a qualitative dynamic immediacy which only I as my center of conscious- ness and you as your center of consciousness can have. I can- not experience your center of consciousness as you do, though I will find good reasons to credit you with the same fulness of dynamic qualitative immediacy in your actual experience as I in mine.

One may ask why the stress is on consciousness, when this is described as so completely absorbed into the qualities experienced. Why not just stress the actuality of the qualities in the ongoing event? The answer will be because there is also a range of nonconscious being that Sartre calls 'being-in-itself.' Being-in-itself has being but not in dynamic actuality; ontologically it is prior to being-for-itself. For the conscious being-for-itself is a spontaneous upsurge from being-in-itself, which is the factuality of the past. It may extend into the environing present (I am not sure of this), but definitely is not in the future, though it is created to become the past by the dynamic activity of the for-itself reaching into the future. It has a determinate influence upon the activity of the for-itself, however, in restricting a person's choices to a certain range of possibilities. There seems to be an echo of Kant's things-in-themselves about Sartre's being-in-itself. The latter is outside the activity of the for-itself, as Kant's things-in-themselves are outside of Kant's phenomena, but it is a restraint upon the activity of the for-itself and something upon which that activity works. Being-in-itself, however, has no intrinsic activity. It simply is. It is, moreover, devoid of both necessity and possibility.

Possibilities arise from the action of the for-itself on the background of the in-itself. For the for-itself possesses freedom, and makes choices within the range of possibilities presented by the in-itself. And here we come upon the pith and marrow of Sartre's philosophy—his doctrine of freedom.[36] One is almost tempted to say that for Sartre, consciousness and freedom are the same thing; they have for him the same origin and are inseparable, only their connotations are different. By thinking of consciousness as freedom, one avoids being troubled by the paradox that consciousness is always consciousness (of) something and yet is not separable from what it is (of). But to say that the field of man's actual qualities of experience is always filled with dynamic action towards possibilities of free human decision, yields no paradox. Yet that is just how consciousness functions for Sartre; it is a constant awareness of man's freedom of choice—and this for Sartre is the peculiarly human contribution to Being. It is the emphasis on this central miracle of Being by which Exis-

tentialism claims to be a Humanism. Only man, apparently,
(no beast) has this endowment.

The for-itself as a free, conscious, act of decision will obviously develop a structure. Actually what it develops is a
purposive structure with anticipations and apprehensions,
means and ends, frustrations and successes, jostlings with the
hard facts of in-itself, and the limited possibilities this makes
available. The many vivid illustrations of the actions of the
for-itself depicted by Sartre are all of purposive situations
and their human significance. In fact, 'situation,' the human
situation, is one of his commonest technical terms.

Since it is the actual situation operating between the past
and the future in which purposive action takes place, the
for-itself requires a temporal duration of some breadth in
which to work itself out. Duration thus characterizes the for-
itself. Sartre never mentions James' 'specious present,' but
this is the sort of thing he refers to. It is the immediately
given living time of human action in process; it picks something up out of the past (indeed a great deal), and feels itself
into the future. It is constantly in a condition of change,
and it is this condition that justifies his frequently repeated
description of the for-itself as "that which is not what it is
and is what it is not." It is, in short, transition. So it never is
in any fixed state like in-itself, but is always ceasing to be
what it is towards being what it is not, as long as it lives.
Sartre finds this a source of constant anxiety and of anguish
when intensely felt (which, he suggests, is most of the time
for any man who reflects on his condition). This is the
condition of man.

He writes, "I can assume consciousness of myself only as a
particular man engaged in this or that enterprise, anticipat-
ing this or that success, fearing this or that result. . . . We
choose the world, not in its contexture as in-itself but in its
meaning, by choosing ourselves. . . . The value of things,
their instrumental role, their proximity and real distance
(which have no relation to their spatial proximity and distance) do nothing more than outline my image—that is, my

choice. My clothing (a uniform or a lounge suit, a soft or a starched shirt) whether neglected or cared for, carefully chosen or ordinary, my furniture, the street on which I live, the city in which I reside, the books with which I surround myself, the recreation which I enjoy, everything which is mine (that is, finally, the world of which I am perpetually conscious, at least by way of a meaning implied by the object which I look at or use): all this informs me of my choice— that is, of my being. . . . Thus we are fully conscious of the choice we are. . . . This consciousness is expressed by the two-fold 'feeling' of anguish and responsibility. Anguish, abandonment, responsibility, whether muted or full strength, constitute the *quality* of our consciousness in so far as this is pure and simple freedom."[37]

The for-itself has now been thickened out considerably. Beginning as an indubitable individual consciousness (of) quality, it is also intuited as free, an upsurge of conscious freedom of decision out of the nonconscious determinate factuality of the in-itself. In the activity of free choice, a range of time is needed—a duration for the possibilities of choice to be first presented, and then felt with anticipation of success or dread. These possibilities of choice develop structure in the for-itself, the structure of purposive action with ends and means and levels of purposive significance in the service of one another with references near or far into the future. And behind these structures of purposive anticipation, is another structure fused with the forward-looking purposive aims: that of the for-itself's significant past, gathered up out of factual in-itself. This latter is the for-itself's 'world' referred to early in the previous quotation: "We choose the world, not as its contexture as in-itself, but in its meaning, by choosing ourselves." I interpret this to mean (and it is a fair sample of Sartre's statements about the 'world' of the for-itself), that the 'world' for the for-itself is not literally the physical world or factual history or whatever else the Being-in-itself may consist of, but the 'meaning' of whatever the in-itself may be for the for-itself in its living activity. It includes the history of the for-itself's free choices throughout its life, carried over into each successive situation where a new choice must be made. It is this 'world' for the for-itself hardened by infiltrations of the stubborn inflexible in-itself which lay out the actual alternatives of free choice (the 'possibles,' as Sartre calls them) for the for-itself in the actual situation it is living through. The quotation lists in detail the sorts of things reflecting past choices of the for-itself that constitute the 'world' of the for-itself, which is that for-itself's own self. In Sartre's words "we choose the world . . . by choosing ourselves." And he adds significantly, "Thus we are fully conscious of the choice we are." This last statement, it becomes clear (especially in his exposition of existential psychoanalysis), Sartre means to be taken somehow literally. For he denies outright that there is anything like the Freudian 'unconscious' connected with his for-itself. Somehow this total 'world' of the for-itself is included in the conscious sphere of the for-itself in its every act of free choice. He would argue: How else could the 'possibles' of choice for this for-itself rise up for responsible decision, as his intuition indubitably discloses that they do? And thereby the anguish, which is the ultimate indubitable evidence of man's freedom.

Thus the for-itself becomes an individual self of complex structure and depth of character. It draws a whole 'world' after it as it lives through the transitory situations that arise continually and calls for responsible decisions which become inevitably part of the 'world' that is itself and will inevitably restrict the possibles of future situations which will also call for decisions.

It is now time to talk about the Nothingness which envelopes Sartre's philosophy, and seems to augment the anguish of the exercise of freedom. The term is dramatic, not to say melodramatic, for it tends to exaggerate the tragedy of his view of life. It is a portmanteau word in Sartre's use of it—and, of course, not only Sartre's but his school's. I began taking down the different meanings of the term in *Being and Nothingness,* and stopped after there were twenty. I will run over a number of his uses—all referring to legitimate things in his philosophy, but with so little in common as better to be relieved of this queer compromising name.

First of all, it refers to the upsurge of the for-itself out of the in-itself. Since the in-itself is regarded as devoid of consciousness and freedom, the spontaneous eruption of the for-itself is in marked contrast with the in-itself. And if the latter is referred to as Being, its opposite could be called Non-Being or Nothing. But 'Nothing' in this queer sense—as an opposite to Being in *its* queer sense (as non-conscious, unfree in-itself) —carries no connotation of voidness in its own self. As we have just seen the for-itself is the richly structured human self in action. All Sartre can mean legitimately is that the for-itself is quite different from the in-itself much as white is quite different from black. But this would take a lot of the drama out of it. Sartre could not so effectively startle us by saying "This nothingness is this hole of being, this fall of the in-itself toward the self, the fall by which the for-itself is constituted."[38] So for him, the whole for-itself as a hole in Being in-itself, is Nothing.

Second, Sartre inserts 'Nothingness' into the activity of continuous change characteristic of purposive action ascribed to the for-itself. The positive opposite in this case seems to be some static being. Since the progressive purposive action of the for-itself is never static, it is nothingness. Duration itself must also by this treatment be Nothingness.

Third, for a different reason, the instant is nothingness. It is squeezed into nothingness by the encroachment of the past on one side and the present on the other.[39]

Fourth, the purposive act itself is contaminated with nothingness, for every expectation or prediction of a future event may be blocked, or prove to be referring to an object that does not exist.[40]

Fifth, in the figure and ground perception, the 'negative' space of the ground is ascribed to nothingness. If I am looking for somebody in a cafe, the figures stand out, the ground is 'nihilated.' Indeed when a figure that has stood out proves not to be the person I am looking for, he too sinks into the ground and is nihilated. "This nihilation is given to my intuition; I am witness to the successive disappearance of all the objects I look at."[41] We all have had this experience. For Sartre this is also an experience of Nothingness.

Sixth, there is a sense of nothingness as what comes before or after the end of an integrated process such as a melody. In terms of the melody, there is nothing more when it is finished, and nothing yet before it began.[42]

Seventh, the future, of course, for Sartre would be a Nothingness: "The for-itself can never be its future except problematically, for it is separated by a Nothingness which it is. . . . The Future qua Future does not have to be."[43]

Eighth, even the past may turn into Nothingness, even the in-itself from which the for-itself upsurged. An experience of the for-itself viewing an expanse of untrodden snow is described by Sartre:

> Its undifferentiation, its monotony, and its whiteness manifest the absolute nudity of substance, it is the in-itself which is only in-itself, the being of the phenomenon, which being is manifested suddenly outside all phenomena. At the same time its solid immobility expresses the permanence and the objective existence of the in-itself, its opacity, its impenetrability . . . that pure in-itself, comparable to the absolute, intelligible plenum of Cartesian extension fascinates me as the pure appearance of the not-me. . . . But if I approach, if I want to establish an appropriative contact with the field of snow, everything is changed. . . . It turns into liquid in my fingers, it runs off, there is nothing left of it. The in-itself is transformed into nothingness.[44]

Now this last may be an ontological slip, a writer's release of expansive enthusiasm on the memory of an emotional scene. Yet the nothingness here attributed to an in-itself is no more diversified than the previous ones—and perfectly understandable as a matter of common experience. What is striking here is solely that so much has been made of the essential

Being of the in-itself and its immunity to Nothingness.

Just one more example of Sartre's diversity of meanings for Nothingness—the ninth. It is by now not surprising to find that in his ontology, mathematical and other such abstractions are nothingness. "Geometrical space," he writes, "that is, the pure reciprocity of spatial relations—is a pure nothingness."[45]

Following the diversity of these meanings, one is almost led to think that nothingness is the relative opposite of something sought or asserted or bounded. If you want salt, everything else is not salt; or if you say "this is salt," all other things are not salt—what is outside the saltshaker is not in it. But any such mild interpretation will not do. There is an aura of tremendous significance about Sartre's Nothingness; it has the presence of a yawning abyss, something fearful and the source of repeated anguish. For him, it permeates existence—that is why he spreads it into all this great diversity of meanings. The inscrutable future and death are the tremendous abysses of Nothingness just ahead, and just behind is the great abyss of Nothingness out of which comes the spontaneous 'absurd' inexplicable upsurge of the for-itself. But besides these are the innumerable cracks and holes of nothingness breaking into the continuity of the for-itself's existence requiring constant free decisions and anxiety.

Nothingness for Sartre is thus much more than the bare diversity of verbal meanings he gives it. It is an ontological entity of major proportions—the very source of freedom and anguish—and established for him with certainty through the indubitability of the feelings of freedom and anguish. Wherever there is anguish, there is Nothingness, and the incontrovertible evidence of my free choice which nothing can overpower. Even if a man is confined in a dungeon, Sartre says in one place he can still freely choose to commit suicide.

We must not conclude, however—from Sartre's emphasis on the existence of freedom and the nothingness that surrounds it—that this is all that goes on in the lived time through which the for-itself endures. For the facts of the past invade the duration of the present and set up restrictions and possibilities. The for-itself must choose among these possibilities, which project consequences into the future, which in turn will become the hard facts of a later past producing still other restrictions and possibilities for the for-itself at a later time. The freedom of a person's choice thus entails a great responsibility. Sartre constantly joins freedom with responsibility: a strong factor of rationality in his philosophy. Those who dub existentialism as a philosophy of irrationality only half understand it.

Indeed the projection of the factuality of the past into the lived time of the for-itself is massive. In a way, the whole past is there in the form of the for-itself's 'world.' Sartre's concept of 'world' is not entirely clear to me even from the great amount that is said about it in *Being and Nothingness*. For there is a sense in which it overflows any person, any for-itself, and a sense in which it simultaneously reflects the perspective, the interpretation, the peculiarity of each individual for-itself. It is somehow both objective and personal (notice, I carefully avoid saying 'private'). I am helped somewhat by the distinction some existentialists make between a person's Umwelt (the surrounding, or roughly, the physical world), his Mitwelt (his social world), and his Eigenwelt (his own personal world). But the Eigenwelt modifies the other two in terms of its own experience; a completely objective world detached for any for-itself is existentially inconceivable—an obvious nothingness. A man's 'world' is his human world pattern, his philosophy of life, his ontological ideal of a sort—hence the appropriateness of the term 'humanism' to the existential philosophy. It never allows itself to get outside of the human situation. As earlier noticed, "situation" is a major technical term for Sartre. That is what the choice of a for-itself is always embedded in, and a situation is always in the midst of a for-itself's 'world.'

We have been absorbed so far in a single for-itself. Yet, as we have seen, the for-itself is included in its Umwelt and Mitwelt as well as its Eigenwelt. We must now consider the

Mitwelt. This is the domain of what Sartre designates as the capitalized Other—the other for-itselfs, persons besides one-self. These are enormously important for the very intuition of the for-itself's own self. One does not get a full idea of one's self except through the eyes of another—except through seeing ourselves as others see us. It is through our social intercourse that we become aware of our personalities. There is much in this phase of Sartre's philosophy that reminds one of the insights of George Herbert Mead.

One of Sartre's most original insights is contained in his analysis of the 'look.' He observed that when you see a man looking at you, you do not see his eyes. You see his 'look.' You pass your gaze right through his eyes to something that comes directly to you with much greater impact than the color or shape of his eyes. Your personality is affected, is touched, by his personality. Two free human for-itselfs find themselves in contact: a supremely signficant human experi-ence. Much of the most appealing and enlightening content of existential philosophy consists in the amplification of this intimate contact of person with person—what might be called the generalized 'look.' Sartre illuminates these situations with a novelist's genius.

One of the most intense incidents of the 'look' is, of course, shame. Sartre has a marvelous description of a person peeping through a keyhole and hearing another person coming down the corridor. The 'look' of that other person suddenly reveals to the shamed one the sly and unseemly character of his act, and of a weakness in his personality. In fact, just the idea of the 'look' does it. Where can he hide himself? How escape? The physical environment and his whole world becomes vivid in the situation. This is a richly humanistic area of Sartre's philosophy; to point it out is enough. And it ceases to be surprising that much of the most incisive existentialist philosophy is to be found in novels and plays written by exponents of the school.

At this point reference should be made to a practical out-come of existentialism on which Sartre places considerable

emphasis—existential psychoanalysis. It is rather revealing of
the salient traits of this philosophy in the very area of human
relationships where it should be strongest. Existential psychoanalysis accepts many of Freud's conclusions, but it rejects
all Freudian features that threaten the freedom and self-
awareness of the person, the for-itself.

It rejects Freud's concept of the unconscious, for if motiva-
tions are repressed and unconscious a person is not free in his
choices. This is, of course, exactly Freud's point. And the
symptoms of the disturbed patient seem so obviously to confirm Freud's hypothesis, that one wonders what substitute
hypothesis the existentialists can offer. Sartre's substitute is a
concept on which he spends a great deal of time—the concept
of bad faith. Freud's concept of the 'unconscious' describes
a split in the personality. The repressed desires are blocked
from coming up fully and undisguised into the area of voluntary conscious decision. Nevertheless they are there in the
personality structure exerting their pressure on the person's
actions and requiring a great deal of the person's energy to
keep them out of conscious view by the mechanisms of repression which are part of a personality's endowment. Sartre
wishes to avoid this split in the personality while still explaining the apparently involuntary actions characteristic of
disturbed persons. He wishes to place the whole matter in the
voluntary area of a person's free choice, and thus retain the
unity of the for-itself with its intrinsic conscious freedom of
decision. He wishes to retain (at all costs) the *responsibility*
of the disturbed person's choices.

In approaching the problem, he makes use of the concept
of lying. In the open, deliberate lie, a person recognizes the
distinction between himself as the deceiver and the other
person as the deceived. But bad faith is a lie to oneself in
which one seeks to deceive oneself. By this concept Sartre
thinks he can retain the unity of consciousness in the midst
of self-deceit. He writes:

> Bad faith implies the unity of a *single* consciousness. . . .
> There must be an original intention and a project of bad

faith; this project implies a comprehension of bad faith as such and a pre-reflective apprehension (of) consciousness as affecting itself with bad faith. It follows first that the one to whom the lie is told and the one who lies are one and the same person, which means that I know in my capacity as deceiver the truth which is hidden from me in my capacity as the one deceived. Better yet, I must know the truth very exactly in order to conceal it more carefully—and this not at two different moments, which at a pinch would allow us to reestablish a semblance of duality—but in the unitary structure of a single project. How then can the lie subsist if the duality which conditions it is supressed?[46]

The plausibility of this interpretation rests, of course, on the analogy of the conditions of lying. The repressions are raised to the level of a voluntary project which a person permits himself to choose. It seems to be implied that the person could choose of his own free will to divest himself of this project and dispel his self-deception. At least he could do this if a competent other person should point out to him the way in which he was deceiving himself. There are circumstances in which this would be perfectly true. But Freud's psychiatric experience offered him cases in which the intensest voluntary desire on the part of the patient was utterly ineffective in discovering the repression and dislodging it. Freud had to seek out other methods of relieving the patient and had to find other causes for repression than voluntary self-deceit, in order to attack the disease effectively.

There is another connotation of the 'unconscious' that bothered Sartre—it seemed to relegate repressions to a mechanistic physiological level. Freud's early training as a physiologist offers some justification for this objection. What the ontological status of a disturbed person's repressed complexes may be is a sensible question and would depend largely on one's world hypothesis. Sartre's categories, as we can already sufficiently see, would have no place for ultimate mechanistic interpretations. But this difficulty would be easily dissolved by describing repressed complexes as fully qualitative repressed immediacies. A split personality would be one with imperfectly integrated fields of consciousness. Why should consciousness in the sense of qualitative immediacy be limited to the central area of voluntary action? When a repressed memory is recovered and brought into the area of central voluntary consciousness, it comes up with all the detailed qualitative immediacy of an unrepressed and so-called conscious memory. There is no difference between the two except that the former was 'repressed.'

A consequence of the denial of the Freudian 'unconscious' is that existential psychoanalysis is limited in its treatments to what can be found in the central voluntary area of consciousness. This leads these analysts in the more severe cases to deal only with the patient's personal worlds, seeking out the sources of personality disintegration in failures of integration in these worlds. They make a great deal of the importance of empathically gaining an intuition of the patient's personal world, and once that is attained, they feel the psychoanalyst is in a position to point out to the patient the inner conflicts from which he is suffering. This is often sufficient. But the restriction cuts the existential analyst off from tracing back in depth to the traumatic incidents in the patient's past history—the repressions produced there, the hidden memories, and the untangling of the drives progressively tangled up since then. The analyst is permitted to work on dreams and their symbolism, since these arise more or less spontaneously; but he is stopped from proceeding deeper in depth. The Gestalt, the pattern, of the patient's 'world' is all he is permitted to work on. Being scornful of anything resembling drive theory as mere hypothesis and lacking the certainty of the immediate deliverances of the for-itself, this view leads one at first to wonder where the dynamics for inner conflicts of the disturbed person comes from. Then one sees it is supposed to come entirely from the spontaneous free upsurges of the for-itself. And this is offered not as theory, not as another hypothesis to be tested in comparison with competing hypotheses like the Freudian, but as indubitable intuition. A wall of intuitive certainty is thus erected against all criticism and further unimpeded research.

This illustration points up the fundamental contrast between the approach of *World Hypotheses* and that of Sartre's existentialism and, I surmise, of the existential philosophy generally. It sets up a wall of certainty localized in the deliverances of the central actual agency of this philosophy in the for-itself, against any contrary evidence or criticism. It disparages the method of hypotheses for its uncertainty. In opposition, *World Hypotheses* disparages the method of certainty for *its* uncertainty. Our view maintains that the doctrine of certainty is a theory of evidence for which the relevant evidence has historically and in practice been overwhelmingly negative. Moreover, it is a theory that in principle is paralyzing to the progress of knowledge and understanding by blocking (or rather attempting to block) all criticism—in which objective it has fortunately been steadily unsuccessful. And yet I think that the philosophy of existentialism is loaded with potential fruitfulness; it seems to contain a deep insight, a suggestion of a fresh root metaphor towards a new world hypothesis of possibly great adequacy.

Suppose we remove the wall of certainty, let the evidences and insights of this philosophy have free rein, and see where these evidences lead for an unrestricted hypothesis. I have noted earlier that the vital illustrations of Sartre's philosophy originating in the qualitative immediacy of what he calls the for-itself are all directed upon the structure of purposive activity as this is qualitatively felt and experienced. He begins by noticing the immediate qualitative feeling of conscious acting going on within a duration that includes a width of past and future in its living present. The act has a dynamics that belongs to itself and is directed towards the future. On further inspection it exhibits a structure: it is set towards a goal and the attainment of the goal lies in a future beyond the duration of the actual present. This condition produces a feeling of suspense, of conation, trying, and anxiety. Actually, this is the feeling of the dynamic tension of the purposive impulse. There are steps to be taken towards reaching the goal, alternative possibilities appear, choices have to be made. Sometimes these choices are difficult to decide upon and anxiety thickens into anguish. A sense of responsibility for the consequences of the choices arises, and the structure of the purpose may be revealed in layers of means and ends towards the ultimate goal. A choice may be frustrated and come to nothing in the aim of the purposive impulse, or it may be successful. If so, it lays down an achievement as a solid fact in the past of the action on which the next step in the purposive action may be made. Such facts build up into a background of established fact. One can make use of these in future purposes. One can deliberately, purposively, explore beyond one's personal range of immediacy for a coherent background of such facts—this is one's personal world. It includes other centers of immediacy, other persons, with whom I in my purposive activities have commerce. It includes nonpersonal objects, tending to be seen and interpreted through my personality, my store of attitudes that manifest themselves in my purposive acts whenever appropriate situations call them forth.

This is as far as Sartre goes. His obsession with certainty and an almost totally undetermined, spontaneous upsurge of freedom as his interpretation of the felt dynamics of his own purposive actions, stops him at this point. But with the wall of certainty down, the evidences Sartre has assembled so vividly up to this point pour over the arbitrary bounds he set and bring to light the whole scientifically discovered environment which is the great achievement of modern man—which indeed man in his common sense has never denied in his constant adjustments to it, nor indeed animals other than man. Among other things that happen when Sartre's wall of certainty comes down is the discovery of his community with other animals. These also have purposes with goals and frustrations. And they do not make such a fuss about their freedom all the time. Animal behavior can now help to illuminate human behavior and *vice versa*. Causation is no longer anathema to human action; it is a source of the stability of human action and character. The solid world of facts gets integrated with the purposive acts of men. There is a problem of just how, but this is an empirical problem open to solution. And in the solution it is not necessary that everything be utterly determined, though it is unlikely that Sartre's many for-itselfs will be as disconnected with the regularities of the world as he wishes to insist they are.

When Sartre's wall of certainty is taken down, there is a great deal of resemblance between his incipient world hypothesis and Whitehead's *Process and Reality*. And I feel that Whitehead's world hypothesis is a big step toward a new type of theory with purposive structure as its root metaphor, or rather what I call 'selective system' of which purposive structure is one important illustration. As earlier said, I call this new world hypothesis selectivism. I am suggesting that existentialism relieved of its dogma of certainty may be taken as another contribution to this apparently new and promising world hypothesis, and that therein lies the legitimate source of its human appeal.

NOTES

1. W. W. Meissner, "The Operational Principle and Meaning in Psychoanalysis," *The Psychoanalytic Quarterly* XXXV, no. 2 (1966), 233–255.

2. *Ibid.*, p. 244.

3. *Ibid.*, pp. 248–249.

4. *Ibid.*, p. 252.

5. Norman Malcolm, "Moore and Ordinary Language," *The*

Philosophy of G. E. Moore, ed. Paul Arthur Schelpp (Evanston, Illinois: Northwestern University Press, 1942), p. 357.

6. J. L. Austin, "A Plea For Excuses," *Philosophical Papers by the Late J. L. Austin,* ed. J. O. Urman and G. J. Warnock (Oxford: Clarendon Press, 1961), pp. 129–130.

7. *Ibid.,* p. 131.

8. *Ibid.,* p. 133.

9. *Ibid.*

10. *Ibid.,* p. 130.

11. *Ibid.,* p. 133.

12. *Ibid.,* p. 134–135.

13. *Ibid.,* p. 149.

14. *Ibid.,* p. 150.

15. *Ibid.,* p. 135.

16. *Ibid.,* p. 136.

17. *Ibid.,* p. 137.

18. *Ibid.*

19. *Ibid.,* p. 138.

20. Anthony Flew, "Again the Paradigm," *Mind, Matter, and Method,* ed. Paul K. Feyerabend and Grover Maxwell (Minneapolis: University of Minnesota Press, 1966), pp. 261–272.

21. Ernest Gellner, *Words and Things* (London: Victor Gallanz, 1959).

22. *Ibid.,* p. 31.

23. *Ibid.* Cf. Antony Flew, "Philosophy and Language," *Essays in Conceptual Analysis* (London: Macmillan, 1956), p. 19.

24. Antony Flew, *Logic and Language,* first series (Oxford: Basil Blackwell, 1951). Second series published in 1953.

25. Friedrich Waismann, "Verifiability," *Logic and Language,* first series, p. 134.

26. Gilbert Ryle, "Systematically Misleading Expressions," *Logic and Language,* first series, p. 21.

27. This article, however, also contains a strong destructive component. It is a fine example of the paradigm case technique, showing up both its dangers and its usefulness. It is put forward as the 'correct' analysis of 'good'—at least, it has been so interpreted by many readers and nowhere mitigates that impression.

The article explicitly in the last paragraph excludes the concepts of 'right' and 'wrong.' "I do not regard them as grading labels," he says. "They function quite differently." Personally, I find 'good' also functions quite differently from grading in all areas of its dynamic connotations connected with desire and pleasure (cf. my two articles: "The Equivocation of Value," *University of California Publications in Philosophy*, 4, (1923), 107–132; and "Standard Value," *Univ. of Calif. Publications in Philos.*, 7, (1925), 89–110). Grading is a cold intellectual procedure of sorting similar to classification. It is indeed one sense of the term 'good.' Urmson does a good (in the grading sense) constructive job in elaborating this particular sense of 'good.' But he does a thoroughly destructive job insofar as he implicitly eliminates 'good' in the dynamic sense of success and delight and its opposite 'bad' in the sense of frustration, failure, and pain. And incidentally, 'right' and 'wrong' are not irrelevant to 'good' and 'bad' in these latter senses, which are as deeply imbedded in common sense and ordinary language as 'grading.' So here is an instance for seeing how the paradigm case device can lead an analysis astray and even into dogmatic proscription.

Another relevant point is that Urmson's analysis of grading could have been worked out just as well without recourse to ordinary language, as a direct empirical study of the grading practices in agriculture, education, the sciences and wherever else it is carried on. Then he would not have been tempted to blur this with other quite distinct meanings of 'good.'

28. It is a concept that has to be used with discrimination. Otherwise it can become a most subtle device of dogmatism. "Triangles are brittle" would be a genuine category mistake as a scientific statement (though not necessarily in poetry). But "sensations are localizable in the brain" is not a category mistake unless one is presupposing a world theory with categories of the Cartesian sort which deny extension to mental contents. It follows that the sensation of a low tone may literally, from the way it feels as well as from cerebral evidence, have more volume than that of a high tone, as William James once pointed out. To dismiss such an hypothesis as a category mistake is stark dogmatism.

All it signifies is that the categorial presuppositions from the controlling world hypothesis of the speaker are different from those
of William James. It can be even more insidiously employed as a
means for a dogmatic insistence on some linguistic interpretation
of a common sense concept—that is, as a device for dismissing out
of hand any description of experience, however well bolstered
with evidence, that appears paradoxical to common sense.

29. Paul Edwards, "Bertrand Russell's Doubts About Induction," *Logic and Language,* first series, p. 68.

30. The destructive ordinary language articles I assign to Ryle's
article in Series I; Findlay's, Macdonald's two articles, Paul's, and
Pears' first article in Series II; the constructive ordinary language
articles to Edwards', Waisman's two articles, Hart's, Wisdom's,
Ryle's article in Series II, Moore's, Pears' second article in Series
II, Austin's, and Urmson's; the nonordinary language analyses
to Will's, Warnock's, MacIver's, Gasking's and Smart's.

31. P. F. Strawson, *Individuals* (London: Methuen, 1959).

J. J. C. Smart, *Philosophy and Scientific Realism* (London:
Rutledge & Kegan Paul, 1963).

Smart says in his preface, "In recent years I have been moving
away from a roughly neo-Wittgensteinian conception of philosophy towards a more metaphysical one, according to which
philosophy is in much more intimate relation to the sciences.
Philosophy, it now seems to me, has to do not only with unravelling conceptual muddles, but also with the tentative adumbration
of a world view" [p. vii].

32. Jean-Paul Sartre, *Being and Nothingness* trans. Hazel E.
Barnes (N. Y.: Philosophical Library, 1956).

33. This statement may be challenged. Ernest Gellner in his
Words and Things presents with a diagram (p. 160) quite an
impressive structure for the ordinary language doctrine. "The
ideas outlined [for linguistic philosophy], and their various sup-
ports," he says, "form a highly integrated (even if not fully consistent) whole, a structure which is so built up that it gives far
greater strength and resilience to each of its parts than they
would have alone" [p. 161]. Antony Flew, however, in his article
"Again the Paradigm," in *Matter, Mind, and Method* repudiates

Gellner's "straw monster." Indeed Gellner obviously constructed it with mischievous intent as an insidious organization unacknowledged and so all the more dangerous. The violent reaction of the linguistic philosophers against Gellner's structure makes one almost believe there may be something in it. However, I tend to agree with the linguists that there is no unity of conceptual system in their multifarious analyses—each article standing on its own. There may be, however, a sort of mystic assumption of a unity in or behind common sense that supposedly guides analyses with an invisible hand.

34. Sartre, *op. cit.,* p. liv.
35. *Ibid.,* pp. liv–lv.
36. Cf. p. 469.
37. *Ibid.,* p. 462–464.
38. *Ibid.,* p. 78–79.
39. *Ibid.,* p. 466.
40. *Ibid.,* p. 7.
41. *Ibid.,* p. 10.
42. *Ibid.,* p. 466.
43. *Ibid.,* p. 129.
44. *Ibid.,* p. 582.
45. *Ibid.,* p. 491.
46. *Ibid.,* p. 49.

OETS KOLK BOUWSMA

was born on November 22, 1898, in Muskegon, Michigan. He took the A.B. at Calvin College in 1922, and the Ph.D. at the University of Michigan in 1928. He was instructor in English at the University of Michigan from 1922–1928; professor of philosophy at the University of Nebraska from 1928–1965; and has been professor of philosophy at the University of Texas since 1965. He was visiting professor at Smith College in 1949–50; Fullbright research professor at Oxford University, England, in 1951; John Locke lecturer at Oxford in 1951; and Woods Study grantee from the University of Nebraska to London, England in 1956. He is a member of Phi Beta Kappa, and of the American Philosophical Association.

In his Philosophical Essays (1965), written in the manner of Wittgenstein whom he first met at Cornell, he has brought together—because of the "incalculable good they might do"—some philosophical pieces written at different times on different subjects. He has also contributed to numerous professional journals and collections.

DOUBLE TALK, JACKIE VERNON AND X

I want in this lecture to remind you of certain curiosities of prose. I may illustrate some of them with pieces of my own invention. This will, of course, strike you as unusual in the work of anyone who has anything to do with philosophy and has some appreciation for the dignity and the high order of philosophical prose. This will be especially the case when you hear some of these pieces. If citing and discussing such pieces were designed to present an order of prose from low to high and to highest, then something of this sort might be considered intelligible. And yet that is not the design I have in mind. I do, however, want to use this and that other piece of prose in order to throw light on some other piece of prose, sometimes written and composed for this very purpose, which looks and sounds like sense but is not. I want to use such pieces of prose in which the illusion of understanding, where nothing is to be understood, is easily dispelled, to help us to the idea of the same sort of illusion where if there is such an illusion, it is, at any rate, not easily dispelled.

When I say that in the case of some prose the illusion is dispelled (and that easily) I do not mean that we are aware as to just how the illusion is dispelled nor how at the outset the illusion is produced. In some of these cases I will make some comments but I am by no means confident that they will be helpful. One thing is certain: there is prose that we all admit makes no sense. And yet I should add that this prose is composed for our enjoyment. If we can get some more or less clear idea of the anatomy of such prose it may help us to see how, in some other cases where there is disagreement not as to whether what is said or written is true but whether it makes sense, we might come to some agreement. It may turn out to be useful that there is prose which makes no sense, but which produces the illusion of sense and of understanding. Of course, the usefulness of this depends upon our agreement that there is such illusion.

I want, if possible, to avoid saying that there is an illusion of sense and understanding when we cannot agree about this, but I do want to say something about how someone's saying this might be understood. Since clarity with respect to the *illusion* of understanding involves clarity, too, with respect to *understanding* it is apparent that this involves a great deal. I will be satisfied to do only a little.

I

Let us begin with a discussion of double-talk. My impression is that though there may be a corresponding double-write, the entertainment value and the illusion upon which that depends requires the resources of face and voice in order to produce the desired effect. And what I have described as double-write will not be written double-talk. The nearest we could get here to something written corresponding to double-talk would be a scarcely legible seeming script which one would then try to make out, to read, but which is illegible in a hyper-sense of illegible. No one can read it; it only looks like legible writing. We need not concern ourselves with that. To begin with, then, we may say that double-talk is used for entertainment. It sounds like talk and enough like talk to tempt one to strain to hear and to understand. It has the rhythm of ordinary speech. It is commonly composed of words in the language one is familiar with—in our case, English. Suddenly it dawns on one that perhaps nothing is being said. In some cases one may suspect that the talk is in some foreign language but then one hears English words again and tries to catch on.

Double-talk is, of course, made up and the person who engages in it may develop a sort of skill at this. Fluent double-talk, no doubt, requires some practice. Such a person must have a good ear and perhaps a good eye for the nuances of spoken English. I am supposing that a double-talker must first compose in writing the double-talk he is to talk. He is under no illusion; he is to *create* the illusion. There may be the momentary illusion that something is being said and there may even be the illusion that so-and-so is being said. The further along the hearers are misled the greater the success of the double-talker—up to a certain point. For double-talk is designed to give itself away. It is a joke, designed to build up an expectation and suspense and then to disappoint it: it turns out to be nothing. Since the author of the double-talk uses English words and endings to make the sounds and rhythms of English sense, it seems that all is there but the sense. What a curious thing it is that there should be double-talk.

Only someone accustomed to English (the words, phrases, sentence structure, rhythms, cadences, etc.) is susceptible to the illusion of understanding. This involves someone who is used to doing in English the sorts of things that we all do, and so this allows for the expectation that the double-talker is doing something too.

Now consider something preposterous. Imagine someone fluent in double-talk, who is himself taken in by his own talk. He will ask in double-talk and he will answer in double-talk. He will discuss and dispute and explain and argue and grow red in the face and pound the table, impatient with another's misunderstanding of his double-talk. And what is even harder to imagine—some would say not so hard to come upon—there might be men who spend their lives at this, engaging in and listening to each other's double-talk, conversing and responding, meshing double-talk with double-talk, generating a community of double-talkers. There might even be schools of double-talk, each with its own characteristic phrases and key sentences and rejoinders to those of competing schools. And there would be yearly meetings at which these talkers come together to talk and to read to each other papers in double-write. And then they would talk some more. Of course, all this is a fantastic notion of mine, and were anything like this to happen it is obvious that this double-talk sounds more like English when you speak or read it and looks more like English when you see it than double-talk ever does. And so it couldn't be double-talk. This is clear from the fact that in this case there is no author of the double-talk who expects that almost anyone who listens carefully will catch on. Double-talk is a joke. But what I am now thinking of is no joke and seems to be about the most important subjects. Those who indulge in this are as earnest as can be. And so powerful is the illusion, that those who hear or come within range of these talkers are charmed and drawn in. They talk too—whatever it is.

Let me review. Double-talk is disguised; it sounds like sense and it looks like sense but it is nonsense. It does not come about by accident, and it is not so well-disguised that one cannot by listening penetrate the disguise. This is, by the way, an interesting point that an ordinary audience soon catches on. It shows how closely the sense of what we say is bound up with what we say, so that subtle variations mark the difference. There is a puzzle here. *How can what seems on the surface to make sense yet make no sense?*

Let us return to the alleged illusion. The illusion consists in a man's thinking that when another man talks—albeit double-talk—he not only talks but he understands what he says, that what he says is intelligible. The man does two things: he says what he says and he does something else. A man may mow the lawn and at the same time catch the grass. There is no doubt about the man's talking; we can all hear him. So the illusion involves something else. Is there something here which corresponds to this man's catching the grass? Clearly one may see someone mowing the lawn and have the illusion that he is also catching the grass. We hear the man talk. And now there must be something else he is not doing at the same time he talks. It sounds like this: with my right hand I do *this* and with my left hand I do *that*. What I do with my right hand leads you to expect that I will do *this* with my left. You expect and then you watch more closely what I do with my right hand and you suddenly realize that I have garbled the motion and you no longer expect me to do that with my left hand. You are disappointed; I do nothing with my left hand. One is here on the verge of saying, "With my right hand I say what I say—which is possible— and with my left hand I think what I think—which is at least more difficult." Curiously, my right hand and my left hand work together. It would not do for me to say with my right hand what I have to say and then to wait a half hour for my left hand to catch up with the appropriate thought. No doubt there are occasions when something like *this* happens. I repeat to myself what someone says and not until I have gone to bed and am ready to sleep does it come to me—my left hand tingling—that you meant that the moon itself is the pie in the sky. Then I go to sleep.

There is no doubt, however, that there is a difference between saying and thinking and saying and understanding. And so there does seem to be room for someone's saying so-and-so and his having the illusion that he had the thought that normally accompanies so-and-so. But no one allows for this in the case of double-talk. The double-talker talks, but as he talks he makes no sense. Or should I say that not only does he not make sense as one might not who tries and fails to make sense, but *he succeeds* in not making sense. Of course he succeeds in not making sense in what might be considered the hard way. For he succeeds at the same time in *seeming* to make sense. He has got to talk and to avoid the common routines of English. In what he is doing he has got to overcome the natural temptation to make sense.

I have now become so involved in the subject of double-talk and in my experiment—which may come to little or nothing—that an example is needed. My example may not be a good one though I can imagine that some good double-talker might make double-talk of it. It occurred to me after I had produced this that it might have been more useful had I begun with an ordinary piece of common prose and then made double of it. That would have brought out in a literal fashion that the base of these extraordinary ventures in prose is the English we are all familiar with. But this piece of double-talk was written without any method.

On the spur of the left foot, the rooster ran headshort against the piano-keys, turned, and the door sprang shut fourteen hands high. Each hand had a little miracle on one finger-tip left by a rich man who came in for a bite of coffee. "After words," said the other man who was nibbling on some bric-a-brac, "there was more banging until a policeman came along and put them in a quadricennial which he failed to bring with him all of a sudden."

"Lilt," he said with a little whistle. And at that very moment she disappeared just as she had been all the while. That made nobody angry and he joined the rest making odd noises such as one, three, five, and so on. But just to get even the other party which was going on sometimes made concurrent intervals with their twins adding twos for any one. When they finished with their twos they began with the alphabet. At that Chanticleer returned to the fence. As for the other man the policeman hurt his feelings with a swing of the ace of clubs and he fell down like a shower of confetti. That left only the girl and she sat there on a tuffet, feeding curds and whey, way down the Swanee River, to a gangster

they called 'The Spider.' Her name was Lucy Locket which
she did as click as she could. Then night fell and spilled
all over.

I assure you that I wrote this with no design, no method,
except to write double-talk. Bearing in mind that what I
have written must bear on its face the semblance of sense, I
can see how it reads like a passage from a story and the sentences are linked by such expression as "each hand" where
the word "hands" occurs at the end of the previous sentence;
"said the other man" where "other" seems to refer to a man
mentioned earlier. In this way the semblance of continuity is
maintained. Another such linking expression is "and at that
very moment." "That," is a reference to what went before,
"to get even," "when they finished," "at that," "as for the
other man," "that left only the girl," "her name," and "then."
Apparently I wrote my double-talk on the assumption that a
piece which is to look and sound like sense (and in this case
the sense of the language of a story told) must show the traces
of continuity. Each sentence, too, has what we may describe
as the rough continuity of the sense of a sentence. And yet I
want to say that all of this is double-talk: the passage makes
no sense.

The problem that arises in connection with this staggers
me and is the problem with which we are occupied here:
*How is it possible that a composition of this sort should be
designed to produce the illusion of sense?* There is this sentence in the *Philosophical Investigations:* "I will teach you
to pass from a piece of disguised non-sense to patent nonsense." We may, I think, describe double-talk as disguised
nonsense. But in this case though there is usually a passage
from disguised nonsense to patent non-sense, there is no need
of a teacher. It might be useful to consider this as preliminary to considering something which it is said is something
like this and much more important.

How is double-talk possible? That is easy. We are all
familiar with plain talk. Anyone can talk or, if you please,

compose plain talk. All one needs to do is to compose a piece which is much like plain talk, looks like and sounds like plain talk, except that it makes no sense. That sounds as though you could take a piece of plain talk and in some way leave the sense out or in some way spoil the sense as though the sense were in some mysterious way in what you composed when you composed the plain talk. We may say that the plain talk makes sense; you put the words together in a certain way and it is there. You mess the plain talk up a bit and it is gone. But it is not like this. Let us say that the sense is not in the words; it is rather like this: You put the words together in a certain way and then something happens in the mind. Here the words; then the thought. But change the order or the combination even in scarcely noticeable ways and then nothing happens but smiles. But in that case, how do you know that nothing also happens no matter how the double-talker smiles? It is well-known to all of us that there is plain talk and that plain talk is not double-talk. But the troublesome part comes in here: *How are we to understand that double-talk makes no sense and plain talk does make sense?* Are we also to say that we can hear the difference? How else indeed? If we allow that we may be under the illusion that the double-talk makes sense, how are we to understand that? Is it as though hearing talk we prepare, sitting on the edges of our chairs, alert with expectation, and then hearing more, we relax?

II

This following may be considered an interlude. I want to notice here another of those curiosities of prose exhibiting once more the virtuosity of our language. In this case I will not compose anything. But I am either going to tell you about such a composition and such a composer or remind you of it. This virtuoso, Jackie Vernon, tells about his adventures with a watermelon. He begins his story with an account of his first meeting with this watermelon—at a fruit stand. He

had been lonesome, far away from home, and he walked
out towards the fruit stand thinking he might pick up an
acquaintance there, and behold! He made a friend. It was a
case of friendship at first sight.

They were both roly-poly and that may have had something
to do with it. At the fruit stand, he caressed the smooth back
of the watermelon, cool and inviting, and the watermelon,
responsive, rolled towards him, nudging his foot. Such a
friendly watermelon he had never met before. He found it
irresistible, picked it up, and held it close under his arm.
The watermelon snuggled, warmed up to him, but neither
said a word. Most watermelons are shy, all blushes within.
He carried his new companion home with him and when his
landlady asked, "What, now?" he introduced her. He said,
"Ma'am, this is my new friend. Be nice to him. He's an
orphan. And he won't make any noise. I need company." His
landlady was a bit upset and did not like the idea of having
a friend like that rolling around the house. Well, there were
further adventures involving some shooting by a segregation-
ist but eventually there was a quarrel and a parting. I think
the watermelon wanted to return to the fruit stand to be
among his own kind.

This composition is obviously not a piece of double-talk
nor is it a piece of plain talk. On the other hand no illusion
of sense or of understanding is involved. No one strains to
hear as though one had misunderstood. On the other hand
neither does one hurry off to meet such a prodigy among
watermelons. The fact is that we delight in such nonsense,
patent nonsense—as patent as can be. What interests me for
the purpose of this paper is the anatomy of this non-sense. I
can use that.

We may describe what I represented as a grammatical
(Wittgenstein's use of the word "grammar") and pictorial
phantasy, explained in this way. There is, let me say, the language of the friend. There may be in the account of the
friend and the friendship, the occasion, the incident, of first
meeting, the day we first played baseball together. Of a friend-

ship we may ask, How did it begin? And then a friendship develops, grows close and warm. Friends come to need one another. There are walks and talks and projects and confidences and expeditions, and so on. Friendships and the ties of friendship grow strong. "And Jonathan made David swear again by his love for him, for he loved him as he loved his own soul" (1 Sam:20). There may be quarrels, dissensions. Job had three friends. "Miserable comforters that you are." Friends part. He moved away, there were a few letters, but then there were only memories. There will never be a friend like him. Hamlet and Horatio, Damon and Pythias, Orestes and Pylades, etc. The essence of friendship could be long. But there is also the essence of watermelon, what can be said about watermelons.

And one might say that the essence of a friend and the essence of a watermelon do not mix. What can be said about a watermelon excludes a great deal and what can be said about a friend excludes a great deal. Now notice what happens in the Vernon phantasy. One goes on talking about this watermelon as one might talk about one's friend. Of course, one does not need a watermelon for this, though one who was ambitious and needed a realistic support might get a watermelon to hang the excluded grammar on. He had better make sure that the watermelon does not kick—for the wrong grammar might be compared to a wrong harness. What I had in mind, however, can be done on paper. Words do not kick. All one needs to do is to go on in the way prescribed, employing this particular language of phantasy. "Yesterday on my way to the forum I met this watermelon. I thought nothing of it but when I turned round and saw that it was following me I took kindly to it. I had no dog at the time (it had run off with a cucumber), and so I thought, well, why not? And so I waited for it to catch up and that is how it all started." A human friend is not a watermelon. Not even a dog is a watermelon. Why did I say that not even a dog is a watermelon? Because in the scale of creatures if we say that man is highest, then, as we know, we may speak of a dog as a friend, a man's best next to the next better. But if a dog reminiscing were to tell me of the days when he scampered and frolicked and tugged and tussled among the vines with its friend the watermelon, wouldn't that dog be on the night club circuit? Never mind; I meant only to mix up the grammar some more.

Why now have I been concerned to bring this to your attention? I wanted first of all to introduce the conception of mixed-up grammar—where it was present—for all to see, where it is deliberate and where, of course, no one is deceived by it. It is a managed mix-up for a certain purpose. You can no more mix up the grammar of these expressions to make sense than you can, in case you lose your friend, substitute a watermelon in his stead. But I do not want to say anything about friends and watermelons. We are to attend here to the uses of expressions, to the language. And here I want to ask a question: *Is it possible that one should be misled into an illusion of sense, and understanding a sentence, the anatomy of which may be in a certain respect like that of: "I made a friend of a watermelon"?* Such a sentence too would be described as a sentence of mixed-up grammar. Since the sentence involved would make no sense and, of course, was not composed to amuse anyone, and yet one was taken in by it, the explanation of this must not be anything on the surface. Now I would like to turn to this.

III

From behind this bearded face and this troubled look he asked the question, "What is consciousness?" And when I did not answer he went on, "What is experience?" Both questions he had no doubt asked before, many times perhaps, never receiving an answer. He might, and I too might then, have looked about us in the room and seen the walls and the windows and the scenes outside the windows and the other students who too heard those questions and which no one could answer. Everyone of us dumbfounded! No one asked, since there was no need then to ask, since anyone could have answered: What is a wall? What is a window? But consciousness? Had someone then asked, What is space? it seems one might have fixed his eyes upon it, between the wall and the window and beyond outside the window, space is what is between all these other things one can see and what we can stretch our arms in and walk about in. But before the question about consciousness one is utterly helpless, stricken, slain. And so isn't the question more like a cry, like a reaching out for a word that no one can give? And may not one in such a predicament feel like an animal walking back and forth before the barriers of its cage?

Consciousness is certainly something. How otherwise could we speak of consciousness, how could we ask the question? Indeed how could we ask the question if it were not consciousness itself that moved us to ask the question? For certainly no one ever asked a question without consciousness. If then we could pull up the question by the roots we should then discover the answer. But would not this be to lose consciousness? And this seems to be the most important question of all since it is a question about what is most important of all.

What could be more important than consciousness? When, accordingly, we look about us in this way with this question directing our looking about, is it not as though all these things we see about us—the walls, the windows, outside, the tower, these students seated here in this room and even the spaces between composing the one space—were all floating in consciousness, the sea of consciousness, without which all these things would disappear in that moment? The question teases us and will not yield. Here we may say we are up against the limits of our needs. A man cannot go beyond asking. If a man asks, What is in the dark? where no light ever shines, he may keep on staring hard and may grow tired. But for him there is nothing to see. To answer the question, What is consciousness? presupposes a point of view beyond consciousness. That should settle it. But man will forever be

climbing walls set around him to keep him in. Man is a pris-
oner furnished in his prison with a book of fascinating names
and they keep him on edge, ill at ease.

So much for the melodrama. Melodrama? Well, drama, at
least. For I do not want to minimize the torment. This reminds me of the following passage from Locke's Epistle to
the Reader of his *Essay:*

> Were it fit to trouble thee with the history of the essay, I
> should tell thee that five or six friends meeting at my cham-
> ber, and discoursing on a subject very remote from this,
> found themselves quickly at a stand by the difficulties that
> rose on every side. [The subject is said to have been 'the
> principles of morality and religion'.] After we had a while
> puzzled ourselves without coming any nearer a resolution of
> those doubts which perplexed us, it came into my thoughts
> that we took a wrong course; and that before we set ourselves
> upon inquiries of that nature it was necessary to examine
> our own abilities, and see what objects our understandings
> were or were not fitted to deal with.[1]

Accordingly, it is obvious that "discussion" and "coming
to a stand," "difficulties on every side," "puzzling ourselves
without coming any nearer a resolution," "doubts which per-
plexed us," etc. have made men unhappy in other times as
well. Locke set out to do something about it. Locke, according to this passage, seems to have thought that a man should
seek *to do what he can do.* But if this is to help any man to
avoid trying to do what is not simply too much for him but
is too much for any man, then someone should tell him what
his limitations are. This may be understood in several ways:
stop trying to invent a perpetual motion machine, it cannot
be done; stop trying to square the circle, it is impossible.
What then are we to do? Something like this: grow asparagus.
The principle is clear enough. If God had made you two feet
taller, he might have given you a giant's work to do. Measure
your height and your strength; don't carry more than a hundred pounds. And if you are living within walls and the walls

are ten feet high and you are six feet tall, there is no use trying to look over those walls.

I should now like to attempt to parody the quotation from Locke.

Were it fit to trouble thee with a history of this essay—which I think it is—I should tell thee that a class of twenty or more students meeting in room 308, and discoursing on a subject not at all remote from the present subject, found themselves quickly at a stand by the difficulties that rose on every side. [The subject was consciousness, and the question was, What is consciousness?] After we had puzzled ourselves a while without coming any nearer an answer so that we could come to some agreement not only concerning the answer but concerning what we were asking, it came into my thoughts that we had taken a wrong course; and *that before we set ourselves upon questions about what consciousness is, we study the question itself and take note of the background out of which that question arose.* Then it occurred to me that it could have arisen only out of the language with which we are all familiar. That is, the man who asked, What is consciousness? must some time have learned the use of such expressions as, What is _____? and must—besides that—have come upon the word "consciousness." How then, out of that background we share and within which we do agree not only in meaning or use but in judgment, do we manage to leap out and leave behind our daily understanding, finding ourselves now distressed with a word and a form of question, with a word we seem no longer to understand and a question we are helpless with?

Now let us return to the question: What is consciousness? First then, remember that this question is asked by someone who is old enough to be troubled in this way. But by the same token he is familiar with the use of the word. I might add that he has never been *taught* the use of that word, much less been furnished with a definition of that word—as though he had use for such a definition. Hence, to begin with I will say that there is something queer about the question and his asking it. That needs explanation.

Now let us answer the question. The answer will reveal that I have been especially favored to have come upon consciousness, as it were, in the flesh. I have examined it, turned it over, bounced it, shaken it, shone lights upon it and I now share the results of my encounter. Consciousness is a weightless plastic, transparent, so that not only do the eyes go right through it but so do our fingers. No one has ever got his finger stuck in consciousness nor ever fixed his eyes for a moment on a point in consciousness. In fact no one has ever located a point in consciousness. Consciousness is invisible, untouchable, inaudible. If anyone were to eat a bite of it, he would not suffer indigestion afterwards. Consciousness is tasteless; and even if one sprinkled garlic over it, one would not smell it. Consciousness is like nothing else one has ever seen, heard, smelled, tasted, or touched, including orchids, the call of the loon, chlorine gas, the finest velvet, or cold marble.

Now that I have written this, I see that it is more like, "I want to tell you about my friend, a watermelon" rather than like double-talk. It has the semblance of intelligibility. It is as though I were thinking of consciousness as a queer sort of something of which I then proceeded to give a description. And I think no one would say that I have given a wrong description, as though there was here and there a mistake in it. And why have I now bothered to give this description? I have done this to oblige. But let me add that I regard the question as inviting just this sort of answer and gave it to suggest just what sort of misunderstanding is involved in the asking of this question. I offered patent nonsense in answer to a question which was disguised non-sense, as a step in the task of clarification. I am, I realize, moving too fast. Let me then say that the foolish answer is given in order to nudge one into examining the question. But how is one to do that?

How strange it is! "Nearer than hands and feet, nearer than breathing" and yet one does not know what consciousness is. You know your hands and you know your feet and you know your breathing. But consciousness, what is that?

You know what it is to lose consciousness. Someone is hit

on the head with a length of iron pipe and he falls. He lies there bleeding and does not move. Bystanders come close; one bends over him and speaks to him, "Frank, Frank." But he does not respond. His eyes are closed. Someone calls for the ambulance, and when the attendants come with the ambulance they remove him on a stretcher and take him to the hospital. Everyone knows this is serious; but no one asks, "What did he lose?"

Later at the hospital he regains consciousness. He opens his eyes, looks around, and asks the nurse, "Where am I?" She explains, "You're in the hospital. You had a fall and hurt your head, and now you must keep quiet." Two days later, much better now, he asks the nurse, "Where are my glasses?" and she answers with a smile, "They are here. You lost those too." He responds, "Too? What else did I lose?" She says, "Consciousness." He says, "What's that?" and she is stumped.

Ruminating, he thinks to himself, "Consciousness, a queer thing. You can lose it but you cannot find it. It's not like money. Money you can lose and look for and find again. It's more like breath. One can be knocked unconscious and when you are thus knocked unconscious you lose consciousness. Breath is like that. You can be knocked breathless and then you lose your breath. So too you regain consciousness and you get your breath again. Paradise lost, paradise regained. There is lost innocence, too, but whoever heard of regaining that? 'Wait till I catch my breath'—one could not say that of one's consciousness. One cannot even *try* to catch that. Is that because it is too elusive? Consciousness, consciousness! Breath one can catch on the surface of a mirror. But where is the mirror for consciousness?"

There are other expressions we are familiar with, such as, "vaguely conscious," "fully conscious," "semi-conscious," "self-conscious," and "conscious." If one has a need for this one can remind oneself of the occasions and circumstances under which these expressions are employed. One can be "utterly unconscious" but not "utterly conscious." And now why have I reminded you of these things you know so well?

I am trying to get you to see that the man who asks what consciousness is, understands as well as any man does what consciousness is. He asks this question under an illusion as to what it is that understanding is. I might say that he is under the illusion that understanding what consciousness is consists in something like having at his disposal a piece of it, a good sample, so conveniently at his disposal that he can take it apart. I am not saying that he will say that this is what he wants. I am thinking of the analogy in the background that forces this question upon him. What is water? Here is a man who has taken it apart. He can tell you.

Let us try to get ourselves and such questions as, What is consciousness? into perspective. As children we learn to speak and to write our native language. We learn to do what our elders do. We learn to ask for more, to run to mama crying, "It hurts." We learn to tell very short stories; to join in singing "Mary had a little lamb"; to boast, "I know 'Adeste Fidelis'; to forbid, "Don't ride my bike," and so on. As we grow older we learn to do more difficult things. We learn to count our money, to write an essay about the flowers in Alaska, to argue about difficult matters in the catechism. We learn to do all sorts of things with our hands and feet. But were we to list the sorts of things we do in speaking, to say nothing of writing, certainly the English tongue would outdo any hands.

Now that I've said this, I'll withdraw it. I'm not sure, but I'll hazard a suggestion: *To understand is to be able to do.* I want to emphasize the "to do" but I'll add speaking, or whispering, or shouting, or crying, etc., under whatever the circumstances are, and whatever in those circumstances the point may be. Dogs bark, but seem not to be as versatile as human beings. In any case no one is likely to deny that all of us, children and adults, can do ever so many things with the English we know. The man, for instance, who asks "What is consciousness?" can with that word in combination with other words tell the police or the doctor about the man who was hit with the iron pipe. *He can do.* I am not denying that to do some of the things men can do (speaking and writing), requires special training; some of these are highly specialized.

If what I have just said is right, the man who asks this question is not asking this because he does not understand. But neither is he pretending. He is under a curious, most curious, most extraordinary, illusion. It is not the illusion that he does not understand. In that case he would not know what to say to the policeman and presumably he would not know what to do in the grocery store. Let me assure you that the illusion involved here is not as serious as this, though it may, depending on how in earnest he is, be a torment to him.

Get this straight. Today he said to the policeman, "Yes, the man was hit with an iron pipe and he lost consciousness." It was not troublesome to him. He could say this, give his report, and the policeman would write it down. Later in the evening, like Descartes at his own hearthstone, he reflects upon the event and what he said. At this point, away from the scene and the time, he asks, "What is consciousness?" as though if at the time he had examined the man he might have discovered what consciousness is. Consciousness goes so fast. At that moment it may seem to him that earlier he was under the illusion of what understanding is. He may say, "I understood and I did not understand." Notice that when he asks, What is consciousness? he cannot say. And surely a man who understands can say. And so he is in trouble, for he spoke freely at the time—"He lost consciousness."

Here then there is a conflict between what we all allow. He recognizes the case. "Of course, the man has lost consciousness and the requirement that he should be able to answer the question, "What is consciousness?" After all, if a man loses his money and someone asks, What is money? this can be shown. And if a man loses his breath, even this could be shown. But if a man loses his reputation or his appetite, that, too (in the aftermath of recollection), is an embarrassment. The word "consciousness" also rises up like an accusation. "You do not understand. You cannot say."

IV

At the outset I said that I wanted to use the analogy with double-talk and the grammatical phantasy and the sorts of questions that may be asked in respect to them to help us to understand the sorts of investigation that may be made in the case of certain other pieces of prose. The point of the investigation is to dispel an illusion of sense and understanding. In this case, however, the illusion is not dispelled by ear since the piece of prose involved sounds and looks too much like sense and under certain circumstances makes sense. Hence hearing it a hundred times may not even lead anyone to suspect anything. The illusion is not dispelled until one contrasts this piece of prose in its present surroundings (which may involve the elaboration of a grammatical phantasy) with that same piece of prose in its native habitat when it breathes and has life. For this purpose I happened upon the question, What is consciousness? which is a natural for all of us. I have in this way tried to explain a certain art or skill, the art of dispelling a certain sort of illusion. I have tried to avoid saying anything about the extent to which we suffer from such illusions. For if there should be a need for this art it is not that only a few of us are in need. In any case it is those and only those who reflect, who think, who are victims of such illusions. For these are illusions of reflection.

I have tried to avoid pretty well the use of the word "philosophy" in this discussion; I have instead confined myself to the discussion of a certain form of illusion and the art of dispelling that illusion. I might also have spoken of the art of creating this illusion; but the fact is that this form of illusion arises not by art but by a tendency to accident. I have in any case avoided the use of the word "philosophy" for a number of reasons. One is that I did not want to alienate at the outset any lover of philosophy who in faithfulness to his beloved might not want to hear. But there is something more important. Philosophy is what is in the philosophy books and there is such variety in these books that I should not want to assume the responsibility for saying something about all those things. Even more important is this: that whatever someone might say about everything has first to be clear when said about some one thing. And that is where I began. I studied what I then took to be the illusion of understanding what consciousness is under particular circumstances. In the same discussion I sought to dispel that illusion. Here at any rate is the art.

I tried to explain what Wittgenstein had tried to do, something strange, difficult, and unfamiliar, by way of something easily understood and familiar. It is certainly true that men before Wittgenstein have been aware that something like what he provided was required; namely, an investigation of how language may mislead us. There was Locke and there was Kant. Locke's investigation was broad and wrong. Kant's was narrow, too narrow, and, I'll say, right. In any case, what I wanted to do, in explaining what Wittgenstein had done, was to give an impression of the distinctions involved. The main idea is this: that in the background out of which the language expressing the illusion arises (and which is our resource in dispelling the illusion) is the language which is intelligible and which we commonly understand. What one has to understand in detail is how the illusion arises—naturally, whoever is under the illusion will not even know that he is under any illusion, though he may be in some trouble— and one has to be able gently and skillfully to lead him both in and out of the illusion. Here of course, special art is required. Here is one approach. Since the idea is to present for our clearer view the workings of our language where these are otherwise lost in the mist, the idea is to begin with the simplest cases—those cases in which a perspicuous view is attainable at once. Here one comes by the idea of the language game which is the servant, the instrument, for getting a perspicuous view wherever we need this. I think that Wittgenstein may accordingly be understood in this way. All the necessary distinctions we need to help us out of illusions of understanding can be found embedded in the language game.

And so, too, the illusions of understanding arise out of forget-fulness of the workings in detail.

It is quite obvious that much more than an awareness of the contrast between the intelligible language and that which expresses the illusion of intelligibility is required to help anyone. It is, however, a beginning. In any case it is helpful in understanding Wittgenstein to appreciate that in trying to figure out just what the relation is between the intelligible and the illusory, he is attempting to see both and to see how one comes to pass from one to the other without noticing any transition. That last is crucial: "Without noticing any transition." In suggesting analogous questions in respect to double-talk and the grammatical phantasy, I intended to be helpful in seeing that this is what Wittgenstein was doing and that he was not going on to indulge in further illusions. In these cases, of course, the double-talker and the writer of phantasy are in full control; they are masters. But in the other case it is as though the language had taken control while the illusion is maintained.

Here the double-talk.	Here the plain talk.
Here the phantasy.	Here the plain talk.
Here the fixed illusion.	Here the relevant language games. Plain.

There are these three contrasts. The first two are interest-ing; the third is not serious. It is more like conspicuous waste which in rich countries there are money and words for. And people to waste too. In any case such illusions require lei-sure. Curiously, double-talk ceases to be of much interest as soon as the illusion is dispelled. But the grammatical phan-tasy may be carried on and on by the source of again-and-again surprises. This may explain some of the fascination with the language of illusion. It too has a sort of order to it, a crazy order, another world, a world to be turned off and on with the turn of a phrase. Drop a word in here, there is a place for it, and create topsy-turveydom. Beware, however, and don't fall into it yourself. On the other hand why not? Your life is dreary. Take your fling.

> How do you make double-talk? There is a method.
> How do you make grammatical phantasy? There is a method.
> How do you create grammatical illusion? There is a method.

Of course, in the first two, one is aware of what he is doing and one can see in the result what the method in any case has been. In the last there is a method too, but it is much harder to make out what it is. It does not show on the surface. One has got to probe.

Now I think I see better than before what Wittgenstein has done and why it had to be done in this way. His task was to dispel a whole order of illusions, illusions which proceed from what he also describes as "misunderstandings" concerning the workings of our language. The problem, at any rate, of those who, like Locke, have felt the need of getting the workings of language into perspective, lies here. One is inclined in doing this to get one's lead by looking hard at language on the page—words, words, words; each word set apart, a unit to be understood by itself. It is as though we should understand one another speaking if we uttered a word, once every minute. And now if we ask what the relation is between the person who utters the word and the word uttered, or between the word heard and the person who hears and understands the word, the answer is given in terms of a relation between the word and what the word stands for. The person who understands is to have both the word and what the word stands for in his mind or somehow before him. "Here the word; there the meaning." It is apparently easy enough to go on under the illusion that in the case of ever so many words one understands in this way. Here the word "tree"; there the tree, the object for which the word stands. Here the name "Elizabeth"; there Elizabeth, the object for which the name stands. But when it comes to such words as "consciousness," "appetite," "reputation," it is hard to look across the table or out of the window to discover seated there or standing in the front yard the objects for which these words stand. Refinements are introduced however.

There was a time when I did not know what a cap is and what a shoe is. And I was not ashamed of my ignorance; I was proud of it—it was a sign of a superior intelligence. I did not share the common slovenliness. The requirements I set for myself were high. At any rate I was not so simple-minded that I thought I knew what a shoe is.

If I am right in this matter, then according to Wittgenstein, some of the problems of philosophy arise out of the need of getting the workings of language into perspective together with what may be regarded as an accidental feature of our written language; namely that words are spaced one by one, which feature misleads us into thinking that we *understand* words one by one. Each word is like a pointing finger and the problem and the task is to trace out the path in the course marked by that pointing finger.

But this is not all one sees as one looks hard at the printed page. There are also sentences. And now, as before one sought the object for which the word stands (a word is a name and there must be the bearer of a name), so in this case the sentence is conceived as related to a fact. A sentence either does or does not correspond to a fact. All sorts of elegant and tantalizing problems are connected with our regarding sentences in this way. No more will be said about this. The main point is that whatever is said with respect to the details, the approach in question views all sentences as functioning in only one way. This is then another source of the problems of philosophy. With respect to the problem of private language, for instance, Wittgenstein remarks that unless we make a radical break with the view that language functions in one way, the issue here will not be understood. The view referred to involves that one speaks of—I will not say "thinks of"—"I have a pain," by analogy with "I see a cardinal." Of course, there have been people who in their excitement have shouted "I see a cardinal" and what they took to be a cardinal turned out to be a red flower on a red rag. No one ever made that sort of mistake with "I had a pain." No doctor ever told a patient, "You made a mistake; it's a red flower." And that is so, even though pain may be represented in the picture by a red spot. Of course, the red spot in the picture might be mistaken for a red flower or a red rag. Let me suggest that the problems that Wittgenstein is most occupied with arise out of the view here referred to, the view that language always functions in one way. Ordinary privacy we all understand: we close the door. But here is privacy of another sort. There is a door which cannot be opened and cannot be shut—a dummy door.

Accordingly, many of the problems of philosophy may be said to arise out of either of these two dispositions treating every word as a name and treating every sentence as a report of some sort. Both give rise to illusions; the first to the object for which the word stands and the second to the fact to which the sentence or the proposition corresponds. And now it seems that to understand the word one must discover that object, and to understand that sentence one must discover that fact and in the more sophisticated cases one must discover the proposition too. In both cases one is inclined to rummage around in the world with antennae which would be the envy of the most sensitive insects—except that insects succeed.

I THINK I AM

The sentence is *Cogito, ergo sum.* For the purposes of this paper I am going to regard that sentence as a summary of the argument in the second meditation. For the understanding of this, one may find helpful the immediate context where Descartes refers to "these thoughts" of the previous meditation, or one may find Descartes' explanation helpful, particularly in what follows his question, "What am I then?" His own explanation in that passage and in others is that the expression "I think" is to be understood as a capsule expression, including in it such expressions as "I imagine," "I decide," "I love," "I believe," and also "I think" (as we use this expression at least some of the time). I have understood this to imply that there are a number of alternative expressions of the *Cogito,* such as *Dubito, ergo sum; Credo, ergo sum; Intellego, ergo sum.* In this exercise I have confined myself to studying the *Cogito* in the restricted form, "I think." I have done this partly because this seems to be the formulation which summarizes the argument in the second meditation, partly because this is the form which fascinates most people (and especially me at the present time), and partly because the kind of difficulties which arise here arise too in the case of any of the other formulations.

In this paper I have tried to do three things. *First,* I have tried to awaken an uneasiness, a suspicion, to stir up trouble concerning both what Descartes does with "I think" and with "I." *Second,* I have tried to focus attention upon how in Descartes' case he comes to do this. There is a tangle of what Wittgenstein describes as "grammatical" confusions. *Third,* I have tried to figure out how Descartes may have thought of this, that is, of "I think."

Let us consider the following. I speak to ghosts, therefore I exist. (When I wrote this I was thinking of Hamlet who was something of a philosopher and who knew of stranger things than Horatio ever dreamed of.) "And what am I then?" A speaking substance who or which stays up nights or gets up just before dawn, "in russet-mantle clad," who or which has ears and a mouth and all the other appurtenances which we know speaking substances to be furnished with, such as lungs, throat, pharynx, and muscles, besides the power and full apparatus required to work and to maintain them, and who or which has a message and a vocabulary to tell an English speaking ghost what he or it can understand.

Now I would not be surprised if you regarded this as preposterous. I do not think you would rush forward with congratulations. It is not as though you were worried and I came forward to reassure you that everything was all right and I was safe. I understand you, however; you think it is preposterous because it is obvious. You might say, "Of course, of course, and don't waste my time." But what now is obvious? Is it obvious to you that I speak to ghosts and so I needn't go on with all that rigamarole, detailing the essence of a speaking substance? Suppose further that you ask me, "Who is that speaking?" Apparently you can't see very well, and I answer, "That was Hamlet speaking." "Hamlet speaking?" "Yes, Hamlet—speaking out of that actor's mouth. Hamlet who has, like poor Yorick, been dead these three hundred years and proving, out of that actor's mouth that he, Hamlet, exists."

And did Hamlet speak to ghosts? Well, at least to one. Out of the actor's mouth, Hamlet speaks. It is good to know. It was such a loss when he died. Let us get this straight: out of this mouth come the words "I speak to ghosts" and yet it's only Hamlet who doesn't exist. And if the words had been "I think" or "Methinks" what then? Out of the one mouth two "I think's." The actor says, "Cogito, ergo sum" and we all say, "Of course, of course." At another time he says, "Cogito, ergo sum" and he adds, "That was Hamlet speaking." Are we to say there's an "I" for the actor but none for Hamlet? But may it not be just the other way round? It is Hamlet who is playing the part of an actor. For Hamlet's "I," "I exist"; and for the other "I," "I don't exist." When now Descartes says *Cogito, ergo sum,* is there any reason why we should not suspect that he is playing a part and that there is some other I-substance other than the one we normally think of when reading Descartes—or perhaps that there is none? At any rate, I have a theory that when Olivier speaks, as we say, or Hamlet speaks, as we also say, no one (at any rate, no one of you, I'll say nothing of myself) can tell whether some soul substance is insinuating itself into the goings on or not. It may, of course, be soul substance A or soul substance B or a legion of them, as many as there are I's, or none at all. This is not to say that Olivier cannot tell or that Hamlet cannot tell, I have a theory but it is just a theory.

Descartes wrote, "Thus I . . . must at length conclude that this proposition 'I am', 'I exist', whenever I utter it or conceive it in my mind, is necessarily true." Does this hold only for Descartes or for actors as well? And what about Hamlet? It strikes me now that if we were to classify Hamlet, it might be appropriate to classify him (or it) as a spiritual substance —no hands, no feet, no head, no organs. And yet Hamlet is certainly not *nothing.*

If I meet you at the door on a cold day, welcome you, and tell you that there is a fire in the grate, you recognize me and understand who it is that is speaking to you. You can see me, hear me, and since you and I speak English you can understand me. We go into the living room and sit before the fire. We have known each other for years. If now in the midst of our conversation and in excitement I tell you that I have made a discovery, namely, *that I think* and that there is absolutely no doubt about it, you might be a bit apprehensive. You might smile. But that would be a mistake; it would only show that you did not understand me. You think I am telling you what you've known ever since we were little boys. How could you not know it? But I am not telling you that; or if I am, I am telling you that as seen now in a quite different and new light. You are naïve. You think I mean by "I think" what we have meant all these years speaking English, and accordingly my now making any such discovery at this late date seems to you absurd. But that is where you are wrong. Perhaps I am not speaking English or perhaps I am speaking English with a difference. It may even be that I am not speaking any language at all, but I know what I mean—if you know what I mean. At least that is what I say. *I?* Who is that? Now don't look at me. I don't mean *me*. Certainly I do not mean anything you can see. Looking will not help.

It is difficult for me to realize that this is something like what it is in Descartes' case. There is Descartes, the spokesman for himself ("I, Descartes"), and then there is another, a stranger, another "I" who gets mixed up in his talk and confuses things. How can I make this plain?

I am first of all going to make some remarks about the use of the word "I." These remarks are commonplace. The use of the word "I" has company, relatives you might call them. It is related to the use of the proper name. "And who are you?" "I am Sonny Liston." It won't do to say "I am I," unless you intend to avoid telling—as Pudding Tame did according to the rhyme, "What's your name? Pudding Tame. Ask me again and I'll tell you the same." But even "I am I" might do, provided your voice came out clear so that by the sound of your voice you let someone know who you are. After all your "I" comes dressed in your voice, a rich bass; or in hers, a pleasant, sultry, velvet, soft and feminine. You may recognize Alice speaking over the telephone. But you can do this only if you already know Alice. Someone says, "Let me help you." You say, "And who are you?" He says, "I'm Sonny Liston." He should be able to help you. Or he says, "I'm the plumber. You called for me." Or he says, "I'm your old friend." In any case, introductions are made in this way. So are grandiose announcements. "It is I, Hamlet, the Dane." The use of the word "I" is connected with the uses of other pronouns. "And who are *you?*" If no one asked that, there would be no occasion to answer, "I am Sonny Liston."

Here are three expressions: "You" in my mouth; "I" in yours; and then there is the expression, "Sonny Liston." I say, "Leave *me* alone" and you are frightened and quit pushing *me* around. So there's "me" too. Sometimes *I* speak for all of *us*. Then *I* say, "We have decided to give all our money to the poor." In this case *I* am said to be the mouthpiece of the group. The group is of one mind and *I* speak for all. It is not, however, my mouth that is the mouthpiece. *I* am the mouthpiece. What is especially nice about this is the connection that is recognized here between the use of the word "we" and a mouthpiece. The mouthpiece does have a mouth. It's "we" in any case. But "I" is not like that. To everyone his own mouth and the one "I" to fill it. You cannot say "I" for me. You must say "you" or "he" or "Sonny Liston." Remarks of a similar sort may be made concerning the written "I" and these other words. Here signature plays an important role.

Now notice how it is with the "I" of the "I think" that Descartes seizes upon. It has no relatives. "I" has no brothers or sisters. When Descartes asks the question, "What am I then?" it is not as though he were echoing the question, "Who are you?" And "I" does not answer, "I'm the plumber" —this "I" has no employment, has no hands—nor "I'm your old friend"—this "I" is solitary, a very private citizen, has no

friends—nor "I'm Sonny Liston"—this "I" is anonymous—
nor "Who do you suppose I am? Don't you recognize my
voice?"—"I" is voiceless, cannot speak above a whisper, nor
below one. So, too, the "I think" Descartes seizes upon is not
to be responded to with, "Good, then you can have the job,"
or "I wish I did." Here there is no company; there is nobody
—there is no body.

In these remarks I have made some point of the fact that
in speaking, the mouth and face and voice have a special role
to play in the use of the word "I." Now I want to suggest that
in reading the Meditations one source of confusion lies in
something like this: There are two "I's" and but one mouth.
Accordingly I want to suggest further that it might be simpler if we could think of the one "I," "I, Descartes," or "I,
Sonny Liston," talking as we normally do, using the common
mechanism of speech, the mouth, and of that other "I" talking as we normally do not, through the ear. I might have
suggested that "I think" be heard as coming out of a crack in
the wall or as out of the air (Ariel) but I still want to maintain some connection with that other "I think" that issues
out of the mouth. Mouth-to-ear maintains that connection.

Try now to imagine this. You have a friend who (as is the
case with most of your friends) goes about in the body. For
years he has been speaking out of his mouth, just as your
other friends do. It's the usual thing. Suddenly one day he
begins talking out of one ear but without giving up talking
out of his mouth. Naturally this startles you. It is grotesque,
like something out of Dante. Sometimes he talks out of his
mouth, and sometimes out of his ear. It's English, all right—
in a way, that is. All the words are English. At first you are so
upset that you can scarcely attend to what is said. You look
at the mouth, attending to what is said, and nervously await
with a sideglance at the ear to hear what's coming from there.
You soon learn, however, to adjust yourself to what you hear
from the mouth, disregarding what you hear at the ear, for
what you might call practical purposes—but not, of course,
altogether. What the ear says is distracting when not divert-

ing. One day you notice that whereas what issues from the mouth continues the same as always (mixing up such things as "There's a fire in the grate" and "I think there's a fire in the grate" and "Where are you going, Johnny?" and "You're a dear," etc.), what you hear from the ear is restricted, specialized. What you hear there always begins "I imagine," "I think," "I doubt," "I hope," "I desire," etc. It's always "I, I, I." There is also this striking difference that whereas in relation to what is said from the mouth there is always some connection with what's going on and you can, as it were, talk back to your friend, in relation to what you hear from the ear you are utterly helpless. Perhaps you have the feeling of eavesdropping on the soul in conversation with herself, though you might on the other hand not regard this as conversation. There seems to be nothing to discuss. At first you did react with your helpless remarks, such as, "You do?" or "Don't be silly" or "Do you mean, there's no fire?" but there seemed to be no communication at all. Of course, you were not at all comfortable talking to an ear. One other day you face up to the situation boldly, as boldly as you can, still feeling a little foolish, and looking straight at the ear, almost as though you wanted to catch its eye, you ask, "And what do you mean I, I, I, think, imagine, hope, etc.?" And at this the shadow of an arm rises and points to the inner ear. You now feel as though you have been speaking to a shadow and though at the moment you look more steadfastly (as though you meant to frustrate that inner ear), you—with your recollection of anvil and stirrup and Eustachian tubes—give up. Certainly *they* can't speak. You give up, resigned to hear English from the ear, which you will never understand.

II

Now how does all this come about? Well, "I think" is indubitable—which in certain cases it is. And so it is with all these other expressions in the capsule. Now it is not so difficult to see what has happened. If we are to represent to ourselves the use and meaning of the expression "I think" (with the reminders of the circumstances in which we use this expression, with the distinctions between you and me and mine and thine in this great wide world, the sun and moon and stars, our present home, and how we have come to use this expression, learning the English language), and if we now reject all this as illusory and cling at the same time to the indubitability of "I think," then we are bound to find a meaning for this expression in what I may refer to as the secret cell. Out of the mouth, your friend speaks English as we all do. Here we understand one another. But out of his ear speaks that other, the shadow of a confusion, the masked indubitability of "I think," or should I say the now naked indubitability of "I think"? And could nakedness be a mask? What is masked is the fact that "I think" now has no context. So another must be supplied. By what? Let us say, by the grammatical imagination. And how then did Descartes spirit away the context of "I think"? By meditation. And on what did he meditate? On the facial resemblances between the language in which we tell our dreams and tell what we have seen and heard and done. The other "I."

I want now to address myself to the question as to how this phenomenon of bilingualism has come about in some greater detail. There is, as you remember, the original "I think" spoken out of the mouth and that other "I think" spoken out of the ear. It is your friend who speaks out of that mouth, and the stranger—mysterious stranger—that speaks out of that ear. I have referred, as you may have noticed, to the mouth-spoken "I think" as the original, and so I propose to describe the ear-spoken "I think" as derivative. I want now to try to figure out how that latter "I think" is derived.

To begin with, bear in mind that there are sentences which, spoken or written, are indubitable and there are others which are not. We have a number of expressions which express this feeling about what we say, or (if you prefer) about our conviction in whatever the matter is. There are such expressions as "of course," "absolutely," "positively," "indeed," "naturally," "without a doubt," "certainly," "surely," and so on. But there are other sentences which when spoken or written evoke a different response. There are such expressions as "Well, maybe," "I have my doubts," "You can't tell," "Unlikely," "It could be," "Nobody knows," and so on. I say, "In Columbus' expedition there were three ships, the *Pinta*, the *Santa Maria,* and one other one—isn't that right?" And now you say, depending upon your impatience at my asking such a question—any school boy knows that—"Of course," or "Go, look it up." But if I asked, "We all know that there were three ships in Columbus' expedition, but wasn't there also one much smaller one that is never mentioned and the name of which we don't know?" Now what about that? The answer might be, "Never heard of it," or "I've got my doubts about that, but of course, I'm no authority." Someone else might respond with, "Yes, there was such a ship. It was a phantom ship and its name was "Delight," named after a poem by Wordsworth. "She was a phantom of delight, but she sank early in the voyage." This last is outrageous disbelief.

Now why have I brought this up? Because Descartes, in effect, regards "I think" as indubitable. And so, like, "In Columbus' expedition there were three ships?" For the moment, let us say, "Yes, like that." And let us add, "But not like that."

And now I want you to notice another less common use of these expressions, a use more familiar to philosophers. There are sentences which may be true and false—let us call these dubitable, since in connection with these the question arises, "Is it true?" And sometimes, at least (depending on circumstances) the answer is, "Maybe," "I doubt it," and so on. There are other sentences which are neither true nor false, and so of course they cannot be doubted either. It makes no sense to say, "I doubt 'Scoot.'" So "Scoot" is indubitable. With "Scoot" this is clear. But with, "Till death do us part" or "Nice day," "You're a little brat" or "I love you, love you, love you" or "Oh, what a beautiful morning!" temptations arise—temptations of a grammatical sort.

Did Descartes then regard "I think" in this way; as rather like "Scoot" and like "nice day"? Let's say "yes," but not at all in the sense that he would himself have said so. Perhaps then we'd better say "No." If Descartes had regarded "I think" as indubitable in the way that "Scoot!" is indubitable, then it would be a rather large mistake for him to infer that "I think" is true just as in case he had regarded "I think" as inedible—there are ever so many inedibles among sentences —it would be a rather large mistake to infer that "I think" is made of wood or stone and hard to chew.

There is a third set of distinctions which in a way has nothing to do with doubt and yet which employs the expressions "dubitable" and "indubitable." It is this: a sentence is dubitable if following the expression "I dreamed" the whole sentence now makes sense. So if you understand me when I say, "I dreamed last night that I was sitting by the fire," then, if I ever call to you "I am sitting by the fire" (no matter whether I am or not), that sentence spoken by me is dubitable. And Descartes seems to say that in that case you'd better be careful—but not in the way of coming to see for yourself. That is no good. The sentence does not change its character by your walking into the living room and catching the warm glow of a would-be fire in that room. Being careful here consists in your mastering your proofs for the existence of the Savior and Protector of all epistemologists in distress— their name is legion.

There are also sentences such that if you begin your sentence with "I dream" and go on with any sentence of this sort that whole sentence will be nonsensical. Such a sentence is "I dreamed that I thought." Roughly the idea is that if you dreamed that you thought whatever it is, then you must have thought it. To dream is to think and later to think otherwise. This is charming but a long story. This sentence "I think" is said to be indubitable.

Accordingly we have a set of distinctions which in various ways is related to the earlier sets introduced. We can see, for instance, that the sentence "I think" may in certain (perhaps rare) cases belong to the class called indubitable in the first set and also to the class called dubitable in that same set. This is because the circumstances or the context enters into the determination. But in other cases "I think" may belong to the class indubitable in the second set. Hence there is ample room for confusion. As far as I can make out we are provided with the following: One cannot dream "I think." One cannot dream the ontological proof either. To dream you must get it wrong. Also, "I think" is true. In this respect it is like no other sentence with which Descartes is acquainted. And what else? "I think" is indubitable in the way in which "Scoot!" is indubitable—neither true nor false. This is, however, too involved for the present occasion. What I wished chiefly to point out is that the seductiveness of what Descartes describes as the certainty of "I think" may be explained in this way: In most uses of the expression "I think," "I think" is indubitable in the way that "Scoot!" is. There is no use arguing with it. And what is more natural, since it is indubitable, than to conclude that it is true—especially since it is sometimes used in such a way that it is true, and furthermore has the form of many sentences which are true. "Yes, I swim."

III

We have now seen that Descartes says that "I think" is indubitable and in what a curious way he comes to say this. However, he has not as yet explained how we are to understand "I think." I suppose that if we were to ask him for examples of the use he was describing he might say that any use would do. In order to make as plain as I can what in effect he does, I want to provide an example and then to treat it as it strikes me Descartes might have done. In an important respect this example is not appropriate. But my point in presenting it is to remind us of the way in which the use of the expression "I think" is tied in with its surroundings. This is required for us to appreciate the fact that in order for Descartes, as he sees it, to present the "meaning" of "I think" which is indubitable he has got to isolate it from all that in its surroundings is dubitable. And that is a great deal.

Let us consider the example. If someone, meeting the great philosopher Kant on Main Street in Konigsberg had asked him what he did for a living, he might have replied "I think." There would have been something or other which led up to this. Perhaps Kant himself began the conversation. Let's suppose a young girl asked him. She is surprised and puzzled at such an answer; can a man make a living by thinking? Her father worked hard as a poor woodman in the forest. Kant watched her with amusement and smiled. When he gave this answer, as he sometimes did, he frequently chuckled, so some people thought he must be joking. They might have asked him what he thought and he could have shown them bushels. They might also have asked him to think a thought for them. The young girl said to her sister: "Do you think he makes a living by thinking?" and her sister shook her head. She said that one might as well make a living by imagining or supposing or wishing. She did not know that some people made a living by guessing. As for Kant himself, there were times when he read what he had written and exclaimed, "Ach, and that's thinking?" You can see in this case that thinking is an expert's business, a thinker's work, and not everyone can do it; it is an ability that requires years of practice.

Now when Kant said "I think," he was right. There is no doubt about it. In fact some people like us might explain to others and to ourselves what thinking is by referring to what Kant did. Pointing to the *Critique* one might say, "If you want to know what thinking is, look at this." And some young man who aspired to be a thinker might read Kant, use him as a model, and after some years try it himself. He might then ask for a job. Someone would ask him: "What do you do?" And he would reply, "I think." The man who asks this understands because he is a thinker too. He says, "Let us see some of your work." In the end they politely tell the young man that he can think, but not well enough. He may have had misgivings of his own. He may have asked himself, "Now is this like what Kant did?" Leaving the question unanswered he may have consoled himself with the thought, "No, it's more like what Plato did."

I propose now to use this to show you in an admittedly crude but figurative way what eliminating the dubitables is like, and I want to do this not in a flash or in the twinkling of an eye, but in a number of steps, gradually, so that we may have a clearer picture of what is involved. A dubitable is anything of which you may have dreamed. In connection with the example I gave we may now do this:

First, let us remove what Kant thought. That means the bushels.

Second, let us remove the young girl's sister, the skeptical one.

Third, that young man and the dons, the young man who read Kant.

Fourth, the surroundings in Konigsberg, and Main Street.

Fifth, the last remaining street on which Kant and the young girl are standing.

Sixth, at this stage the young girl and Kant remain suspended in the air, let us remove the girl.

Seventh, only Kant remains. Remove Kant, all except the mouth still saying, "I think."

Eighth, remove the mouth but let the motions of the mouth remain with the sound of the voice.

Ninth, remove the motion gradually, like the smile of the Cheshire cat. Let it recede gently and with it the voice diminishing to a whisper and finally to nothing.

Tenth, let the sky come falling down like snow and melt away.

What remains is "I think," all dubitables having been removed. But "I think" remains—not the words, but the wordless fact. Descartes' sentence is, "Nothing in the world exists—no sky, no earth, no minds, no bodies." And so I could go on, "Nothing in the world exists, no bushels of thoughts, no sister, no young student, no dons, no Konigsberg, no Main Street, no young girl, no Kant, no Kant's mouth, no motions of his mouth, no voice, no sky."

I have represented separating out "I think," (the indubitable), from all the dubitables, such as, "That young girl is asking the great philosopher Kant what he does for a living," as a matter of rubbing out the whole world so that nothing is left. That, however, may be misleading. Let us regard what is done rather as some form of transformation. Let us imagine then that by the waving not of a wand but of an argument, we transform the whole wide world into mirror images which have remained fixed in their places after the mirrors have been removed. There are no originals of their images. All the "accidental" features of what make them mirror images have been removed. They are regarded as the stuff of which dreams and seeing are made. And now in relation to these images, all this "stuff," there is a shadowy figure, a shade without a face, not a human being, the thinker. This is that "I" of the *Cogito,* the "I" whose dream is composed of the world and all, including Descartes. They are "I's" dream. It must be clear then that if Descartes says "I think" and does not mean "I, Descartes," the "I" he has in mind might better be called I_2—to make sure that there's no mistaken identity. How Descartes gets to know about I_2 and what I_2 thinks has been what I have sought to explain to myself.

How now are we to represent the life of I_2? Life? Well, something. Bear in mind, then, that where all is mirror images there are no mirror images. For what are they to be images of? So I_2 cannot recognize an image as the image of anything. He cannot, for instance, come to say, "It's a rabbit," for where would he get the idea of a rabbit? I_2 might better be represented as a viewer of abstract paintings, who has long forgotten that there are other sorts of paintings. Hence I_2 just looks, or rather does whatever a shade can do. This is what I_2

does. At most, I_2 thinks, "I think" or "I see." Previously I described I_2 as a dreamer, but I think now that was a mistake. For a dreamer (as Descartes thought of him) has a great deal of confidence, and recognizes a rabbit when he sees one. Of course, he makes mistakes. But Descartes' "I_2" is one who has learned his lesson. I_2 has been subdued by a humiliating examination. I_2 lets the chiaroscuro go by. At most we can allow that I_2 still has the impulse to say, "A rabbit" but in "I's" cowed state, "I_2" never gets beyond gaping and uttering "A-A-A"; but the word "rabbit" is stayed. The point is that where there is no distinction between "It's a rabbit" and "It seems to be a rabbit," the word "rabbit" has ceased to have any meaning.

And here is one last suggestion. The "I" of "I think" is an "I" embarrassed and upset by the argument of the first meditation, dumbfounded by its new surroundings, composed of nothing but elusive and delusive presentations. It neither believes nor doubts nor imagines nor supposes nor sees nor fears nor guesses, though it has a suspended capacity for doing all these things. And that is what "I think" is, suspended capacities. Fortunately, one capacity remains to it: the capacity for the ontological proof. Without this all would have been lost.

ANSELM'S ARGUMENT

"For why do we have our philosophers if not to make supernatural things trivial and commonplace."

(Kierkegaard)

They say that to unscramble an egg is very difficult, that even with all the king's horses and all the king's men one is likely to fail. Imagine, then, how much more difficult it must be to unscramble the scramble of a dozen eggs! In this case, with even the help of all the kings themselves one can scarcely hope to succeed. And yet that is something like what I propose to do: to restore out of the scramble, a number of eggs, whole and sunny-side up. The scramble I have in mind is the ontological proof, the most bewildering and tantalizing, and neat and compact bit of scramble in the history of philosophy. The only piece that rivals it for complexity and apparent simplicity is the argument of Berkeley. They are both magnificent in both respects, and Anselm's argument looks least like a scramble.

The following summary of the argument may serve to guide the course of the discussion. Nearly all of this will be quoted. The argument is presented by Anselm in the course of a meditation which begins, "And, indeed, we believe that thou art a Being than which none greater can be conceived." This sentence contains the key phrase in the argument. He goes on, "Or is there no such nature, since 'the fool hath said in his heart, There is no God'? But, at any rate, this very fool, when he hears of this Being of which I speak—a being than which none greater can be conceived—understands what he hears, and what he understands is in his understanding; although he does not understand it to exist."

After a paragraph of explanation, he goes on:

Hence even the fool is convinced that something exists in the understanding, at least, than which nothing greater can be conceived. For when he hears of this, he understands it. And whatever is understood is in the understanding. And assuredly that than which nothing greater can be conceived, cannot exist in the understanding alone. For suppose it exists in the understanding alone: then it can be conceived to exist in reality; which is greater.

Therefore, if that than which nothing greater can be conceived, exists in the understanding alone, the very being, than which none greater can be conceived, is one, than which a greater can be conceived. But obviously this is impossible. Hence there is no doubt that there exists a being, than which nothing greater can be conceived, and it exists both in the understanding and in reality.[2]

These are the sentences I am going to explore. And I submit once more that no more splendid headache has ever been composed. Aspirin may help a little, but I want to try something different.

This investigation is extremely complicated. Accordingly, I thought it might be useful to provide a guide concerning what I propose to do. I intend to look closely at the following sentences:

1. "We believe that thou art a being than which none greater can be conceived."
2. "The fool hath said in his heart, there is no God."
3. "This very fool . . . understands what he hears."
4. "What he understands is in his understanding."
5. "That than which nothing greater can be conceived cannot exist in the understanding alone."

If we look closely at these sentences, we may see how Anselm, as he goes on, gathers in and compounds difficulties. The amazing thing is that out of the confusion woven of fourteen darknesses Anselm should have made one pure ray of light. Such density, and yet such translucence!

I

I want first to discuss the sentence: "And, indeed, we believe that thou art a being than which none greater can be conceived." We may notice to begin with that this sentence, like the other sentences in the discourse, is addressed to God. With this in mind one might consider it strange as though one intended something like, "We believe it but is it so?" We may, however, discard this as of no particular significance since the address to the deity pertains rather to the form of the meditation. Anselm is musing and Anselm is devout. But the sentence may be troublesome in some other way. The form "We believe" may remind one of the form of the sentences which make up the Apostles' Creed which begins "I believe. . . ." They do not, however, go on, "I believe that. . . ." They continue, "I believe in. . . ." "I believe in God, the Father, Almighty Maker . . ." But we know in any case that Anselm is not, as in the congregation, making a confession of his holy and undoubted Catholic faith. He is not in the church, there are no candles, this is not the hour of prayer. Anselm is standing at his desk, thinking, writing, trying to get the words in order. In any case the form of these words is not right for the confession. But neither is Anselm meditating out of some Cartesian frame of mind, testing his belief, straining for a doubt to be induced, for a belief shaken. There is no intention to go on, "But may we not be deceived?" When Anselm goes on to ask, "Or is there no such nature?" this is not to be taken as an expression of Anselm's doubt. We know that he had no such doubts. Anselm's question is to be regarded rather as the occasion to present the proof.

And how are we to understand what Anselm is doing? We must remember that Anselm has for a long time been engaged in attempting to devise a proof—neat, clenching, final, clicking—a proof in one quick trick, nothing clumsy, nothing bumbling. And how now would one go about this? Would he borrow a hint from Euclid? Most likely Anselm had no clear idea as to how he would go about this and most likely, too, how he did go about it became clear to him only when he had hit upon the proof itself. At any rate, at some time during his musings the sentence we are busy with occurred to him and we can see how in the sequel it served him. It provided him with a phrase which he employed as something like a definition. I still hesitate to call this a definition since in the sequel it seems to serve rather like a description. In any case my question is as to where Anselm got that phrase, for though Anselm may have been the first to employ it as he did and certainly the first to have written the sentence "We believe that thou art . . .", he may not have invented the phrase itself. This is also apparent in the introductory words "We believe," which suggests that no one would question what follows. The phrase I have in mind is "the being than which none greater can be conceived." It is accordingly from what Anselm treats as common belief that he goes on to lift this phrase. My question can now be restated: Out of what context did Anselm lift that phrase before he incorporated it as a part of the statement of belief? I do not mean that we will discover precisely this phrase in some familiar surroundings, but I do mean that we may discover some phrases enough like this so that we can understand what language is involved here. Once we have discovered this, we can then see the phrase in its natural surroundings, alive and full of joy, and we can also see the same phrase in unnatural surroundings, lifeless and joyless. Later we may see it in the guise of a living thing, together with the help of other illusions providing it the semblance of a moving thing, jerks in an argument.

As you can see, I am taking for granted that the phrase in question (or some phrases very much like it, familiar, breathing, full of spirit) can be found. The reason for this is that I cannot otherwise explain the strong hold this sentence must have had upon Anselm, nor the assent of so many generations of readers of Anselm's proof. The roots of this and of this common assent must lie deep in the language with which Anselm and all these people are so well-acquainted. And where now should we look for this? Here again it will be useful to keep in mind that Anselm is a Christian, monk, and archbishop, and that he is busy with a proof for the existence of God. This would certainly involve (proof being what it is), that at the outset he would seek out what to him would seem a clear formulation of the concept, God. I do not mean that Anselm would have weighed the matter in this way and considered in some precise fashion what he was about. Nevertheless, I want to suggest that what Anselm is doing may be clearer to us if we think of him as trying to get into perspective the meaning of the word "God" under the special limitation of doing this for a certain purpose. If a definition is required for proof, then that will be the form which the perspective will take. And now where would a Christian look for this? Where but in the Scriptures? Now I do not mean to say that there are any definitions in the Scriptures nor even that Anselm directs his search in this way. He takes what may strike us as a shortcut; namely, to what he regards as a statement of what we Christians all believe. But since we are all Christians and the Bible is our book, this must be where we are led to discover this language. Of course, I do not mean that what Anselm provides as a statement of belief is a statement of belief. It serves Anselm, however, as a sentence holding in perspective some part of the meaning of the word "God," but in such a way as to embody profound confusions and to lead on to even greater densities of the same.

I propose now to go on to find the surroundings of this phrase in several books of the Scriptures, but especially in the psalms. In this way I expect to exhibit this phrase as a slightly altered fragment of the language of praise. Once this grammatical detail is digested, we may come to see what a surprisingly strange piece of work this argument is. It may help to remark that in the light of this, Anselm's sentence, "We believe that thou art a being than which none greater can be conceived," may be regarded as arising out of a distorted reading of the words of praise. If everything had been kept in order, Anselm might have written, "We all praise thee, O God, at the top of our voices, shouting, Thou art great, O Lord, Our God," but this would have been praise and itself quite useless for his proof. And now I want to pass on to remind us of some of the language of praise after a few introductory remarks about this language.

Praise is common; so is invective. There is fulsome praise, generous praise, hollow praise, insincere praise, half-hearted praise, faint praise. We praise God. We praise men. Sometimes praise is spontaneous. "Bravo! Bravo!" Sometimes we set a time to praise, a special occasion, with a dinner to honor. "Let us now praise famous men." "We come to bury Caesar and not to praise him"; but we praise him all the same. A man may be "damned with faint praise." There is a ceremony of praise; the banner is raised high. So is the football hero—he is lifted up. The place of honor is a raised place and the praised sit at the high table. With praise go honor, laurels, decorations, singing telegrams, all hail! And there is singing ("For he's a jolly good fellow"), shouting, blowing of horns, ringing of bells, fireworks, confetti, flowers. With joyful brass sounding and shouting, paper streaming, the gay and loud, the bursting rockets, the umbrella of stars, the glory of the praised is showered upon the blessed. And there is eulogy, the words well-spoken, remembering virtues and deeds: they are glorious, and we all join in the exultation. Once they were bigger than man-size, and we'll not forget but praise them. Praise is verve, it is delight, zest, and jubilation. It is the finery of our spirits in noise and color, in the sound of the trumpet and in song, shouting for joy in the blessedness of what is high and noble. Praise is articulate wonder and exultation, a making merry, celebrating the presence or the memory of heroes.

I am sure that I should not have written about praise in this way had I not just lately refreshed myself with the language of praise in the psalms. These writers were, of course, praising God. And what praise it is! Compared to their praise, all other praise is tepid. Here the spirit rejoices. What jubilation and ecstasy! I know of nothing today rivaling this in intensity, that exuberance of the spirit, that extolling of what is high. Here we sing, we praise, we are glad, we bless, we magnify, we exult, we extol, we make a noise, we raise our hands, we dance, we sound the trumpet, we play on the psaltery and harp and with cymbals and dance, with stringed instruments and wind, and organs, and upon the loud cymbals and the high sounding cymbals. What were Bach and Handel doing but praising God?

And now I should like to review some of the language of praise. I have chosen these particular instances as reminders we need in order that we may discover the surroundings of the phrase "the being than which none greater can be conceived." Here are a few:

King Solomon to King Hiram: "And the house which I build is great; *for great is our God above all gods.*"

And here is King David: "Wherefore *thou art great,* O Jehovah God; for there is none like thee, neither is there any God besides thee, according to all that we have heard with our ears." Compare this and the foregoing with Anselm's "Thou art a being than which none greater can be conceived," Anselm gilding the praise of King David.

And here are some sentences from the psalms:

Great is Jehovah and *greatly* to be praised . . . (Ps. 48)

Jehovah reigneth; let the people tremble;
He sitteth above the cherubim;
Let the earth be moved.
Jehovah is great in Zion. (Ps. 99)

Bless Jehovah, O my soul.
O Jehovah, my God, *thou art very great.* (Ps. 104)

Great is Jehovah and *greatly* to be praised.
And his *greatness* is unsearchable. (Ps. 145)

I have selected these particular cases of the language of praise to stress the role of the word "great" in praise. In the book of Acts it is the Ephesians who cry out: "Great is Diana of the Ephesians." There are also such expressions as "great above all other gods" and "very great," and "great and terrible" and "his greatness is unsearchable." The use of the superlative is common. So we have "neither is there any God beside thee," "a great King above all gods," and so on. And so, too, "a being than which none greater can be conceived."

There are other words which serve in much the same way that the word "great" does. Here, for instance, is the word "high." "It is a good thing to give thanks unto the Lord and to sing praises unto thy name, O most high" (Ps. 92:1). And in the same psalm, "But thou, Lord, art most high forevermore." Here we also have the superlative "most high." Also, "The Lord is high above all nations and his glory above the heavens" (Ps. 113:4). The use of the superlative in praise is common both in Scripture and otherwise: "too wonderful for me," "the peace that passeth understanding," "beyond all estimate," "indescribably lovely," "beyond words,' "incomparable," "peerless," "as the heavens are high above the earth, so are my ways higher than your ways, my thoughts than your thoughts," "more than words can tell," "impossibly noble life," "unbelievably fine." By this time it should be unmistakably clear that Anselm's phrase is derived from the language of praise.

Now let us ask: And what would have happened to Anselm's proof if instead of his happening upon the sentence, "Thou art a being than which none greater can be conceived," he had happened upon "Thou art a being than which none higher can be conceived," or "none more glorious"? Perhaps it would have made no difference. Here, however, is a sentence from Shakespeare of somewhat the same sort: "O wonderful, wonderful, and most wonderful wonderful; and yet again wonderful. . . ." And now what if Anselm had happened upon, "Thou are a being than which none is more wonderful wonderful and yet again more wonderful beyond all that can be conceived." Would the proof have gone on as in the proof we know? There would perhaps be room for the same misunderstanding.

Let me try once more. The word "Ah!" is certainly an expressive term, expressive of awe and delight, a sort of inarticulate praise. We sometimes ask, "What are you Ah-ing about?" An attentive face and an open mouth go with this. The equivalent of Anselm's sentence will now be something like, "Thou art a being than which none more Ah-ed about or more to be Ah-ed about is conceivable." Ah-ing and praising are human reactions.

There are two further points to be made in connection with the language of praise. First, there are variants of the language of praise which (unlike those mentioned earlier and involving the word "great") would never mislead one in the way in which "God is great" may have done. It is the function of these sentences as expressions of praise which we must keep in mind. One is, "O magnify the Lord with me" (Ps. 34:3). How does one magnify the Lord? By singing out in this way. One may also magnify the Lord by singing out, "Great is Jehovah, our God."

Here are others:

> Be thou exalted, Lord. (Ps. 21:13)
> I will extol thee, O Lord. (Ps. 30:1)
> Let the Lord be magnified. (Ps. 35:2)
> Blessed be the Lord God of Israel. (Ps. 41:3)

O, let the nations be glad and sing for joy. (Ps. 67:6)
Sing unto God, ye kingdoms. (Ps. 68:32)
Clap your hands, all ye people. (Ps. 47:1)

The point of introducing these variations of the language
of praise is to help us to understand by way of what original
misunderstanding Anselm may have gone on with the phrase
under investigation as he did. The earlier set of sentences
have the form of indicatives—"Great is Jehovah," etc. When
removed from their surroundings and cooled for the purpose
of proof, they may be mistaken for sentences about God, as
though they furnished information or descriptions. But they
are no more statements or descriptions than the sentences just
quoted. Those by their imperative form prevent at least that
misunderstanding. The sentence, "Great is our God above all
other gods" is not to be mistaken for such a sentence as,
"High is the Empire State Building above all buildings in
New York." Or is it? I'm afraid so.

And now I want to make the second point. We have so far
identified the surroundings of that phrase and of similar sentences as psalms but we have not indicated what those surroundings are. The surroundings I am concerned to notice
are these; namely, that the psalmist praising God, remembers
what God has done. Here is a nice example from Psalm 103:

> Bless the Lord, O my soul, and all that is within me bless
> his holy name. Bless the Lord, O my soul, and forget not all
> his benefits; who forgiveth all thine iniquities; who healeth
> all thy diseases; who redeemeth thy life from destruction;
> who crowneth thee with loving kindness and tender mercies;
> who satisfieth thy mouth with good things; so that thy youth
> is renewed like the eagle's, etc.

And here is a part of Psalm 104:

> Bless the Lord, O my soul. O Lord my God, thou are very
> great; thou are clothed with honor and majesty; who coverest
> thyself with light as with a garment, who stretchest out the

heavens like a curtain; who layeth the beams of his chambers in the waters; who maketh the clouds his chariots, who walketh upon the wings of the wind; etc.

These may serve to illustrate the common pattern of the psalm of praise. There are the commonly introductory sentences of praise and then continuing in praise, the remembrance of what God has done or what God does. "Remember his marvelous works that he hath done; his wonders and the judgments of his mouth . . ." (Ps. 105).

I have now made these rather elaborate explanations of the sentence "Thou art a Being than which none greater can be conceived" in order that we might see it in its surroundings, along with the shout and the joyful noise and the reminders of what God has done. It is to be spoken in the voice of praise. And the phrase "the being than which none greater can be conceived" may also be understood in these surroundings. If, however, Anselm first lifts the sentence out of its surroundings and then goes on to lift the phrase out of the sentence (and we remember that a sentence or a phrase is to be understood only in its surroundings), we may anticipate that this is where Anselm's troubles, which do not *seem* like troubles, first begin.

And now in the light of all this I should like to return to Anselm's sentence, "We believe that thou art a being than which none greater can be conceived." And how are we to read this? Why, in the same way in which we might read, "We believe that we are glad and sing for joy," or "We believe that we shout Hallelujah unto thy name," or "We believe that we delight in thee, O Lord God of Israel." And need I now add that this is strange? Surely this is neither praise nor belief but a confusion.

And what in this instance has Anselm done? Clearly, he has lifted out of the shouting surroundings, "with a great shout," a shouting sentence. But now there is no shout. And where is the wonder now, the delight, and the thanksgiving? Gone with the shout. "We believe that we thank thee, O Lord."

And of course there is no dancing, no clapping of the hands. And what have the little hills to do with this that otherwise were singing for joy? All that we have now is praise on ice, the denatured words of praise, dead. And where are those other surroundings, the remembrances of deeds so wonderful, from which the spirit of praise was transfused? They are all tucked away in the book, forgotten, irrelevant. And now imagine Anselm. He writes down the sentence, "We believe that thou art a being than which none greater can be conceived." At least that is settled. He looks at it hard or he repeats it to himself and sees in it now nothing like the climax of acclaim, but a discovery. So that is what God is. Of all beings conceived and conceivable, none is greater than God. And that is a fact. Praise on ice—some praise, that is—looks like ever so many matters of fact.

No doubt, I have written enough to show what I regard as the confusion involved here, but I have said nothing as to how this same sentence must have struck Anselm nor what might have led to this. Hence, I should like to go on with this.

As far as I know, Anselm provides us with no explanation. Hence, all we can ask is: What would a reasonable misunderstanding in this case be? And here the sentence may give us some help. "We believe that thou art a being than which none greater can be conceived," looks like the summary of the results of a series of comparisons. (The expression of praise is nothing of the sort.) There is a building in New York City than which there is none in New York City that is taller. Perhaps there is one on the drawing boards, among the conceivables. But what now are being compared? It seems that *beings* are being compared. But this would, I think, be misleading. We had better say that we are comparing conceivables, and a special class of conceivables; namely, the class of conceivable beings, or rather the class of conceivables, called "beings." But how are we to compare conceivables? We know well enough how to compare horses. There are horse shows and judges of horses at horse shows. Blue ribbons are awarded to the finest horses. There are, no doubt, scores for prance, and scores for stance, and scores for dance, and so on. There are poultry shows, dog shows, cat shows. And at the animal fair there may be a first and grand prize for the finest animal in the fair. This cow is a finer beast than any cat at the fair. For all I know, a tiny white mouse might win the prize; presumably, there is a way of estimating these things. But comparing conceivables cannot be managed in that way. There is no "conceivables fair." Or is there? But it is not simply that conceivable beings are to be compared, for they are also to be arranged in some order of what is called their greatness. Concerning this order, it is said that there is some last conceivable in the order of the progression, beyond which no greater conceivable is conceivable. And that does not mean that some inconceivable does come next.

And if one should ask, "But what are these conceivable beings?" let me suggest that there are conceivables such as "now" and "if" and "one" and "ask" which are certainly conceivable but certainly not as conceivable beings. Some conceivables are beings and some are not. Conceivable beings are "pebbles," "fleas," "stars," etc. In respect to some words, sentences of the form, "It is round," "It is a flea," "It is a pebble," etc., make sense. Each of such sentences is a part of what is meant here by a conceivable of the sort called "beings." If we are satisfied with this, it should speed us on. At least we have enough trouble. In any case I will now hasten to provide a list of conceivable beings, and in the order which some will certainly consider the right order. It will follow more or less the order of evolutionary generation from lesser to greater: a stone, a mite, a horse, a man, Shakespeare, an angel, Satan, Zeus, God. Perhaps it will also now be clear that by a *conceivable* in the case of each of these words, is meant whatever may be said about any stone, any mite, any horse, etc., respectively. So by the conceivable being, "stone," is meant whatever may be intelligibly said about any stone. And now if someone were to say about a stone, that it is a being, not than which none greater can be conceived, but that it is a being than which some being greater than it can be conceived (namely, a mite) perhaps this would be understood. Whatever someone did mean by this I suppose that he would have to explain this by way of what is said about stones and mites, respectively. I wish that I knew in detail how this explanation would run. It seems that some sort of comparison would be involved, upon which one would then say, "And so the mite is higher than the stone." There are shadows here. Albert Schweitzer has reverence for the mite—it is alive—but not for the stone. "Higher" here might then mean no more than that he, Schweitzer, has reverence for the mite but not for the stone. A stone is a stone, but a mite is a mite. The mite is alive, but that the mite is alive must not be regarded as involved in some argument. Nor is it a defense.

Never mind that. If we look upon Anselm's sentence in this way, it must be in the higher reaches of this progression that the main interest lies. Let us suppose that we have gotten on with our conceiving and our comparing of "beings greater than" to Zeus. Zeus is greater than Satan (Is he?) and Satan is greater than the angel Gabriel. (Is that how Milton represents Satan?) And now comes the climax: God is greater than Zeus. At this point the progression ends. Any further conceivable conceived will have to be placed down lower in the order. (It just occurred to me now that there may be some difficulties in this. The conceivable being "God" is defined by what is said of God in the Scriptures—"theology as grammar.") If the place of the conceivable, God, is determined by way of the comparison of what is said of God with what is said of some other conceivables, then the place of the conceivable "God" must await the results of conceiving and further comparisons, and so must remain uncertain. In this way, that God is "the Being than which none greater can be conceived" will itself be no part of what is involved in the conceivable, will be no part of theology. It is then as though Anselm examined "Zeus" and then examined "God" and as a result of this examination Anselm came to make this discovery. This may serve at once to remind us that God is great, and as great as you please is no discovery at all, and that Anselm is mistaking the sentence of praise for that of fact.

It may be interesting in the course of this fantasia of order to notice what determines that Zeus' place is higher than that of Satan. And here is a suggestion. Zeus is quite impressive. He says, "Go to now, ye gods, make trial, that ye may all know. Fasten ye a rope of gold from heaven, and all ye gods lay hold thereof, and all goddesses; yet could ye not drop from heaven Zeus to earth, Zeus, counselor supreme, not though ye toiled sore. But once I likewise were minded to draw with all my heart, then should I draw you up with very earth and sea withal. Thereafter would I bind the rope about a pinnacle of Olympus and so should all those things be hung in air. By so much am I beyond gods and beyond men." And here is another sentence, "And loud as nine thousand men or ten thousand cry in battle when they join the strife of war so mighty was the cry of the strong shaker of the earth sent forth from his heart and great strength he put into the hearts of each of the Achaeans to strive and war unceasingly." Notice that Zeus boasts himself "beyond gods and beyond men." I will not continue the comparison with Satan. Satan, we know, "made himself equal with God" and suffered the consequences. I am introducing the idea of this comparison only in order to try to figure out some more or less plausible misunderstanding of Anselm's sentence.

Suppose now that someone were to remind Anselm of his sentence and of what Zeus could do and were now to put the question, "And is not Zeus that being than which none greater can be conceived?" Then how will Anselm answer? He might have quoted a passage from Isaiah, "Therefore the redeemed of the Lord shall return, and come with singing unto Zion; and everlasting joy shall be upon his head; they shall obtain gladness and joy; and sorrow and mourning shall flee away. I, even I, am he that comforteth you; who art thou that thou shouldst be afraid of a man that shall die, and of the son of man which shall be made as grass; and forgettest the Lord, thy Maker, that both stretched forth the heavens and laid the foundation of the earth; and hast feared continually every day because of the fury of the oppressor as if he were ready to destroy? And where is the fury of the oppressor?" And with this, as I am now representing Anselm's hybrid sentence, Anselm (by comparing what is said about Zeus with what is said about God, two conceivables conceived) will have shown himself that God is greater than Zeus.

Perhaps this will be better. Just as there are psalms in the Scriptures praising God, so too there were psalms, or the equivalent, in Hesiod or Homer, praising Zeus. The psalms to Zeus would be composed after much the same fashion as those in the Scriptures: "Great is Zeus, the earth-shaker; Great is Zeus, the cloud-gatherer, etc." Someone familiar with Homer might easily compose such psalms. And now imagine Anselm in Paris reading first some psalms from the Scriptures and then reading some psalms from among the praises of Zeus. Then he would turn to his listeners, "Now which is greater, our God or Zeus?" And all his listeners would reply, "Our God is greater." But what if there were four who replied, "Zeus is greater!" What then? Anselm, presumably, would say that there must be some misunderstanding and he would read the psalms again. And once again they would say, "Zeus is greater!" And Anselm would exclaim, "Is it greater that Zeus should draw up gods and goddesses with the very earth and sea on a rope of gold and hang them all up in air from a pinnacle of Olympus than that God should return the redeemed of the Lord with joy unto Zion and that he should stretch forth the heavens and lay the foundations of the earth?" And they would look puzzled and say that they did not even understand what he was saying. If now Anselm went on insisting that God is not only greater than Zeus but greater than any being conceivable, would not this exhibit a misunderstanding on his part? This suggests questions like: Is the sentence, "God created the heavens and the earth" intelligible? Or, how is that sentence to be understood? But the chief lesson once more is that concerning the misleading nature of "greater than." For as it enters into what I regard as a form of misunderstanding, whether it be Anselm's or not, it is treated as though one could show that this or that was greater. It is as though one could compel praise as one can press upon someone a conclusion.

And now I can imagine someone asking: But why are you making such a fuss about this? This deserves an explanation.

I was busy with Anselm's first sentence, "We believe that thou art a being than which none greater can be conceived." I tried first of all to exhibit the absurdity of this, the mixture of the grammar of the sentences of praise with that of the grammar of the statement of belief. To Anselm, the sentence obviously seemed far from absurd. It must have seemed to him that what he was saying was beyond all question—which indeed it was—and yet that it made sense to say that we believed it. The question, accordingly, was this: How was Anselm misunderstanding the sentence "Thou art a being than which none greater can be conceived"? That is, by way of what grammatical analogy can we understand what he was doing? And I said that he was regarding this fragment of the language of praise, which is indubitable, which it makes no sense to doubt, as a statement of the results of a comparison. The sentence is similar to sentences which do state such results. Accordingly, this sentence will seem indubitable, and yet, as the statement of the results of a comparison as subject to error. I tried then to give an account of how one might come to think of this, the comparison of conceivables. It must be remembered that I am not trying to give any account of what Anselm's thoughts were at the time he was writing this piece, nor am I trying to give such an account as Anselm might have given had he come to answer questions. Anselm has himself left us a mere sketch and that is in part what makes his argument so neat. What I am trying to do is to provide those resources which lie hidden in the background of the language which may help us to see what led Anselm to say what he said. For this purpose I have at times had to engage in fantasy, but this was only in order to get the language into perspective.

But there is one special reason why I have had to elaborate the way in which we might think of Anselm's regarding the sentence, "Thou art a being than which none greater can be conceived." I have already referred to this as the reasonable or plausible misunderstanding and I have done this deliberately. For there is another misunderstanding of the same sentence (or a part of it) which enters more directly into the argument, and which I prefer to describe as utterly unreasonable and implausible, explained only by that excess of zeal which Anselm had for proof. I regard it as a plausible misunderstanding that Anselm should have supposed that he discovered God was greater than Zeus by a review of the praises of each. But I regard it as an almost incomprehensible misunderstanding that Anselm should have supposed that in the same way he discovered that God is not a mere idea or an image or a sensation. The explanation for this must wait. Let me suggest this further: the confusion which we meet at the outset I regard as transitional. It is transitional in relation to the other confusion which operates in the argument proper.

II

Now I should like to go on to consider Anselm's reflections on the understanding of the fool. Anselm says, "Or is there no such nature, since 'the fool hath said in his heart, There is no God'."

The sentence, "The fool hath said in his heart, there is no God" interests me not alone because of what Anselm does with it but because a study of the psalm in which it is found, the surroundings of the sentence, reveals something surprising about the meaning of that sentence. And anyone who has a taste for the niceties of language may relish this. Anselm assumes that since "the fool hath said in his heart there is no God" that "the fool when he hears of this being of which I speak understands what he hears." But the psalm does not support this construction. It does not even support assuming that when the fool hears a psalm intoned that he understands this. If the fool is a Hebrew fool who has as a boy been taught out of the Scriptures and has every year taken his part in the Passover feast and has asked the ceremonial question, "What mean ye by this service?", then he would understand a great deal. But even though he did understand the psalms and had once taken part in the singing and been one of the musicians, this would not involve his understanding Anselm's "a being than which none greater can be conceived." Even if we assume the fool understands it, it is clear from the argument that he did not understand it in the same way that Anselm did. And what fools among us understand it? But what I had in mind to point out was that the psalm involves nothing concerning the literacy or illiteracy of the fool. The fool is an unrighteous man. And when the psalmist writes that "the fool hath said in his heart" this is not to be understood as meaning that the fool said this to himself, nor that when he is asked what he has said in his heart that this would mean anything to him or that he could tell. It is the speaking of his misdeeds which is the saying in his heart. He utters misdeeds and they are speeches out of the fullness or the emptiness of his heart. Actions speak neither Hebrew nor English. There is a version here of, "By their fruits ye shall know them." So the fool's deeds show, not that he is saying to himself "There is no God" but that he does not believe, that he neither keeps God's commandments, nor fears God.

The psalm begins with the line already quoted, "The fool hath said. . . ." But it goes on, "They are corrupt, they have done abominable works, there is none that doeth good" and it continues, "They are all gone aside, they are altogether become filthy," they "eat up my people as they eat bread." I am emphasizing this detail in order to point out another instance of Anselm's lifting out of its surroundings a sentence which in these surroundings has a use which is quite different from that to which Anselm now adapts it. In this case it may not make much difference since there are also fools who noisily proclaim "There is no God," others who mutter this to themselves hiding their unbelief, and still others whose deeds speak—perhaps even such deeds as contradict their mouths. Anselm's fool is a literate fool, but he is not the fool of this psalm.

Let us then consider: There is a fool and he said "There is no God." Anselm tells us nothing about this fool, what the occasion was on which he said this, what troubles he has had, etc. We cannot even tell from what Anselm says whether it is precisely the fool's saying this that makes him a fool. "The fool" in this case is a barren concept. So we will have to make up our own fool. These necessities are laid upon us by our working with a mere sketch. Concerning this fool, Anselm does not tell us merely that he understands what he is saying when he says "There is no God" but that "this very fool when he hears of this being of which I speak—a being than which none greater can be conceived—understands what he hears, and what he hears is in his understanding." I want to try to get this in perspective.

Let us suppose that this fool is a renegade Jew and the time is that of the capitivity. He remembers well how it was at home when he was a boy and at his grandfather's house, the reading of the book, his grandfather poring over the Talmud, the candles in the house, the feast of lights, the unleavened bread, and the Sabbaths when no servant worked and no ox and no ass pulled anything. He remembers, too, as a boy hearing the choirs intoning psalms in the congregation, the same choirs intoning now their disenchanted hopes. It is all very sad now. He sees the foreign soldiers in the streets and thinks of other days when his father walked so proudly. Times have changed; it has been very hard. His grandfather has been dead now a long time, his father and mother are gone and the family has been scattered so he never sees them any more. Among his own people he has few friends and most of them, too, have departed from the old ways. Abraham, Isaac, and Jacob, and Samuel, Joshua, and Moses, and Saul, David and Solomon—these names still bring tears to his eyes. "They are my people." A man is not a stone. But the God of Abraham, Isaac and Jacob? There is still a congregation in the town, men of faithful memory who are diligent each Sabbath day, keeping themselves and the Sabbath holy. Sometimes he stands at the door where they meet and he listens to the reading, those stirring and terrible chapters from Exodus and Deuteronomy, and he hears the injunction, "Only take heed to thyself, and keep thy soul diligently, lest thou forget the things which thine eyes have seen and lest they depart from thy heart all the days of thy life; teach them to thy sons and thy sons' sons." And he hears again of "the mountain that burned with fire" and of "the darkness, clouds, and thick darkness" and of "his voice out of the midst of the fire." He is distressed, both sad and angry. He has neither sons nor sons' sons, and if he did what would he teach them? He no longer believes. He is desolate, tender with memories but without hope. God, too, is only a memory. And when he hears the psalm, "Bless the Lord, O my soul, and all that is within me bless his holy name. Bless the Lord, O my soul, and forget not all his benefits," he stands grim at the door, looking in upon those old men in their little black caps. But he does not enter. He turns and walks hurriedly away.

III–IV

I have now presented to you Anselm's fool. He has heard the words of Moses, the words that once made him fear, and the words of the psalm once heard in blessing and still sweet to his ear. Of this fool Anselm says, "This very fool when he hears . . . understands what he hears. . . ." And surely Anselm is right about that since that is just the sort of fool I have presented. How could he not understand seeing he was brought up as he was. Anselm continues, "understands what he hears and what he understands is in his understanding; although he does not understand it to exist." And now what are we to make of this?

The fool stood at the door and he heard the words of the chapter from Deuteronomy and the words of the psalm, and he understood those words. He was moved by them, attracted and repelled. Wistful he listened; and yet when the injunctions were sounded, "Hearken," and "Keep therefore and do them," "Take heed to thyself and keep thy soul diligently," "Take heed unto yourselves, lest ye forget," and when he heard the pleadings and the wooings and the threatenings, he neither hearkened nor heeded nor feared. Yet he knew well enough how those pious old men with their long beards received those words and how they kept them in their hearts and how those words ruled them and how they raised their spirits and comforted them as a refuge in their calamities. But when they invited him in to join them in remembering, in prayer, in praise, he shook his head and would not, could not. God to heed, to obey, to fear, to remember, to hearken to! What is God? "A shout in the street." And he turned away, miserable, guilty, numb. A man now turning against his youth! And had he not for years heard those words, and been taught, and taken his part at the feasts and the commemorations? The shout of Abraham, Isaac, and Jacob!

The question is as to what Anselm means by saying that the fool understands what he hears. But first let us take notice. The men in the congregation might be said to understand in a way in which the fool does not. They remember what God has done; they receive and obey the commands as God's commands; they heed and fear God; they praise God and they pray; they also bring their offerings. He, the fool, does not and cannot do any of these things. And yet he understands what they are doing, remembering, heeding, obeying, fearing, praising, and praying. Apart from his once having taken part in all these, these have their analogues in human relationships. All these people in the congregation are like people who are devoted to an unseen king, a government in exile or in their exile, and the fool understands that. But the fool has said in his heart and at the door, "The King is dead."

So Anselm says that the fool "understands what he hears." And I suppose that if we asked him how he knows this, he might explain in the way in which I have already indicated we might. "Of course, of course, the fool understands. Wasn't he brought up to understand?" and so on. But now the language begins to thicken. "The fool . . . understands what he hears and what he understands is in his understanding." Let us now first ask whether when Anselm noticed that the fool "understands what he hears" he also noticed that the fool had something in his understanding and it turned out to be what he understands? Did Anselm look twice—once to find that the fool understood, and then once more to discover what was in the fool's understanding? We will not attempt any answer to this question. Instead, let us see whether we can figure out just what it is that is said to be in the fool's understanding. Consider then that the fool understands the words:

> Great is Jehovah and greatly to be praised.
> And his greatness is unsearchable.
> Thou art a being than which none greater is conceivable,
> O Lord.

He hears these words and he understands them. What he understands is in his understanding and it is the words he understands. So the words are in his understanding. This may seem to be all right, but it is nevertheless wrong, even if the words are in his understanding. Where are the words? They are in the book, in the mouth of the reader, and the fool might have stored the words in his memory. All the same, Anselm was not speaking of the words even though it is words the fool understood and what he understood was in his understanding. How do I know? Well, Anselm goes on to say, "although he does not understand it to exist." It seems obvious that if we asked the fool (who understands what he hears) whether what he hears is in his understanding, he would not say that what he hears does not exist. He is not that sort of fool. He has heard the words written above and so has everyone else. But what then? Well, what else is there? There is the meaning of the words, of course. If the fool has heard those words and understood them, then he may, for instance, be able to explain how he understands these words and what he then explains is the meaning. You cannot explain the meaning of a word or words unless there is the meaning of the words, and where would the meaning be but in the understanding? What does a man do who explains the meaning but doesn't tell you about what he has there? So when a man understands the words, obviously there are words which may be on the page but there is also the meaning of the words which is certainly not on the page. "Here the words, there the meaning." Where now? In the understanding. The meanings must be accessible and convenient to anyone who is to explain them. I do not suppose the meanings need to be there all the time even when the words are far away or nowhere in sight or hearing. But they must be there when you understand the words. This seems to be undeniable unless one intended to say that they might be in some place, also readily accessible, but not in the understanding. Still the understanding seems as good a place as any.

In the quotation above, beginning, "Great is Jehovah," there are some twenty or more words and each has a meaning. And when the fool hears these words and understands them, there are twenty or more meanings of those words in the fool's understanding. There is nothing startling about this, and I had no intention of surprising anyone with this. What I wanted to point out is that there are words and meanings here in which Anselm has no interest at the moment. And if we had selected some other portion of Scripture which the fool also understands, this would be clearer still. He would, for instance, not be interested in saying that the meaning of the word "sons" or "mountain" or "darkness" or "cloud" is in the fool's understanding. If now we remember that the fool said, "There is no God," then we may realize that what Anselm meant to say was that when the fool hears the word "God" or "Jehovah" or "Lord," then the meaning of these words is in his understanding. This may help to explain how Anselm goes on, as he does, to say "although he does not understand it to exist." This may still strike one as strange since what the fool presumably does not understand is that the meaning of the word "God"—which he understands, and which he has in his understanding—still does not exist. There is the word "God" and there is the meaning of the word "God." There is also something which Anselm refers to as "it." Now what could that be? It seems preposterous to think of the fool as one who understands the word "God," and yet when you ask him whether he understands the word he says that the word has no meaning; that is, that "it" does not exist. So once more, what is "it"?

Before going on with this I want to say something about the meaning of the word "God." Anselm is a Christian and accordingly when he is busy with the meaning of the word "God," the meaning with which he is concerned must be regarded then as Christian; namely, that embodied in the Scriptures—"theology as grammar." The Scriptures are also described as "the word of God," and accepted by Christians as a revelation. Here God declares himself to men and reveals his love towards men, seeking to draw them unto himself. There is great variety in the ways in which God has pursued these purposes as the variety of forms and style in the books of the Bible makes plain. This is the role of the Scriptures as a sacred book. But there is something else pertinent to our present investigation. If anyone is interested in getting into perspective the meaning of the word "God" among Christians, his resource must be the Scriptures. Anyone who in Anselm's time or our time understands the word "God" will know what sentences involving this word make sense and which do not make sense and he will in this have been guided by and nurtured in the language of the Scriptures. Generally, this will involve religious education both in literature and in practice—singing, ritual, sermons, sacraments, feasts, etc. Accordingly, if the fool understands what he hears, as a Jew or as a Christian this will involve that he, having been brought up in the Jewish or the Christian religion will be able to distinguish between sense and non-sense in respect to what people say and do employing that word. Heresy is Christian or Jewish non-sense. And now the point of what I am saying is that to understand a word is to have an ability, the ability to speak and to write the language in which that word occurs, and to understand others who speak and write. The understanding of a Christian consists in his ability to employ the word "God" in his Christian practice, in prayer, in praise, etc. And the fool? He has no more than the ability to distinguish sense and non-sense when he stands at the door and hears. He knows the Scriptures, too, and listens with understanding. But he neither remembers as those do who are inside, nor does he praise God nor pray nor confess nor offer gifts. He can also explain to others.

Now let us return to Anselm. Anselm said that the fool understands what he hears. He adds that what the fool understands is in his understanding. The fool has the meaning and he grasped it. And that is what is in his understanding. But if we now mean (when we say that the fool understands) that he is scripturally literate, that he has a certain ability with respect to that language, that he is able to do so and so, then it seems that Anselm has said something like what he might say of a man who could lift heavy weights, namely, that he had lifting weights in his arm. This might be picturesque language but it would be a mistake if one expected to find anything but muscles, etc., in the strong man's arm. Accordingly, it now seems that if Anselm intended to explain to us what he meant by saying that the fool understands what he hears, he might better have told us that the fool can (in respect to the words he has heard) tell us what in the service led up to their speaking these words, what special circumstances are involved as in the case of the Passover Feast, what the attitudes of the people in the congregation were (kneeling, bowing their heads, or raising their hands), and what came after —language has surroundings. But once again, if Anselm had said this then the addition "although he did not understand it to exist" would be incomprehensible. There certainly is no reason for supposing that the fool would deny that he could give these explanations.

We should now be in a position to understand what has

led Anselm to say what he says. The fool understands the words he hears, so he is doing two things. He hears the words and he understands. Hearing and understanding are different, but now as the words are to the hearing, so the meaning is to the understanding. Understanding might be thought of as a special internal form of hearing. And now what could the meaning be? Well, in the case of the word "God," however it may be with other words, the answer is clear. The meaning of the word "God" must be what the word names, so God is the meaning of the word "God." Perhaps we can also see how Anselm regarded the state of the fool's understanding. The fool understands the word "God" and so he must have something in his understanding. The fool does not deny that he has something in his understanding. Since he is Anselm's fool, he may agree with Anselm that if he understands a word, then the meaning of that word must be in his understanding, and it must be what the word is a name of. So too with the word "God." But there are now apparently two sorts of things which bear the names which are words one understands. One says of things of the one sort, that they do not exist; of the other sort, one says that they do exist. The fool, accordingly, has in his mind the meaning of the word "God," it bears that name, but he classifies it wrong. He says that it belongs to the class of those things in his understanding which do not exist. Anselm tells us nothing about how either the fool or Anselm manages to make this distinction, nor how the fool ever came to make this mistake.

There is something very important here for this discussion. In connection with such expressions as "the abominable snowman" and "the monster of Loch Ness," or "the suspected murderer of the man who died in a fall" and "ghosts" and "whooping cranes" and "passenger pigeons" and "the inhabitants of Easter Island" and "descendants of Julius Caesar" (each of which is a "name" and has a meaning), one might make a classification. There would be those of which one might then say that they exist and those of which one might say that they do not exist. In connection with this one could also go on to indicate by what sorts of investigations one came to make these distinctions. If then the meaning of the words "exists" and "does not exist" are to be understood in just such surroundings, the question arises as to how we are to understand not only Anselm (who says that God exists), but also the fool (who "does not understand it to exist"). If the fool should explain this latter by saying that he does not understand what Anselm is saying when he says that God exists, since the word "exists" has the surroundings of "the abominable snowman" and "ghosts" and "whooping cranes," etc., then he would seem to have the advantage. It may be well here too to remember that the fool of the psalm makes no such classification as is attributed to the fool of Anselm's argument. It is his deeds that utter his unbelief. He is not represented as making a mistake in sorting out his ideas.

V

We are now at this point. The fool has something in his understanding called "God." He classifies it as belonging to the class of things that do not exist. Anselm is now ready to correct him. In this case, whatever the fool may do in the case of "whooping cranes," all he needs to do now is examine what he has in mind, or should I say examine the name? With Anselm's help he is to substitute for the word "God" the expression which Anselm lifted from the psalms, namely, "the being than which none greater can be conceived." Once he does this he will reclassify what he has in his understanding. That is, he will see at once that "the being than which none greater can be conceived" exists.

Presumably, this will help the fool only if he understands this expression. Does he understand it? Of course. He has understood it all along and also when he stood at the door of the meeting place. He understood it then as a slightly mutilated fragment of the language of praise. It is among the sentences like, "Bless the Lord, O my soul." So he understands it all right even though he never pours out his soul in blessing. Let us see what this comes to. Suppose that the fool recites Psalm 145 for Anselm. It begins, "I will extol thee, my God, O King"; and then are the lines, "Great is Jehovah, and greatly to be praised." The psalm continues with the praises of God's mercies and of his "wondrous works." So he certainly knows what the surroundings of this phrase of Anselm's are. His understanding before did not incline him to join the congregation then, and to be reminded of it now does not either. The difficulty obviously arises out of his not sharing Anselm's misunderstanding. Let us see how this goes.

The fool has the meaning of the word "God" in his understanding. But the fool does not realize what it is he has there. So Anselm tells him that he has a being there, "the being than which none greater can be conceived." Now the words of praise are going about in the guise of a description. We have earlier seen out of what more or less plausible comparison this illusion might arise. But we have now introduced them into a situation in which this plausible comparison will be of no use. For how would the fool be moved from his position, change the classification, by reminding him of other greatness, the praises of Shakespeare and Milton's Satan and Zeus? Praise is praise, but that does not mean you will find Zeus on Olympus.

Now I want to return to Anselm's words.

> Hence even the fool is convinced that something exists in the understanding, at least, than which nothing greater can be conceived. . . . And assuredly that than which nothing greater can be conceived cannot exist in the understanding alone. For suppose it exists in the understanding alone: then it can be conceived to exist in reality; which is greater.

Here again we meet that previously noticed classification. There are first of all existences in the understanding. We have already noticed some instances of these. And now there are the two sub-classes, those which exist in the understanding alone, and those which exist in the understanding and also in reality. But how are we to think of "existences in the understanding alone"? Shall we suggest that this must be done by introspection? Think of the abominable snowman which you most likely think does not exist anyhow and then see what the existence in your understanding is like. He is a very large creature, half bear and two-thirds man, who walks on four feet that leave the footprints of only two, who eats storms and is always seen disappearing. Let me suggest then that an existence in the understanding alone is a mere idea and a mere idea is an image. Perhaps we could say that a sensation, too, is an existence in the understanding alone. Now then we might explain the classification in this way: There is a class composed of images and sensations. Sensations clearly exist in the understanding alone. There are no sensations in the sky nor in a stone. I am now inclined to say that images, too, exist only in the understanding. Where else could images exist? And yet one gets the impression that many of these existences in the understanding exist also in reality. And so it would seem that these existences in the understanding are not images. What now could exist both in the understanding and in reality? Why, a universal. Might not a universal exist in the image which exists in the understanding, and also in the cat on the fence which is in no one's understanding, but in reality?

I asked what sort of something this is in the fool's understanding. And I should like to remind you that the question is misleading. I was inclined to say that the fool has a grammatical mistake in his understanding, but that would not be quite right. The whole phrase "something in his understanding" is a grammatical mistake. Accordingly, our question should be: What sort of grammatical mistake is this? This now is a partial description: Anselm is thinking of the meaning of an expression, the function of that expression as a thing, and of the understanding as a place, and accordingly we get "something in the understanding." Now superimposed is another confusion, a difference in somethings in the understandings (meanings); namely, the difference between somethings that "exist in the understanding alone" and "somethings that exist both in the understanding and in reality, perhaps, the difference in the meaning between such expressions as "the abominable snowman" and "ghosts" and the meaning of such expressions as "horses" and "cows." Now comes the question: What sort of something is this—what sort of meaning is this—that the word "God" has? Since the fool has this something (meaning) in his understanding, the question is now understood in this way: Is the word "God" a word with the meaning such as that of such words as "abominable snowman" and "ghosts" or such as that of such words as "horses" and "cows." Regarded in this way, the fool says that it has a meaning, a kind of something, such as the expression "abominable snowman" has; but Anselm says that it has a meaning, a kind of something, such as the word "horses" has. And it is this that Anselm proves.

Now notice: If we say that the meaning (the something) of the expression "abominable snowman" exists in the understanding alone, we might think of this as an image. Images exist in the understanding alone. If Anselm should ask himself what the meaning of that expression is, he would look into his understanding and find the something; namely, the image of the snowman. But if we went to the Himalayas to look for the meaning of the expression, he would not find it. So the meaning of that expression exists only in his understanding. And what now about the meaning of the word "horse"? Well, again, he looks into his understanding, and there it is—the image of a horse. And does it exist in the understanding alone? No indeed; he went out into the stable and there he found the meaning of the word "horse" eating oats. So the meaning of the word "horse" exists not only in the understanding but also in the stable. This is one way of understanding Anselm, and I do not know a better way of understanding Anselm's misunderstanding.

And now we also have a way of understanding Anselm's misunderstanding of the fool. The fool understands the word "God." He looks into his understanding and then he finds the meaning of the word "God." Will it do to say that the meaning of the word "God" is an image? At any rate it is a something. Now the fool asks himself: Is the meaning of the word "God" in my understanding alone? and he decides to find out. He visits the Himalayas, he goes to the stable, he scans the heavens with a telescope. He cannot find the meaning of the word "God" anywhere but in his understanding. So he concludes that the meaning, "the something" of the word "God" exists only in his understanding. Now notice that Anselm does not say, "But you have not looked in the uttermost parts of the sea," or "east of the sun and west of the moon." Such investigations would in any case be too tedious for Anselm. Anselm needs something quick as lightning. And so we get the proof. With this, I want to add, he also abandons the surroundings of the word "exists."

Notice now the proof. I said that the fool understands the word "God," but he says that the meaning of the word "God" exists only in his understanding. Anselm induces him to substitute for the word "God," "a being than which none greater can be conceived." It is not clear to me how this is done, whether Anselm intends that these expressions mean the same or whether the latter is intended only to describe the something in the fool's understanding called "God." I think it must be the latter. This introduces a new confusion. There is first something, namely, the meaning of the word "God," so we describe it. What we actually have are two expressions—the word "God" and the expression "a being than which none greater can be conceived." The meaning of these expressions is related, for instance, in the psalms. But the meaning of the latter is not to be regarded as a description of the meaning of the former. It is simply that in praise of God men may employ the latter.

By way of compounding confusions we have arrived at this: that the fool has in his understanding something; namely, a being than which none greater can be conceived. Now the question is as to whether a being than which none greater can be conceived *can* exist only in the understanding. It is obvious that the abominable snowman, I mean the something which is the meaning of that expression, *can* exist only in the understanding. But then no one ever said of it that it was a being than which none greater can be conceived. If anyone ever did say that about the something in the understanding (which is the meaning of the expression "the abominable snowman"), then, of course, he would no longer say that it could exist only in the understanding. It simply cannot. That would follow in this way: If I say that anything, snowman or God, is a being than which none greater can be conceived, I mean that it cannot exist in the understanding alone but must exist both in and out of the understanding. Suppose that Anselm would explain this sentence in this way: If I say that anything, snowman or God, is a being than which none greater can be conceived, then it will certainly be preposterous of anyone to ask me whether what I am so excited about is just in my understanding. If the fool were given the first explanation, he would simply have to deny that he meant anything of the sort by "God is a being than which none greater can be conceived," which is obvious enough, too, since he already said that this something exists in the understanding alone. And if you ask him what he did mean, he might refer you to Psalm 103. There you will find the being than which none greater can be conceived, and it exists in my understanding and in other understandings perhaps, but in understandings alone. And if Anselm urges upon him the second explanation, then he may say that if there are people who are so excited about what they have in their understandings then it may be preposterous for them to say that it exists only in their understandings, but that he is not that excited, which once again is shown by the fact that he still says that the something exists only in his understanding.

*   *   *

This is the intelligible basis of Anselm's argument. There is a man also called a fool who stands at the door of the meeting place and hears the Scriptures read. He understands it but he pays no heed. He says, as it were, "There is no God."

He goes home and about his business. Perhaps in another year he will return to hear the reading again. Out of this simple situation and what I venture to call a magic formula Anselm manages to fashion a proof.

Now, let us see what Anselm does. Anselm notices that the fool stands at the door and hears what is read and that he understands. So far it is the same as in the other case. But now we have an addition. He sees that the fool has something in his understanding. He asks the fool, "What is that you have in your understanding?" The fool falls in with this and says, "O, nothing, just something in my understanding." Anselm recognizes this as a mistake and goes on. "You have Godot in your understanding, don't you?" And the fool says, "Yes." "Well," continues Anselm, "if you describe Godot as Godot who cannot be just something in your understanding, then you will see that you made a mistake when you said 'O, nothing, just something in my understanding.'" "But," asks the fool, "why should I describe Godot in this way?" And now Anselm says, "Because, as you know, all the people praise him so. They cry out to Godot, 'Thou art a being than which none greater can be conceived.' So that's what you have in your understanding." To which the fool replies, "And so that's it. I have something in my understanding and all the people shout about it and say that it is not something just in my understanding. But what has their praising it and saying this got to do with my saying that it is not just something in my understanding? Let us put it this way: I have something in my understanding. People ask me what it is and I say, 'O, nothing, just something in my understanding.' But other people when they hear the word which occasions my having something in my understanding when I say this, do not say this. I ask one of them: 'What do you have in your understanding?' And he begins praising it. And when I go on, 'And is it just in your understanding?' he says, 'What do you think I am, a fool?' and he goes on with his praises. But it doesn't lead me to praise anything. And when people now ask me, 'What do you have in your understanding?' I say as I said before 'O, nothing, just something in my understanding.' If someone asks: 'But haven't you heard?' I say, 'Yes, yes, I've heard everything. What others say and do, hearing what I hear, doesn't affect me. I'm a decent citizen. But I don't sing praises to what I have in my understanding. I'm a plain unbeliever. I'm not even waiting for Godot.' "

In order to make up this conversation I have had to get the fool to enter into the confusion concerning something just in his understanding. But I have permitted him freedom from the confusion concerning the language of praise.

I am not getting along very well with this, but perhaps I have given it up anyhow. I do want to take one more look at "he has something in his understanding but he doesn't know what it is." (He says that it is in his understanding alone but that is not so.) What is the analogy here? A man walks with a limp. Someone asks, "You have something in your knee?" The man replies, "Yes, something in my knee." The other asks, "And what is it?" And the reply is, "O, just something in my knee." The conversation goes on, "Just something in your knee? Not a bone, for instance." The man smiles. "O, no. I mean a pain. If you have a pain in your knee, it's just in your knee, and if it's in your knee, it can't be anywhere else. If it were somewhere else, it wouldn't be the pain in your knee. So I said it was just in my knee."

"But aren't you making a mistake? Let me examine your knee." And he pulls a needle out of the man's knee. "See," he says, "you were wrong. It wasn't just in your knee after all since I've pulled it out." The man is flabbergasted. "And I was sure I had a pain in my knee and it's turned out not to be a pain at all but a needle. How could I have made such a mistake?" Anselm now explains, "I said you had something in your knee greater than which none is conceivable, so you might have known it wasn't a pain, seeing ever so many things conceivable—such as a needle or water—are greater than a pain. Anything which is just something in a knee, like a pain, is obviously not as great as something which can be

not only in a knee but which can also be drawn out of a knee
—'which is greater.' "

I was pretty sure I would not be able to do it.

The common form of the psalm of praise in which there
may be something misleading is this: there are the introductory sentences of praise, and then follow the remembering of
the wondrous works. The introductory words are like a fan-
fare, the great shout; there is no logical connection. One
would be misled if he thought that from the introductory
words of praise he could now go on to infer that God must
have done so-and-so, or that the introductory words were a
summary and whatever there was summarized could be
inferred. The summary, then, the words or sentences of
praise, would be an abbreviation of what followed in greater
detail. This is a mistake. The psalm contains no argument
and no conclusions. One praises, remembering. One shouts
the sentences of praise and then goes on remembering, praising. But in his argument Anselm treats the introductory sentence of praise either as a sentence from which one can infer
what God is being praised for, or (as I suggested), a summary. But one might then more reasonably suppose that one
could infer all the rest of the psalm from the introductory
words of the psalm. This would save one's remembering. But
actually nothing can be inferred. If one is acquainted with the
form of the psalm, then if one hears someone or a group, in
the service, beginning with the introductory words of the
psalm, then one may know how they will go on, since one
knows the psalm. This is rather like knowing the form of a
sonnet. It may be that the form "Because . . ." and "For . . ."
is what misleads in this case. It is certainly clear that in his
argument Anselm is misconstruing the words of praise by
trying to deduce from the sentence, "Thou art a being than
which none greater can be conceived" what he must have
regarded as a necessary part of the reason for saying this. But
there is no such necessary reason and no reason at all. In the

psalm there are no reasons even if one might give as a reason some part of what is in the psalm if one was called upon to justify one's praise. But the remembering is not a justification. The remembering is praise.

Anselm's proof is sometimes formulated in this way. "I have the idea of a most perfect being, and if I have the idea of a most perfect being, then implied in this is the idea that the most perfect being exists." Now what are we to say about this? To have the idea of the most perfect being is to understand this expression "the most perfect being." If someone understood this, he also would be able to identify the most perfect being if it were offered. So, if someone pointed to a stone and asked, "Is this it?" the person who understood this expression would be able now to say whether it was or not. Let us suppose that he would say, "No." Then other things would be pointed to and the same answer would be made, "No, that's not it." That he understood it would not in the least involve that at sometime someone would point to something and that he would then say, "Yes, that's it." All that would be involved is that if it ever were presented, he would be able to identify it. But his now being able to do this would not involve that it is available for this.

In general it is a part of the grammar of ever so many concepts that so-and-so or a so-and-so exists. If one understands the concept, then one understands also so-and-so exists. Consider the expression "most perfect woman" or "most perfect man." Let us suppose that these expressions have a meaning and that someone understands them. With some experience now he might say, "There is no such being as the most perfect woman or the perfect woman. There is no perfect woman. Any woman has some defect, a mole, for instance, or a sharp tongue or a clumsy thumb." But there is provision for "The most perfect woman exists." You may say, "I have found her."

On this account of the matter the mistake lies in mistaking one's ability to identify the most perfect being for one's saying that the most perfect being exists, mistaking this grammatical feature of the word for an assertion.

But the primary mistake is to assume that the sentence "God exists" is a part of the grammar of the word "God." That Anselm should attempt to prove this makes it appear that it does come in somewhere apart from the proof itself. But where then?

"I have the idea of a most perfect being."

"Well, what is it?"

Then he tells you; he quotes Psalm 103. What better, indeed, could he do? So that is his idea. Let us suppose he quotes it as what the psalmist sings. Then you ask him, "And has he forgiven your iniquities? And has he healed your diseases?" And he smiles, and says, "My iniquities, what are they? And as for my indigestion I take Tums which quiets my complaining."

I want once again to try to review.

The sentence of praise is, "Thou art a being than which none greater can be conceived." Now Anselm, overhearing some worshipper in the temple, beginning this psalm, and realizing that this is the man Reuben, a righteous man, says to himself, "Now there is a man who believes and who remembers day by day what God has done, that he has made the world in six days and that the heavens declare his glory, and what he has done for his people and what in particular he has done for Reuben." Anselm could do this only if he knew the form of the psalm.

Now consider the case as Anselm thinks of it.

There is the fool, and not a devout man at all. He mutters to himself: "Thou art a being than which none greater can be conceived," but he is not in prayer. He is not addressing God. He never prays. He says this and frowns. Perhaps he says, "Bah!" Now Anselm overhears him. It is clear enough to Anselm that the fool is a fool. And so, though he may allow that the fool understands these words—otherwise why does he frown so?—Anselm cannot now infer that the fool, like Reuben, believes and remembers day by day what God has done, and so on. He neither believes nor remembers, and, of course, if he does not believe, what should he remember? All the same, Anselm makes a point of saying that the fool understands the sentence he repeated, which may well be. And now what would this be like that the fool should understand this sentence? Well, why should he not understand it in the same way that Anselm himself understood it when he heard Reuben, the righteous man, intone with reverent attitude those same words in the temple. The fool might also make a comment about Reuben, the righteous man, who believes and remembers what God has done. The fool could not do this, of course, if he were not acquainted with the psalms, the psalms of praise. Naturally, there is a difference in the way in which Anselm listens to Reuben, taking it all in reverently just as Reuben himself engages in the psalm itself praising. In this case too the fool hears, and shakes his head and frowns. Here, then, we have a clear case of what one would mean by saying that the fool understood the sentence which he repeated and which he overheard as he passed the door of the temple.

But this is not at all how Anselm goes on to write of the fool's understanding that sentence. Whereas I have tried to present the meaning of that sentence by way of the surroundings of that sentence in the life of the psalmist who utters it, Anselm looks at meaning, and in this instance, at the meaning of the phrase "a being than which none greater can be conceived" in an obviously different way. If the fool understands that phrase then there must be *something,* namely, the meaning of that phrase in the fool's understanding. So far as I can make out, he thinks of that phrase as a description of the something in the fool's understanding. I take it that the movement of the proof depends upon this way of regarding the phrase, in the first place as a description, and of understanding as a having in the understanding the something which is described by that phrase. The rest is a matter of figuring out the meaning of that phrase which then the fool does not understand. It comes to this, then: that the fool who is said to understand this phrase and has the meaning, the something, in his understanding, still does not understand what it is he has in his understanding. It seems, accordingly, that the fool understands the phrase sufficiently so that the something is in his understanding but not sufficiently so that he also realizes what the something is that he has in his understanding. It is almost as though he had not examined closely what he has there. But at the same time he cannot examine what he has there without the help of the phrase whose meaning that something is.

Now notice how Anselm goes on. The fool admits that he has something in his understanding and, of course, that it is "the being than which none greater can be conceived." But now he is represented as saying that it exists in his understanding alone. Let us see what contrast is involved here. The fool, of course, could have gone on repeating to himself the whole of the psalm which he heard Reuben, the righteous man, intone in the temple. When Reuben does this, Reuben is praising God, as we have seen. And what is the fool doing? Well, we might say that the fool is ridiculing Reuben or that he is gnashing his teeth, showing his displeasure or expressing his displeasure at the thought of Reuben or of any man praising God for making such a world and such people in it. In any case there is nothing for the fool to react to or against but people like Reuben. Only in this way can we see the fool alive. Has there ever been a fool who said, "I understand the phrase 'the being than which none greater can be conceived' and so I have in my understanding the something which is that *being but it exists* in my understanding alone?"

Consider in any case how we might think of this. The fool says, "The being than which none greater can be conceived exists in my understanding alone." Now Anselm asks, "And what being is this?" To this the fool replies, "The being who made the world in six days and rested on the seventh day, the being who called Abraham out of Ur of the Chaldees, who saved believing Noah and his family from the flood, who led the people of Israel out of Egypt, who keepeth Israel, who forgiveth our iniquities, who healeth all our diseases, and so on." The fool gives Anselm the rigmarole. And now Anselm asks, "And that being exists only in your understanding?" to which the fool replies, "Of course." And now how is Anselm to go on? He might have gone on, "Surely God is great, and greatly to be praised for his mighty works. And the psalmists have sung God's praises for having done all these things. But haven't you forgotten somthing?" To which the fool responds, "Well, what?" And now Anselm says, "Haven't you forgotten that that being exists in your understanding? Isn't that wonderful?" Now the fool grows impatient. "I thought you were asking me what being this is that I have in my understanding and now you expect me to add among other things that the being in my understanding is in my understanding? In any case I do not think of the being in my understanding as somehow to be rejoiced at because that being graciously consented to come into my understanding from outside my understanding. There is in any case nothing in my understanding but the meaning of all those sentences I recited to you."

Let me try to see through this. The meaning of the word "God" is seen in perspective in the language of the Scriptures. If the fool is literate he may be able to recite the relevant passages. If now Anselm had asked: "And do you pray to God? Do you fear God? Do you believe in God?" the answer might have been, "No. There is no God." But this must not be taken as a reaction to God. It is a reaction to men who do believe. But Anselm is treating "There is no God" as though this were a reaction to God himself. This is what comes of treating the meaning of the phrase as though this were a something in the understanding, God in the understanding.

"As great as can be conceived."
"Greater than which none can be conceived."
"Greater than which none can be in the understanding alone."

Where are concepts? In the understanding alone. So we have a concept than which no greater concept can be conceived, or can be in the understanding alone.

The difference between I see it and I imagine it. So try to imagine God.

NOTES

1. John Locke, *An Essay Concerning Human Understanding* I, ed. Alexander Campbell Fraser (New York: Dover, 1959), p. 9.

2. St. Anselm, *Proslogium,* 2nd ed., trans. S. N. Deane (Chicago: Open Court, 1962), pp. 7–8.

INDEX

Absolute Idealism, 124–127
Abstraction,
  the third degree of, 82
  of the first principles of being,
  92
Adequatio theory of truth,
  its foundation, 83
  a theory of *human* truth, 996
Aesthetic criticism, 162
Analytic philosophers, and speculative metaphysics, 31
Analytic philosophy, 2, 3–4, 24,
  30–34
Anguish, 194, 195–196
Anselm, St. 19–20, 252–293
Augustine, St., 60–61, 66, 76, 82,
  96, 99
Austin, J. L., 14
  his approach, 14
  and "linguistic phenomenology," 32
  and performative statements,
  115
  and linguistic philosophy, 116
  and sense-datum theorists, 136
  and ordinary language, 173–177
  Pepper's comments on, 173–181
  sources for analyzing "excuses,"
  176–180
  and the "job principle," 180–181
  and other minds, 185
  and "excuses," 208
Ayer, A. J., viii, 1, 2, 7–11, 100,
  171–172

Bad faith, 202–203

Being,
  as a genus, 46
  its analogical structure, 91
  as known, 92
Being-in-itself, 193
Being than which none greater can
  be conceived, 19–20, 253–254
  and Anselm, 255, 257–263, 268
  source of, 259, 262–263, 268
Berdyaev, N., 97
Bergson, H., 127
Berkeley, G., 10, 40, 102, 122, 130–
  138, 192, 252
Berkeley's denial of matter, 124–
  125, 132–145
Biology, 66–67
Boswell and Johnson, 132
Bouwsma, O. K., viii, 1, 17–20, 212
Bradley, 54, 126
Brentano, Franz, 27
Broad, C. D., 136

Cajetan, 91
Carnap, 113, 147
Categorial frameworks, 2
  and metaphysics, 2–3
  categorizations of the universe,
  37
Categorial metaphysics, 37
Categories,
  and a world hypothesis, 12, 155
  of the highest kinds, 37
  and root metaphors, 155–156
"Category mistake," 40
Certainty, 153, 189
Chestov, 46